The
Hiker's Guide
to **Montana**

The
Hiker's Guide
to Montana

Edited by Bill Schneider

Falcon Press Publishing Co., Inc.
Billings and Helena, Montana

Library of Congress Number 79-55480

ISBN 0-934318-01-8

Manufactured in the United States of America

Published by Falcon Press Publishing Co., Inc.
P.O. Box 731, Helena MT 59601
Cover photo by Bill Schneider

More guides from Falcon Press

The Hiker's Guide to Montana is the second in a series of recreational guides planned by Falcon Press. *The Floater's Guide to Montana* was released earlier in 1979 and is currently available at bookstores and sport stores statewide.

The Floater's Guide introduces river-lovers to Montana's 26 most popular floating streams and includes vital information on water conditions, access points, hazards, fishing, and history.

The third in the series—a guide to fishing Montana's famous trout rivers—will be out in early 1980. Anglers interested in expert advice on fishing the trout-laden rivers won't want to miss this guidebook.

Order *The Floater's Guide* or extra copies of *The Hiker's Guide* from Falcon Press, P.O. Box 279, Billings, MT 59103. And watch for future installments in this series.

Acknowledgements

Editing any book runs into lots of work, but editing this book would have been quite impossible without the kind help of so many people.

First and foremost, I must thank the contributors who provided most of the hikes. Without them, *The Hiker's Guide to Montana* would not be. Although their by-lines follow their contributions, I want to again acknowledge their help by listing them here: Wayne Avants, Don Berg, Bill Brown, Pat Caffrey, Bruce Chesler, Mike Comola, Frank Culver, Bill Cunningham, Art Foran, Herb Gloege, Linda and Tom Hurlock, Loren Kreck, Joe Mussulman, Dave Orndoff, Bob Oset, Mike Sample, Elaine and Art Sedlack, Elaine Snyder, Fred Swanson, Larry Thompson, and John Westenberg. If you bump into any of these good folks on a mountaintop somewhere, please thank them for making *The Hiker's Guide* possible.

Perhaps as important as the text are the excellent maps. For these, thank Gary Wolf, an accomplished cartographer with an extra endowment of patience.

Many of the photos are courtesy of the U.S. Forest Service. I especially thank the helpful public servants at the Regional Forester's Office of Information in Missoula. However, Forest Service personnel from ranger districts throughout Montana helped in various capacities. Other photos in the book come from the cameras of Bruce Chesler, Art Foran, Joe Mussulman, Doug O'looney, Tom Hurlock, Harry Engels, and Mike Sample.

T&R Engraving of Denver did an excellent job in the difficult task of photographing topographic maps from the U.S. Geological Survey. And of course, the USGS itself deserves thanks for making the maps in the first place and allowing their reproduction.

Ed Godlevsky of New Era Typesetting in Helena somehow mastered the tedious and time-consuming job of setting the book in type. Lithography is by Worzalla Publishing of Stevens Point, Wisconsin. Gary Little of Billings provided the art for the title page. My wife, Marnie, and Cindy Christin put in long hours to weed out all the typographical errors.

As you can see, it takes much more than an editor to finally complete such a project.—*Bill Schneider*

Contents

Foreword

Hiking is for everybody / 1

Introduction

Touch the Land Lightly / 3 • Make it a Safe Trip / 5 • Hiking Bear Country / 7

The Hikes

Northwest Peak / 10 • Hoskins Lake / 12 • Boulder Lakes / 14 • West Branch of the South Fork of Big Creek / 16 • East Branch of the South Fork of Big Creek / 18 • Fish Lakes Canyon / 21 • Parsnip Creek / 23 Roderick Mountain / 25 • Pellick Ridge, Ross Creek / 27 • Cedar Lakes Loop / 31 • Baree and Bear Lakes / 34 • Moran Basin, St. Paul Peak / 36 • Leigh Lake / 38 • Three Lakes Peak / 41 • Hub Lake, Ward and Eagle Peaks / 43 • Illinois Peak / 45 • Bonanza Lake, Lost Creek / 47 • Blodgett Canyon / 49 • Overwhich Falls / 53 • Blue Joint / 55 • Stoney Lake, Dome Shaped Mountain / 57 • Legend and Spud Lakes / 59 • Welcome Creek / 61 • Stuart Peak, Twin Lakes / 64 • Rainbow Lake / 67 • Pioneer and High-up Lakes / 70 • Bobcat Lakes / 73 • Hollowtop Lake / 75 • Lake Louise / 77 • Trask Lakes / 79 • Humbug Spires / 81 • Murr Canyon / 83 • McDonald Peak / 85 • Summit Lake / 87 • St. Mary's Peaks / 89 • Morrell Falls / 91 • Crater Lake / 93 • Jewel Basin / 95 • Columbia Divide / 96 Logan Creek / 98 • Ousel Peak / 100 • Great Northern / 102 • Stanton Lake / 104 • Marion Lake / 107 • Nyack Loop / 109 • Akokola Lake / 112 • Pikamakan and Dawson Passes / 115 • Iceberg Lake / 118 Gateway Pass, Gateway Gorge / 120 • Our Lake / 124 • South Chinese Wall / 126 • Halfmoon Park / 129 • Gates of the Mountains / 131 • Red Mountain / 136 • Mount Helena Ridge / 138 • Crow Creek Falls / 140 • Manley Park / 143 • Elkhorn and Crow Peaks / 146 • Edith/Baldy Basin / 149 • Bear Trap Canyon / 151 • Spanish Peaks / 154 • The Helmet / 156 • Lizard Lakes / 160 • Hilgard Basin / 162 • Ramshorn Lake / 165 • Hyalite Lake / 167 • Emerald and Heather Lakes / 170 • Big Snowies Crest / 173 • Crazy Mountains / 176 • Cottonwood Lake / 181 • Middle Fork, Lost Fork of the Judith / 183 • Highwood Baldy / 187 • Bear Paw Baldy / 189 • Pine Creek Lakes / 191 • Elbow Lake, Mount Cowan / 192 • Lake Pinchot / 194 • Aero Lakes / 197 • Rock Island Lake / 200 • Tempest Mountain and Granite Peak / 202 • Sundance Pass / 206

Afterword

The Wilderness Challenge / 209

Appendix

Always check the checklist / 212 • Finding maps / 214

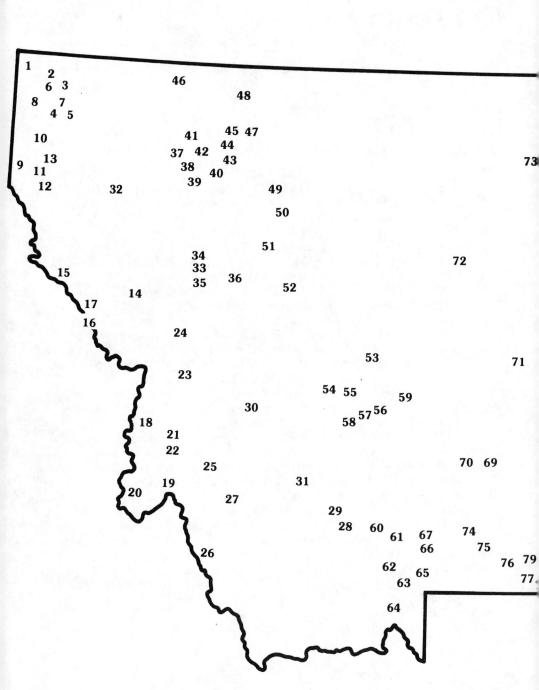

Hikes Throughout Montana

Use this map to generally locate hikes in your general vicinity. Then, use the detailed maps later in the book and other maps to find the trailhead.

68

0

Foreword

Hiking is for Everybody

Although we occasionally hear claims that only the young and rich elite use wilderness, quite the reverse is true. Families spent many pleasurable nights camping far from vehicles. And day hiking (or "walking for pleasure" as agencies sometimes call it) is undoubtedly one of the most popular forms of outdoor recreation.

The people who make such statements must do little, if any, hiking or they surely would see young, old, large, small, rich, and poor—all thoroughly enjoying the back country trails. Hiking and backpacking are available to all ages, sexes, and sizes. It only requires a small amount of physical conditioning (which everybody should have anyway) and a minimal amount of equipment.

That's right—a *minimal* investment. Hiking and backpacking *can* be expensive like any other sport *if* one chooses to make it so. On the other hand, it can be one of the most economical forms of outdoor recreation—especially with day hiking which requires nothing except a pair of hiking shoes that are probably already in the closet.

For overnight trips, more expense is required. But even this can be a small investment. The cost of one, two-week vacation, staying in motels and eating in restaurants, would be sufficient to outfit an entire family for backpacking. And this equipment can be used year after year. Once a small initial investment is made, hikers can see millions of acres of spectacular, roadless country without spending another penny on equipment. They only need a few dollars for food and for transportation to the trailhead. After the trailhead, it's free.

Not only is hiking free in the economic sense, but also free of the stress and regulation of modern America. Once on the trail, hikers can forget (albeit only temporarily) the tension of their work, the Internal Revenue Service, the unpaid bills, the noise and pollution—it's all behind them for a few hours or days. They can't even hear the bad news on the radio.

Hiking provides an escape—a chance to smell only natural odors, to hear the wind whistling through mature pines, a mountain stream whisper by or

1

Backpacking clowns. Bill Schneider photo.

the elk bugle, to hook a native trout instead of a hatchery-raised catchable, to see the sunset across a mountain lake or a mountain goat race across cliffs man would need climbing gear to negotiate, to drink from a gin-clear stream, and study vegetation that evolved without man's influence.

All this is here for the taking. Fortunately, Montana offers plenty of opportunity to do so.

Hikers can, of course, figure out their own trips by talking to local hikers or agency personnel and searching through topographic maps. But to make it easier, we published this guide. It contains enough hikes for a lifetime of back country thrills.

We've included hikes from almost every roadless portion of Montana. Although we have trails from the more famous areas such as Glacier National Park and the Bob Marshall and Mission Mountains wilderness areas, we've been careful not to forget the many splendid areas that haven't gained a national reputation—yet.

We've also included hikes for all kinds of hikers—beginners, families, experienced backpackers. In fact, most of the hikes are short, day hikes— usually well-suited for families or inexperienced hikers. Since we've picked hikes from throughout Montana, one of the trailheads is most likely only a short drive.

Also, we feel the *way* this guide was written makes it particularly valuable. Instead of relying on the experience of one or a small group of hikers, we've listed the favorite hikes of veteran Montana hikers—people who wish to share their experience with others, hoping that new users will appreciate and fight to preserve these areas. The topographic maps included with each hike add the final touch to the already detailed and accurate descriptions. With this guide, hikers shouldn't have any trouble discovering and enjoying wild Montana.

Happy hiking.—*Bill Schneider*

Introduction

In Montana, the potential for hiking seems almost endless. So any hiking guide can only include a small minority of the hundreds—perhaps thousands—of spectacular hikes. However, each of these hikes can be viewed as only an introduction to another hiking area; there are, of course, many more lakes, mountains, alpine basins and trails in the area to lure the hiker back the following summer.

The contributors to this guide have hiked these trails recently and recorded the directions in this book. But even more recent road or trail construction or natural phenomena could have changed something. This is why the a source of updated information accompanies each hike.

The maps are good reproductions of sections of USGS Quads and can provide many details to the course of the hike. In the book, the scale is always on the south side of the map—whether it lies horizontally or vertically on the page. Although you can probably get by without taking other maps in addition to those in the book, it would be better to do so. They will be especially helpful in identifying distant landmarks not included on the small maps in the book.

Unfortunately, there aren't topographic maps for every hike in the book, as some sections of Montana aren't covered by USGS Quadrangles. In these cases, the Forest Service map was used. Likewise, FS maps were used when a hike tranversed both 7.5 and 15 minute quads.

Touch The Land Lightly

Compare your favorite hiking area with your living room.

You don't mind visitors. Often, you invite them. But you want them to treat your home with respect.

If you have six obnoxious visitors who put their cigarettes out on the floor, spill drinks, and use foul language, your living room has, in your mind, exceeded its carrying capacity. And these visitors will leave lasting marks.

On the other hand, if you have a dozen quiet, polite, neat guests, the thought that your living room is being overused never enters your mind. And after they've gone home, there is no sign of their presence.

Using wilderness can follow the same theme. There is a large capacity as

3

long as everybody behaves. But a few thoughtless or uninformed hikers can ruin it for others. An important addition to the checklist on page 212 would be proper wilderness manners. Don't leave home without them.

Most hikers treat wilderness gently, but some aren't aware that they have poor manners. Often, their actions are dictated by outdated remnants of a past generation of wilderness campers who cut green boughs for evening shelters and beds, set up camp close to alpine lakes, built fire rings, dug trenches around tents, etc. Twenty years ago, these "camping rules" may have been okay. Today, they leave unacceptable, long-lasting scars. Such behavior can no longer be tolerated.

The wilderness is shrinking, and the number of hikers is mushrooming. In fact, use has increased by more than 300% in some western wilderness areas in past years. In some national parks, it has increased even more. Without question, some camping areas show unsightly signs of this craze.

Thus, a new code of ethics is growing out of necessity to cope with unending waves of hikers—all wanting a perfect wilderness experience. Indeed, they should have it and probably can have it *if* all hikers educate themselves on proper and courteous use of fragile country.

As a general rule, touch the land as lightly as possible. Canoeists can look behind them and see no sign of their passing. The next canoe party has no idea another canoe is around the next bend. It should be the same with hiking and backpacking. Leave only memories and good times behind.

Nowadays, nobody dares litter—in or out of the wilderness. This means everything, including orange peels, flip tops, cigarette butts, and gum wrappers. Leave nothing, regardless of how small it is, along the trail or at the campsite.

Try to camp below timberline. Alpine areas are delicate and require special care. Often, it's only a short hike to a good campsite below timberline.

Also, keep your camp off the shoreline or streambank. Take alternate routes to water to avoid leaving a beaten path.

Hikers seek solitude and silence, so avoid making loud noises that may disturb others. This is only common courtesy.

Be very careful with food wastes to prevent unsightly messes and bad odors. If fires are allowed, burn food wastes. Throw cans and foil into the fire to burn off food scraps and odors. Then before breaking camp, dig them out of the ashes and pack them out.

Likewise, burn fish viscera if fires are allowed. If fires aren't allowed, wrap fish viscera and leftover food in plastic bags and carry it out or at least to the next fire area. Never throw fish viscera into mountain streams and lakes.

Waste water from boiling foods should be poured around the perimeter of the fire to keep it from spreading. This also protects natural vegetation. Wash dishes and clothing well away from streams and lakes and carefully discard dish water, such as in a small sump hole that can be covered with soil later. Never wash dishes in a mountain stream or lake: a glob of instant oatmeal is almost as ugly as an aluminum can on the bottom of a crystal-clear lake or stream. If you use soap, make sure it's biodegradable.

As with food wastes, be careful with human wastes. If toilet paper is used, burn it or carry it out. Thoroughly bury human wastes to avoid any chance of bad odor. This is an excellent reason to carry a lightweight trowel. Obviously, wastes must be kept away from lakes and streams.

Perhaps fires cause more damage than any part of back country camping. In many areas, avoid fires completely. (Sometimes regulations prohibit fires.) This goes double for alpine areas where wood is scarce and aesthetic and topsoil is sparse.

If a fire is allowed and appropriate for the campsite, dig out the native vegetation and topsoil and set it aside. Don't build a fire ring with rocks. When breaking camp, douse the fire thoroughly, thoroughly scatter or bury the cold ashes, and replace the native soil and vegetation.

Another acceptable method is spreading several inches of mineral soil on a flat rock to avoid fire-scarring the rock. Later, scatter or bury the ashes and expose the rock—which should still look natural.

Build fires away from trees to prevent damage to root systems. Keep them small. And widely disperse any partly burned wood.

Don't make a mess tearing apart trees to get firewood. Don't use a saw or axe on a tree and leave a lasting scar. And never build a fire ring or light a fire near a reflector rock which will be permanently scarred.

Take a bath by jumping in water and then moving away from water to lather yourself. Rinse off by pouring cans of water over your body. This allows soap to biodegrade quickly as it filters through the soil. Of course, use only biodegradable soap.

Avoid cutting switchbacks. And leave "souvenirs" for the next hiker to see; don't carry them out.

Finally and perhaps most important, strictly follow the pack in-pack out rule. If you carry it in, you must consume it, burn it, or carry it out.

Make it a safe trip

Perhaps the best safety advice has guided scouts for many decades—be prepared. For starters, this means carrying survival and first aid equipment, compass, and topographic map—*and* knowing how to use them.

Perhaps the second best advice is to tell somebody where you're going and when you plan to return. Pilots must file flight plans before every trip, an excellent safety rule that can be used by hikers. File your plan with a friend or relative before taking off.

After those two points, safety advice can go on and on. There are probably other tips besides those listed here, but if hikers adhere to the following suggestions, they should have a safe trip.

- Watch the weather, being especially careful not to get caught on a ridge during a lightning storm or at high altitude by a snow storm.
- Be super careful with fires.
- Check the long-term forecast to avoid extended periods of cold, often snowy, weather.
- Don't hike at night.
- Never split up in the back country; always keep your party together.
- Avoid temptations to swim across cold, alpine lakes.
- Stay on the trail unless you are a very experienced hiker.

Survival kit

Compass, whistle, matches in waterproof container, candle, surgical tubing, emergency fishing gear, 60 feet of six-pound line, six hooks, six lead shot and six trout flies, safety pins, copper wire, signal mirror, fire starter, aluminum foil, water purification tablets, space blanket, and flare.

First aid kit

Sewing needle, snake bite kit, 12 aspirin, antibacterial ointment, two antiseptic swabs, two butterfly bandages, adhesive tape, four adhesive strips, four gauze pads, two triangular bandages, 12 codeine tablets, two inflatable splints, moleskin, one roll of three-inch gauze, and lightweight first aid instructions.

- Don't slide down snowbanks with cliffs or rocks at the bottom.
- Know the symptoms and treatment of hypothermia, the silent killer.
- Study basic survival and first aid before leaving home.
- Don't eat wild mushrooms or other plants in the back country unless you are positive of the identification.
- Find out as much as you can about the hike, especially any potential hazards, before you leave.
- Never hike alone.
- Don't wait until you're confused to open your topo map. Follow it as you go along, starting from the moment you start up the trail.
- Don't exhaust yourself or weaker members of your party by trying to travel too far, too fast.
- If you get lost, don't panic. Sit down and relax for a few minutes while you carefully check out the topo map and take readings with the compass. Confidently plan your next move. Thousands of hikers have spent unplanned nights in the woods and survived. A few—usually those who panicked and ran wildly around—didn't survive. If you've followed the rules and left your "flight plan" with somebody, they will be looking for you in the morning.
- If your hike calls for fording a large stream, take special precautions to cross safely. Remove your socks and put your boots back on. This makes for more secure footing on the slippery streambottom. Avoid the current's full force by keeping sideways to the flow. Slide—don't lift your feet one at a time, making sure that one foot is securely anchored before seeking a new hold with the next one. Go slowly and deliberately. Some hikers use a walking stick or branch for additional support.
- In general, don't take any chances while in the back country such as climbing cliffs, jumping over objects, challenging shaky tree "bridges" over streams, etc.
- Last, but definitely not least, stay clear of all wild animals, and this

Fording streams such as the Middle Fork of the Flathead—one backcountry hazard that requires extreme caution, especially when children are along. Bill Schneider photo.

goes triple for bears. In Montana, bears—particularly grizzly bears—present a hazard not faced by hikers in most other states. If hikers learn about bears and use proper backcountry etiquette, bear country can be very safe. (The following chapter, compiled from interviews with authorities on bears and reviews of most of the literature on the subject, contains the basic information necessary to make hiking in bear country as safe as possible.)

Hiking bear country

General. Be cautious and alert. Stay together. Never hike in bear country alone. Watch for bear sign and be extra careful when you find it. Leave your dog home. (Your pet may be "man's best friend" at home, but not in the wilderness where it could attract a grizzly.) Report all bear incidents to local authorities.[1]

Hiking. If you see a bear at a distance, make a wide detour on the upwind side so the bear can get your scent. If a detour isn't possible, slowly back down the trail until safely out-of-sight. Then, make lots of noise (the more, the better) and slowly and noisily make your way up the trail again. The bear should be gone when you get back to your earlier observation point. If the bear is still there and you can't safely get around him, abandon your trip.

Although it isn't a foolproof method, making noise while hiking helps avoid bears. Many hikers hang bells or a can of pebbles from their packs or belts. As a general rule, the noisier, the safer. Metallic noise seems more effective than human voices which can be muffled by natural conditions. Also, it's difficult to keep up steady conversation during long hikes.

Camping. Be careful and neat with food and garbage. Keep a clean camp. Don't camp in sites obviously frequented by bears. If you see a bear or fresh sign where you intend to camp, pick another campsite.

If possible, camp near tall trees that can be easily climbed. Sleep some distance from your campfire and cooking area. Keep food and garbage out-of-reach of bears at night (such as suspended between two trees) and away from your sleeping area. Keep food odors off clothes, tents, and sleeping bags. Avoid fresh, perishable, or "smelly" foods (i.e. bacon, lunch meat, sardines, etc.).

Burn combustible trash if regulations and natural conditions allow open fires. Burn cans and other incombustibles to remove odors. Then, dig them out of the ashes and pack them out. Never bury trash in the back country. If you can carry it in, you can carry it out.

Don't clean fish near camp. Burn fish entrails, if possible. Never leave them around camp. The smell of fish can attract bears. Camping at popular fishing sites requires extra caution.

Special precautions for women. Stay out of grizzly country during menstrual periods. Avoid using perfume, hair spray, deodorants, or other cosmetics. There is some evidence that bears are attracted and even infuriated by these scents.

The confrontation. Most important, try to remain calm. Never panic and run. You can't outrun a bear. And by rapid retreat, you may excite the bear into pursuit.

If the bear stands his ground and doesn't seem aggressive, stand still. If he continues the unaggressive behavior, back very slowly and quietly down the trail until out-of-sight.

If the bear looks aggressive, start looking for a tree to climb. If the bear moves toward you, get up it fast *if* you're sure you have enough time. Make sure it's tall enough to get you out-of-reach. Most such confrontations are with grizzly bears; only grizzly cubs can climb trees.

Before starting for the tree, drop something like a pack or a camera to distract the bear. Stay up the tree until you're positive the bear has left the area.

If you can't get up a tree, play dead. Curl up and clasp your hands over the back of your neck in the "cannonball" position. This takes courage, to say the least, but it's preferable to serious injury.

Physical resistance is, of course, useless.

---

[1]Keep in mind these are merely general rules. They're probably the best generalities anywhere, but as always, it's dangerous to generalize. Certainly, there is no concrete formula for avoiding confrontations or for what to do when you are confronted. Dr. Charles Jonkel, upon reviewing these rules, suggested trying to evaluate each individual situation based on these general rules. And by all means, Jonkel emphasized, "try to avoid an encounter."

Hypothermia

Be aware of the danger of hypothermia—subnormal temperature of the body. Lowering of internal temperature leads to mental and physical collapse.

Hypothermia is caused by exposure to cold, and it is aggravated by wetness, wind, and exhaustion. It is the number one killer of outdoor recreationists.

The first step is exposure and exhaustion. The moment you begin to lose heat faster than your body produces it, you are undergoing exposure. Two things happen:

• You voluntarily exercise to stay warm, and your body makes involuntary adjustments to preserve normal temperature in the vital organs. Both responses drain your energy reserves. The only way to stop the drain is to reduce the degree of exposure.

• The second step is hypothermia. If exposure continues until your energy reserves are exhausted, cold reaches the brain, depriving you of judgment and reasoning power. You will not be aware that this is happening. You will lose control of your hands. This is hypothermia. Your internal temperature is sliding downward. Without treatment, this slide leads to stupor, collapse, and death.

To defend against hypothermia stay dry. When clothes get wet, they lose about 90 percent of their insulating value. Wool loses less heat; cotton, down, and some synthetics lose more.

Choose rainclothes that cover the head, neck, body, and legs and provide good protection against wind-driven rain.

Understand cold. Most hypothermia cases develop in air temperatures between 30 and 50 degrees Fahrenheit.

If your party is exposed to wind, cold, and wet, think hypothermia. Watch yourself and others for these symptoms: Uncontrollable fits of shivering; vague, slow, slurred speech; memory lapses; incoherence; immobile, fumbling hands; frequent stumbling, lurching gait; drowsiness (to sleep is to die); apparent exhaustion; and inability to get up after a rest.

When a member of your party has hypothermia, he/she may deny any problem. Believe the symptoms, not the victim. Even mild symptoms demand treatment.

• Get the victim out of the wind and rain.

• Strip off all wet clothes.

• If the victim is only mildly impaired, give warm drinks. Get the person into warm clothes and a warm sleeping bag. Well-wrapped, warm (not hot) rocks or canteens will help.

• If victim is badly impaired, attempt to keep him/her awake. Put the victim in a sleeping bag with another person—both stripped. If you have a double bag, put the victim between two warm people.

• Build a fire to warm the camp.—*U.S. Forest Service*

The Hikes

1 Northwest Peak

General description: An easy, scenic uphill walk for almost anyone.

General location: Forty miles north of Libby in the northwest corner of the state, 3.5 miles from Idaho and 2.5 miles from Canada.

Maps: Northwest Peak USGS Quad and Kootenai National Forest, Yaak Ranger District.

Special attractions: An old lookout cabin on the peak, views of the Northwest Peak Scenic Area and on a clear day, the Canadian Rockies.

For more information: Write the District Ranger, Yaak Ranger District, Kootenai National Forest, Troy, MT 59935 or call (406) 295-4717.

Northwest Peak (elevation 7,705) is the central attraction of a high mountain ridge, the most striking portions of which are included in the Northwest Peak Scenic Area, an official designation of the Forest Service. Under this designation, the area's unique qualities are recognized and protected.

The area is seldom visited, simply because most people have never heard of it. Those that have hesitate to drive that far. But it's a great opportunity if you're in northwestern Montana with a half-day to kill.

The main access, Pete Creek Road #338, heads north off State Highway 508 two miles west of Yaak. After finding this paved road, drive 13 miles north and then turn left (west) onto the West Fork Road. After two miles, turn right onto the Winkum Creek Road. Climb seven miles on this road. At 6,100 feet, you'll find the trailhead on the left (south) side of the road at the edge of a clearcut.

There are streams farther up the road if you want fresh mountain water; there isn't any on the trail. This area usually has more than its share of snow, so wait until July to conquer Northwest Peak.

The trail follows a skid trail through the clearcut for about one-fourth mile before slipping into deep timber. The trail is marked with new signs, so it's easy to follow.

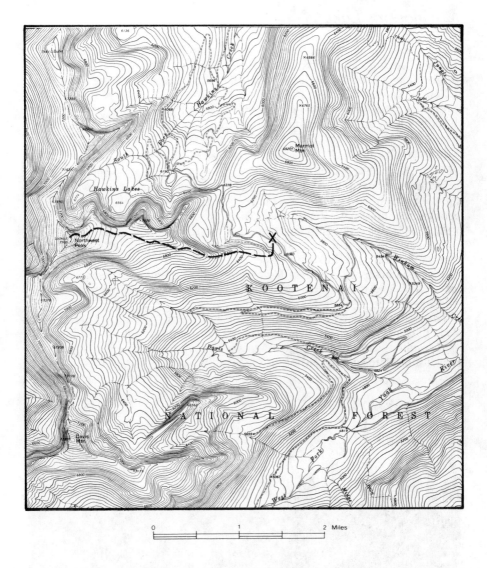

Northwest Peak

The trail climbs for two miles to the top of the peak, the last one-fourth mile consisting of open, talus rock. At the top is an old, unmanned lookout cabin, complete with rusty pans and other nostalgic artifacts. The terrain drops down to alpine lakes on three sides of the peak.

The ridgetop to the south invites hikers, if you have time. The views are extensive, with the Cabinet Mountains to the south and the Canadian Rockies far to the north.

It's an easy place to pass time without being in a hurry to do something or go elsewhere. —*Pat Caffrey*

11

2 Hoskins Lake

General description: An easy round trip to a mountain lake.

General location: Thirty-five miles north of Libby in the Purcell Mountains.

Maps: Bonnet top USGS Quad (somewhat outdated) and Kootenai National Forest, Yaak Ranger District.

Special attractions: A low-elevation, mountain lake with good fishing accessible by a short, well-maintained trail.

For more information: Write the District Ranger, Yaak Ranger District, Kootenai National Forest, Troy, MT 59935 or call (406) 295-4717.

Take the Pipe Creek Road north of Libby for about 33 miles until the road forks right to Vinal Lake. Take Vinal Lake Road #746 (which isn't shown on Bonnet Top USGS Quad) for about nine miles or until you're about three miles past Vinal Creek. Here, you will find Forest Service trail #162 to Hoskins Lake on the right side of the road.

Vigorous hikers will have a hard time calling this a "hike," as it's less than a half-mile to Hoskins Lake. However, for small children or less experienced hikers, it's perfect for an enjoyable day hike or "camp out." It takes only five minutes to reach the lake if you don't stop to smell the wildflowers.

The well-maintained trail has plenty of water along the way. There are no steep hills or hazards, and bear danger is almost nonexistent.

Mosquitoes can take the edge off this hike in the early summer, so it's best to wait until late summer or fall to see Hoskins Lake.

Hoskins Lake in the proposed Mount Henry Wilderness. Tom Hurlock photo.

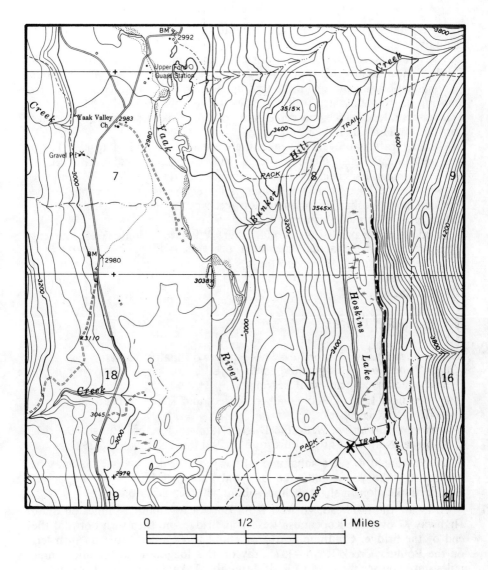

0   1/2   1 Miles

Hoskins Lake

There are actually two lakes—a large lower lake with nice-sized cutthroat trout and a small, marshy upper lake. Because of the good fishing, the lower lake is more heavily used, but not overused, mostly by local hikers. However, the upper lake offers an excellent opportunity to be alone with the wilderness.

A representative western larch forest, with some very large trees, surrounds the lakes. Deer and moose are frequently seen. Grouse are common, and a lucky hiker might spot an osprey or common loon near the lower lake. Some of the more common wildflowers include wake robin, shooting star, wild rose, Pacific trillium, queencup beadlily, and rock clematis.

A few hikers continue north past the lakes and go down Bunker Hill Creek. Simply follow this trail past the upper lake and stay with it for about one mile until it junctures with the trail up Bunker Hill Creek. Then, turn left, ignoring the unmaintained trail that goes to the right up Bunker Hill Creek. This makes a loop, since you come back to Vinal Lake Road about 1.5 miles north of the Hoskins Lake trailhead.

Although rarely an overnight hike, there are several good campsites. There is a developed Forest Service site at the lower end of Hoskins Lake. However, most backpackers prefer camping at the wooded FS campsite halfway up the lake where the fishing is better. You can also camp at the foot of Upper Hoskins Lake about 100 feet west of the trail. This spot gets little use, as it isn't a FS campsite.

Hoskins Lake is part of the Mount Henry Wilderness Study Area. Current management for the actual lake area prevents roading and logging and motorized recreation. However, the FS plans to log the hillsides east and west of Hoskins Lake, starting about 300 feet above the lake. —*Linda and Tom Hurlock*

3   Boulder Lakes

General description: A short, easy hike into two subalpine lakes.
General location: Thirty miles north of Libby or seven miles west of the
 bridge across Koocanusa Reservoir.
Maps: Boulder Lakes USGS Quad (outdated) and Kootenai National Forest,
 Rexford Ranger District.
For more information: Write the District Ranger, Rexford Ranger District,
 Kootenai National Forest, Eureka, MT 59917 or call (406) 296-2539.

If you wanted to see a subalpine lake without vehicle access, this may be the easiest hike you could take. It's only about 1.5 miles to the Lower Boulder Lake along a slight incline—about 440 feet elevation gain.

To locate the trailhead, go west from Eureka for about 14 miles on State Highway 37 over the Koocanusa Reservoir Bridge and then turn north at the end of the bridge. Continue north for about three miles until you turn left on the Boulder Creek Road #337. Stay on this logging road for about nine miles until you see the road to Red Mountain. Take the left fork here and go about two miles past this junction and turn right on the small road one-half mile past a sharp switchback. Follow this road for 1.5 miles until it ends and trail #91 takes off to the right. (If you find yourself driving on the level for miles, you've missed the last road junction, as the road levels off after the turn-off to Boulder Lakes).

The trail is well-maintained and after one-fourth mile stays in the woods all the way. Just before the lake, this trail forks. Go left, as the right-hand trail continues to Purcell Marsh. (This last junction isn't shown on the Kootenai National Forest map.)

Bring drinking water; it can be very dry until you reach the lower lake.

The feeling of remoteness can be found on this hike, but not until after

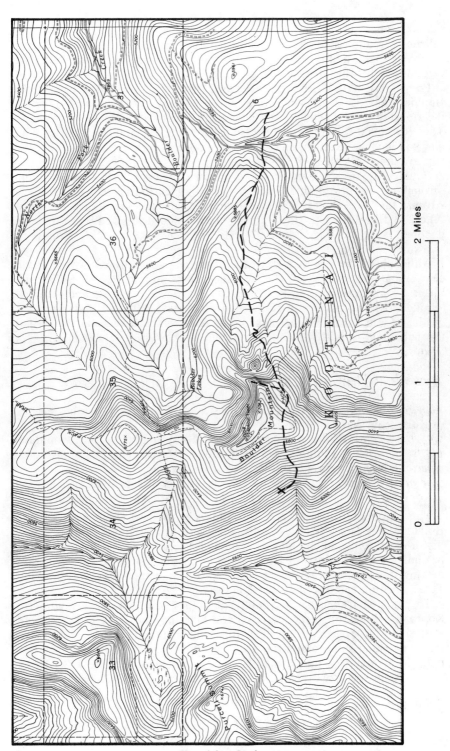

Boulder Lakes

the first one-fourth mile which goes through a clearcut. Also motorized vehciles are allowed on this trail throughout the year. The threat of bear trouble is slight, and mosquitoes aren't a significant problem. Midsummer is a good time for this hike.

For experienced hikers, there is an interesting side trip. From Lower Boulder Lake backtrack about one-fourth mile and take the trail #91 west to the ridgetop at the head of Basin Creek which is about a 500-foot climb. Then, drop 900 feet to Purcell Marsh. Here, you will find few signs of man, and you have an excellent chance to see moose. It's an extra five-mile round trip to Purcell Marsh from Boulder Lakes.

Boulder Lakes country hosts the same diversity of wildlife found throughout northwestern Montana—deer, black bear, moose, elk, etc. Around the lakes, hikers will find beargrass, glacier lillies and a variety of other wildflowers. On the Purcell Marsh side trip, you can find the uncommon alpine bog kalmia. Lower Boulder Lake has fair fishing for pan-sized cutthroat.

Although this is usually a day hike, there is an established Forest Service campsite at the lower lake. A few backpackers stay at Purcell Marsh, but this is a primitive campsite. Both sites have sufficient firewood and water.

Like Hoskins Lake (page 12), Boulder Lakes and Purcell Marsh are part of the Mount Henry Wilderness Study Area which may soon have roads throughout it—unless, of course, enough people object. —*Linda and Tom Hurlock*

4   West Branch of the South Fork of Big Creek

General description: An easy, day hike perfectly suited for families because of the scant elevation gain.
General location: Fifteen miles north of Libby in the Purcell Mountains.
Maps: Banfield Mountain USGS Quad and Kootenai National Forest.
Special attractions: Easy hike that very few hikers use.
For more information: Write the District Ranger, Rexford Ranger Station, Kootenai National Forest, Eureka, MT 59917 or call (406) 296-2539.

Most Montana hikes have at least one steep hill to climb and the West Branch of Big Creek is no exception. The hill, however, is a short one, only half-a-block long and climbing only about 75 feet. Moreover, it's at the very beginning while you're still fresh. After that, the trail winds along a slow-moving mountain stream which is frequently interrupted by beaver dams. Total elevation gain is only about 250 feet.

To find the trailhead, go about eight miles south of the bridge across Koocanusa Reservoir (near Rexford) and take the Big Creek Road from the west side of the reservoir. Follow this logging road west for about seven miles, swinging south along the South Fork of Big Creek for another eight miles to a three-way junction half-a-mile south of tiny Horse Lakes. Take the left-hand road past the marsh and continue for another four miles to the end of the road. (The last three miles are quite rough.) The trail takes off at the end of the road.

The trail can be reached more directly from Libby by following the Pipe Creek Road 15-20 miles north from Libby to the junction a mile past the

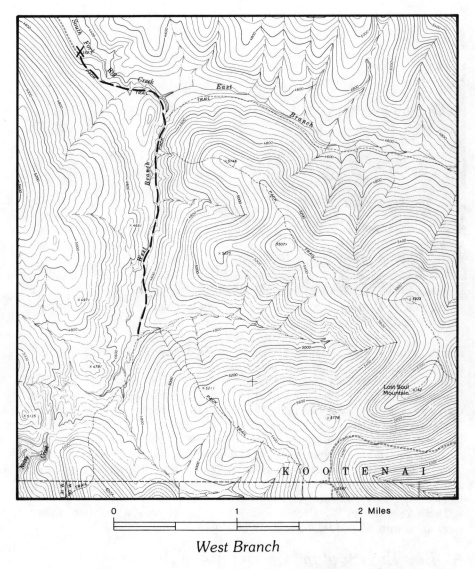

West Branch

Pipe Creek campground. Take the right-hand fork up the East Branch of Pipe Creek for about six miles to a "T"-junction. Turn right and go another mile and turn on the South Fork Big Creek Road at the three-way junction by Horse Lakes, and continue to the right past the marsh and four miles to the end of the road where the trail begins.

After winding along the stream for about three miles, the trail is no longer maintained. By not going past the third trail junction (southeastern corner of section 28), you can avoid the unmaintained portion of this hike.

Late summer and fall are best for this hike. Earlier in the season, the trail

The South Fork of Big Creek in the Kootenai National Forest. Tom Hurlock photo.

can be quite wet and boggy. And mosquitoes can make the early summer hike unpleasant.

Since the hike is only six miles round trip, it's nicely suited for families. However, very few hikers use this trail. Even with frequent stops to watch the beavers, a slow hiker can make this trip in four hours.

Motorized vehicles aren't allowed on this trail from April 1 through November 30. The area seems remote, with the signs of man disappearing once you're 100 yards from the road. Fishing is fair for smaller cutthroat.

Few hikers make this an overnight backpack. But if you're so inclined, camp at the juncture of the East Branch and West Branch of Big Creek. It has lovely, grassy campsites and a few good fishing pools.

The hike traverses Big Creek/Gold Hill Roadless Area where two timber sales are proposed. —*Linda and Tom Hurlock*

5 East Branch of the South Fork of Big Creek

General description: A moderate, day hike into a seldomly used and ecologically unusual area.

General location: Fifteen miles northeast of Libby in the Purcell Mountains. Mountains.

Maps: Ural and Banfield Mountain USGS Quads and Kootenai National Forest, Rexford Ranger District.

Special attractions: A very moist site—unusual for Montana.

For more information: Write the District Ranger, Rexford Ranger Station,

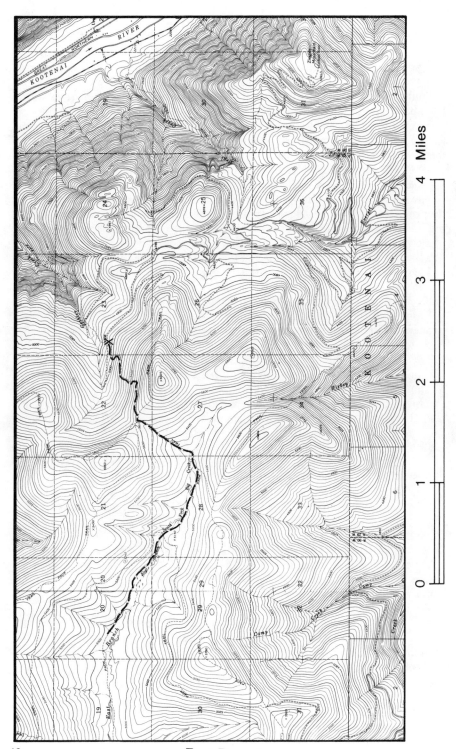

19

East Branch

Miles

0 1 2 3 4

Kootenai National Forest, Eureka, MT 59917 or call (406) 296-2539.

This hike is similar to the West Branch of Big Creek (page 16), except for one addition common to most Montana hikers—a big hill. This hike is still easy, but it has one 700-foot ridge to climb.

Find the trailhead by driving east from Libby to Libby Dam, then north for about 12 miles along the west shore of Koocanusa Reservoir until you turn left (west) on the Bristow Creek Road. Follow the Bristow Creek Road for about two miles until you see Road #4874. Take this road north along the west side of Everett Creek. Go about six miles, crossing Ural Creek, to Trail #70 heading up Geibler Creek in the west side of section 23. The trail is marked with red "blazes."

The trail starts at about 4,900 feet and goes over a 5,600-foot ridge before dropping down to 5,300 where it starts leveling off and turns west to follow the north side of the East Branch. Big Meadow, perhaps the scenic highlight of this hike, lies at 5,000 feet, about two miles past the ridgetop. From here on, the trail crosses a number of small streams and meadows.

There is a clearcut about one-fourth mile from the trailhead. But you can see where the trail takes off from the right edge of the clearcut, about halfway up, by following the painted red arrows.

From that point, the only sounds are nature's own. Like the West Branch of Big Creek, very few hikers use this trail—even though it's just right for families and beginners.

This is an eight-mile round trip that usually takes about five hours. Water is available along the trail, so there's no need to carry your own.

The trail is adequately maintained, but can be very boggy in the early summer—bad enough to make waterproof boots necessary. Mosquitoes are also abundant during early summer, so most hikers wait until late summer or fall for this hike. Motorized vehicles are banned from April 1 through November 30.

Although black bears are common in the area, bear/hiker conflicts are almost unknown. The area also has a large moose population as well as beaver, muskrat, barred owl, deer, mink, pine martin, spruce grouse, ruffed grouse, and many smaller birds. It's excellent for observing wet-site wild flowers like trillium and false hellebore. Also expect to see beargrass and Canada dogwood.

Most hikers take only one day to make this trip, but it can be an overnight backpack. The best campsite is in the northwestern corner of section 28 where an unmaintained trail crosses the East Branch trail. Firewood and water are plentiful, and the campsite is dry. However, fishing is marginal, as is the case throughout this hike.

An interesting side trip leaves the main trail at the junction on the ridgetop. Follow the side trail less than a mile to the northeast corner of section 27 and go through the openings shown on the Ural USGS Quad sheet to a 6,025-foot knob. From this high point, hikers get a scenic perspective of the entire area, including the Cabinet Mountains on the east horizon.

Perhaps the top attraction of this hike, however, is the gentle valley with meandering stream and wet meadows, the last such site remaining unroaded in the Kootenai area of northwestern Montana. On top of that, it's easily accessible to hikers.

The Forest Service has logging plans for the area around the trailhead, so check with the Rexford Ranger District for a status report before taking this hike. —*Linda and Tom Hurlock*

6 Fish Lakes Canyon

General description: One of the easiest and most scenic 12-mile hikes in Montana.

General location: Thirty air miles north of Libby on the east side of the Yaak River.

Maps: Lost Horse Mountain, Mount Henry, and Yaak USGS Quads and Kootenai National Forest, Yaak Ranger District.

Special attractions: A 50-foot waterfall and a chain of five lakes in a rugged, low-elevation canyon.

For more information: Write the District Ranger, Yaak Ranger District, Kootenai National Forest, Troy, MT 59935 or call (406) 295-4717.

To some, Fish Lakes is an overnight camp out. To others, it's a full day's hike. But to every hiker, it's one of the most scenic and diverse trips they've ever taken.

To find the trailhead, take the Pipe Creek Road north from Libby. Follow it for about 31 miles until you turn right on Vinal Lake Road #746. Vinal Creek trail #9 takes off to the east about six miles up this road. (This trail isn't shown on the Lost Horse Mountain USGS Quad.)

The trail is well-maintained, has plenty of drinking water, and gets rocky

The southernmost lake in a chain of lakes in the Fish Lakes Canyon, part of the proposed Mount Henry Wilderness. Tom Hurlock photo.

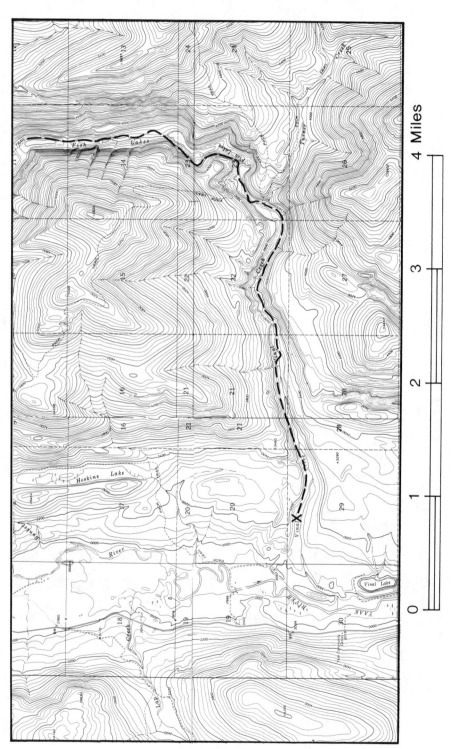

Fish Lakes

only along a few talus slopes. Elevation gain is a mere 600 feet to the northernmost lake.

It takes an average hiker 12 hours to make the complete round trip. However, if you only want to see South Fish Lake, the first in the series of five, the trip should take eight hours. This makes the Fish Lakes Canyon suitable for almost any hiker—families with children to veteran backpackers.

Forest Service regulations prohibit morotized vehciles from May 1 through October 31. The area is quite remote—except at the north end of the canyon where a few signs of man (i.e. clearcuts in the distance) are barely visible.

Wildlife and wildflowers abound and are characteristic of northwestern Montana—moose, deer, black bear, wakerrobin, Canada dogwood, clematis—to name a few. Wild roses line Vinal Creek in great abundance.

Bear danger is low, but mosquitoes can be vicious in June and July. Take this hike anytime during the summer or fall.

For overnighters, there is an undeveloped campsite at Turner Falls, about 3.5 miles into the hike at the mouth of the canyon. It's so close to the falls that the roar of the crescendoing water dominates everything. It has firewood and dry spots to pitch tents.

There is a similar campsite at the foot of South Fish Lake, the second and largest of the chain. This has a great view and good fishing.

South Fish Lake perhaps has the best fishing in the canyon—with nice-sized cutthroat and rainbow. However, you can also fish Vinal Creek for cutthroat, rainbow, and eastern brook trout, Middle Fish Lake for pan-sized cutthroat and North Fish Lake for smaller cutthroat.

Perhaps the most outstanding feature of the hike is Turner Falls. But even without the falls, this would be one of the most beautiful hikes in Montana. Here are five mountain lakes strung through a narrow, rugged canyon lined with a quiet forest of large cedar and larch trees.

Equally remarkable, however, is the fact that this area possibly won't be set aside from development even though it's part of the Mount Henry Wilderness Study Area. Like many other roadless areas in the Kooteani National Forest, timber cutters want to keep this forested valley "from going to waste." Perhaps a letter from hikers explaining the value of such a place in its natural state might mean a better future for Fish Lakes Canyon. —*Linda and Tom Hurlock*

7 *Parsnip Creek*

General description: A very short, easy hike.
General location: Twenty miles northeast of Libby in the Purcell Mountains, halfway between Libby and Eureka.
Maps: Inch Mountain USGS Quad and Kootenai National Forest, Rexford Ranger District and Libby Ranger District.
Special attractions: Fine example of old-growth cedar woods just off the beaten path.
For more information: Write the District Ranger, Libby Ranger District, Kootenai National Forest, Route 2, Box 275, Libby, MT 59923 or call (406) 293-7741.

Parsnip Creek could be described as something besides a hike. Perhaps it would be more appropriately called a good place for a walk in the woods. Actually, it would be perfect for a weary traveler to take a short stroll to calm the nerves.

To find the trailhead, drive east from Libby on State Highway 37 and turn north and go about 20 miles up the west side of Koocanusa Reservoir. Watch carefully for a turn up Parsnip Creek. This road, which turns southwest, isn't shown on the maps. It leaves the highway about one-fourth mile north of trail #70.

Follow the Parsnip Creek Road until it ends. The trail takes off on the lower side of the road right where it ends.

Although back from the stream slightly, the trail follows Parsnip Creek for about one-half mile, then it climbs steeply uphill. Hikers usually stroll up the trail to the point where it turns uphill enjoying wildlife and wildflowers, then return. Even with the slow pace, the round trip takes only an hour.

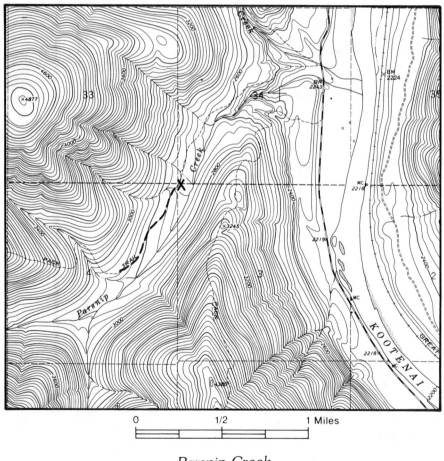

0   1/2   1 Miles

Parsnip Creek

There is virtually no elevation gain. Bear trouble is slight. Mosquitoes aren't a problem. And water is available all along the trail.

Very few hikers camp out on this trail, but a few have stayed at a fair campsite at the end of the road.

Parsnip Creek is part of the Big Creek/Gold Hill Roadless area which the Forest Service hopes to log in 1983. —*Linda and Tom Hurlock*

8   Roderick Mountain

General description: A strenuous day hike.

General location: Twenty miles north of Troy.

Maps: Sylvanite USGS Quad and Kootenai National Forest, Troy Ranger District.

Special attractions: Eye-opening scenery from the top of one of northwestern Montana's tallest peaks.

For more information: Write the District Ranger, Troy Ranger District, Kootenai National Forest, Troy, MT 59935 or call (406) 295-4693.

To find the trailhead, drive west of Troy on U.S. 2 for about 12 miles

Black bear, common in most Montana mountain ranges. Harry Engels photo.

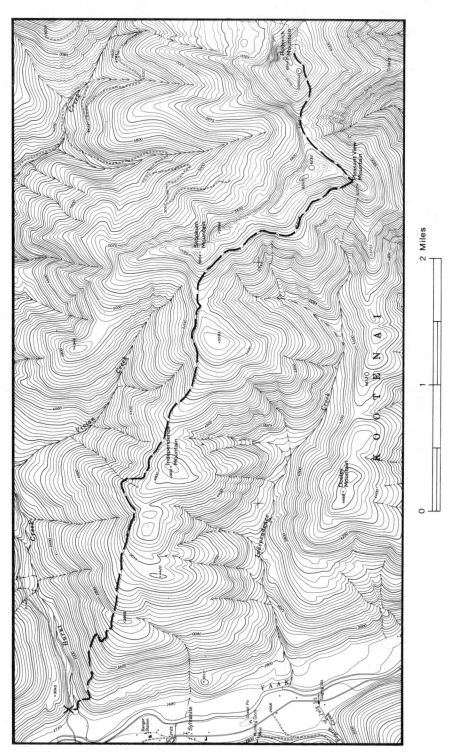

0   1   2 Miles

Roderick Mountain

until you turn right on the paved Yaak River Road. After ten miles, watch for the Sylvanite Ranger Station in a clearing on your right. Go less than one mile past the ranger station and turn right on the Burnt Creek Road #472. The Roderick Mountain trailhead (trail #193) is on your right less than one-half mile up the Burnt Creek Road.

A word of caution: The Forest Service is rapidly developing the timber in this area, so new roads are continually under construction. If there is any confusion on the location of the trailhead caused by new road construction, drive back to the Sylvanite Ranger Station and ask for updated instructions.

The trail is somewhat rocky and faint in spots, but still easy to follow. Although the trail cuts through deep timber most of the way, there are plenty of open parks with expansive vistas.

It's a gradual uphill pull all the way, going from 2,720 to 6,644 feet in seven miles. The first two miles are the toughest.

Although there are a few springs and intermittent streams, this is essentially a dry, 14-mile round trip. Bring plenty of drinking water.

Snow usually leaves the area by mid-July. So anytime in late summer or fall is right for climbing Roderick Mountain.

Actually, you climb three mountains on this hike. At about the four-mile mark, you traverse the western slope of 5,954-foot Skookum Mountain, and a mile later, the trail goes almost to the summit of 6,107-foot Pleasant View Mountain. Although impressive, these two peaks are belittled by Roderick Mountain.

Although few hikers make this an overnighter, you can camp at the base of Roderick Mountain. There are a few springs here, but you are still smart to bring your own water instead of depending on these springs.

From the top of Roderick, you can look north into the very remote country of Sheepherder, Flattail, and Papoose drainages which are trailless and support a struggling population of grizzlies. This takes the keen edge off a wonderful hike since much of this country has been allocated for timber development. —*Mike Comola*

9 *Pellick Ridge, Ross Creek*

General description: A day or overnight hike for experienced hikers, or if two cars are used, a rugged two or three-day, point-to-point hike.

General location: Thirty-five miles southwest of Libby in the West Cabinet Mountains (Scotchman Peaks).

Maps: Smeads Bench, Heron, and Sawtooth USGS Quads and Kootenai National Forest, Cabinet Ranger District.

For more information: Write the District Ranger, Cabinet Ranger District, Kootenai National Forest, Box 97, Trout Creek, MT 59874 or call (406) 847-2432.

Hikers who don't mind rugged, dry walking and appreciate wild scenery and solitude should like this trip. Pellick Ridge is the pristine, southeastern spur of the Scotchman Peaks and forms the scenic western backdrop to the Bull River Valley.

A Forest Service trail follows its crest for ten miles to an abandoned

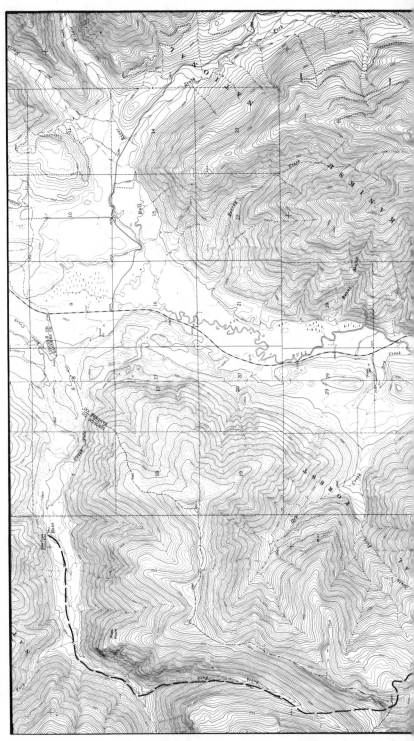

Pellick Ridge

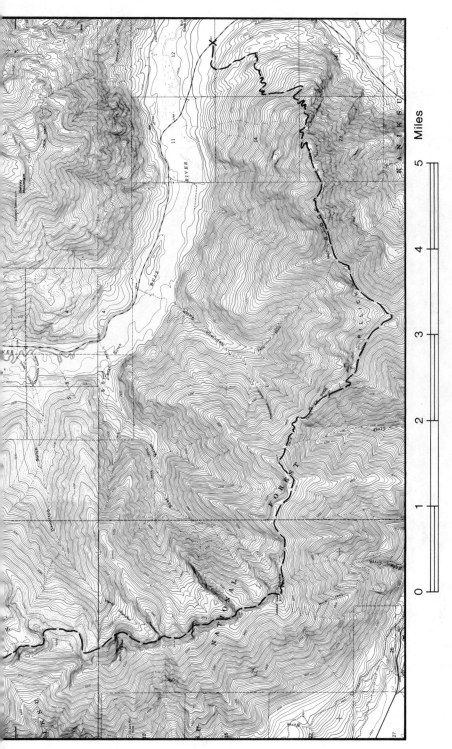

Miles

0   1   2   3   4   5

lookout on Squaw Peak. Views of the Cabinet Mountains, the Bull and Clark Fork Valleys, and Lake Pend O'reille in Idaho are superb.

The hiker stands a good chance of seeing deer, elk, bear, bighorn sheep, and mountain goat. In addition, the southern slopes of the ridge have an abundance of dry-site wildflowers.

To get to the Pellick Ridge trailhead, take State Highway 200 about 40 miles west from Thompson Falls, through Trout Creek, to the junction with Highway 56. Follow Highway 56 (marked Highway 202 on older maps)

Bull elk still in velvet. Harry Engels photo.

north for nine miles to the signed trailhead on the west (left) side of the road.

The six-hour walk (twelve miles) to Squaw Peak gains 3,000 feet. Take plenty of water, particularly if you're camping. There are sub-alpine basins below the northeast side of the ridge that have water and possible campsites. However, once off the ridge, the terrain becomes very steep and brushy, so don't expect easy going or an abundance of level camping spots.

You can return to your car from Squaw Peak on the same route, or walk to a second car by way of the Napoleon (#1035) or Star Gulch (#1016) trails, both of which drop down into the Bull River Valley. Napoleon Creek trail takes off to the right two miles before Squaw Peak, as Star Creek does three-fourths of a mile before the mountain. The trailheads join up with Highway 56, 13 and 14 miles north of State Highway 200 respectively.

However, by far the best one-way trip entails leaving a second car at the Ross Creek Cedars Scenic Area, 15 miles north on Highway 56 from the Pellick Ridge trailhead, and four miles west on the well-marked Forest Service road.

Leaving a car at Ross Creek enables an experienced hiker to strike off north from Squaw Peak for six, trailless, ridgetop miles to Sawtooth Mountain. Although the going is very rugged, the viewing is excellent and solitude assured. Be on the alert for elk and mountain goats or even one of the few grizzlies still in this area. Scramble up Sawtooth Mountain for a panorama of the heavily glaciated upper Ross Creek drainage.

Passing around Sawtooth Mountain from the right brings the hiker to the South Fork of Ross Creek. Another option is to wind around Sawtooth Peak and drop into the Middle Fork of Ross Creek. Follow either of these forks downstream for approximately six miles to the Ross Creek Cedars and your car. Only the last four miles will be on a trail; dropping down to the valley floor requires some difficult bushwhacking.

The very wild Ross Creek drainage contains some of the most beautiful forests in the state. However, this hike is strictly for woods-wise hikers with topo maps and compass.

Although the Pellick Ridge and Lower Ross Creek area had broad support in the Forest Service's wilderness review process, the Forest Service has dropped most of those areas from the proposed 84,000-acre Scotchman Peaks Wilderness. Ross Creek and Pellick Ridge offer high quality wilderness recreation and are important to the integrity of the Scotchman Peaks area. Unfortunately, it is now possible that Pellick Ridge and Lower Ross Creek will be developed. The American Smelting and Refining Company (ASARCO), for example, has begun exploratory drilling at Ross Point in the South Fork of Ross Creek that provides year-round mountain goat habitat.—*John Westenberg*

10   *Cedar Lakes Loop*

General description: A long day or overnight loop for experienced hikers.
General location: Ten miles southwest of Libby.
Maps: Scenery Mountain USGS Quad and the Cabinet Mountains Wilderness
  Map.

Cedar Lakes in the Kootenai National Forest. U.S. Forest Service photo.

Special attractions: On clear days, spectacular views of the Cabinets, Glacier National Park, Canadian Rockies, Selkirk Mountains in Idaho, the Purcell Mountains, Scotchman Peaks, and Kootenai Falls 4,000 feet below.

For more information: Write the District Ranger, Libby Ranger District, Kootenai National Forest, Route 2, Box 275, Libby, Montana 59923 or call (406) 293-7741.

For those interested in a fairly demanding hike that can provide many scenic rewards, this trip is ideal.

From Libby, take U.S. 2 west for four miles to the Cedar Creek Road. Turn left (south) onto this road and follow it about six miles until it ends at the trailhead.

The 16-mile hike requires a 4,300-feet gain in elevation and most of the walking is on waterless ridgetops. It begins with an easy one-mile walk up the Cedar Creek Trail (closed to motorcycles) to its junction with the Scenery Mountain Trail. Take this well-maintained trail north, then west for approximately five dry, uphill miles to Scenery Mountain. The views get more spectacular as you go, and an open forest of large ponderosa pine further improves the scenery. Most of the trail is on a ridgetop with cool breezes and few insect pests.

The view from Scenery Mountain is superb, particularly when looking down on the jade-colored Kootenai River. Kootenai Falls, the largest remaining falls in Montana, and the China Rapids Area upstream can be seen 4,000 feet below. Kootenai Falls is the site of a proposed hydro-electric facility which would divert most of the water from the falls, through underground turbines and would back water three miles covering the China Rapids.

From Scenery Mountain continue west on an unmaintained trail that generally follows the ridgetop for three miles to Grambauer Mountain.

Here, the view expands to include Lake Creek and Lower Kootenai Valleys and the Scotchman Peaks. From Grambauer Peak, head south along the main Cabinet Divide. After a mile of ridge walking, veer slightly to the left, leaving the ridgetop. Bushwhack until intercepting either Lower Cedar Lake or the trail leading to it. Along the way, stop to fill up in some of Montana's largest huckleberry patches.

Both Cedar Lakes have campsites, but avoid those suffering from abuse and overuse—except perhaps to clean them up.

The loop is closed by following the Cedar Creek Trail through a beautiful forest back to the trailhead. Less experienced hikers can make this a 12-mile

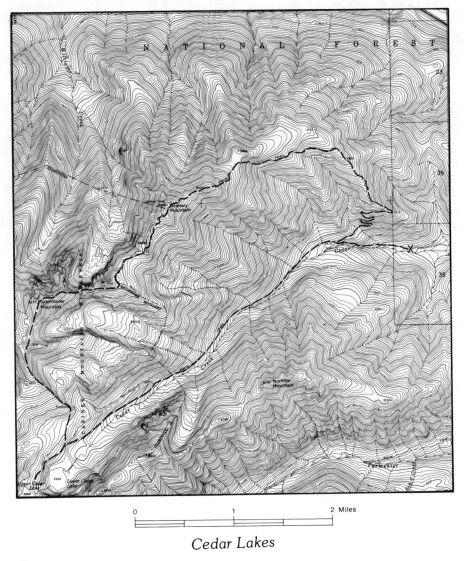

0   1   2 Miles

Cedar Lakes

round trip by retracing their steps back to the trailhead from Scenery Mountain.

Grizzlies are present in the Cabinets, but sighted less frequently at this northern end of the range. Black bear and many more wild animals are common, however.

Clear weather adds to the enjoyment of this hike. Late August and September is the best time. The bugs are mostly gone, and the shorter, often rainy, days of late fall haven't begun.

The entire trail to Scenery Mountain lies outside the Cabinet Mountains Wilderness, and the Forest Service has refused to study it as a possible addition to the wilderness. —*John Westenberg*

11 Baree and Bear Lakes

General description: A long day hike or leisurely, three-day backpack.
General location: Thirty miles south of Libby in the Cabinet Mountains.
Maps: Goat Peak and Silver Butte Pass USGS Quads and the Kootenai National Forest's Cabinet Mountain Wilderness Map.
For more information: Write the District Ranger, Cabinet Ranger District, Kootenai National Forest, Box 97, Trout Creek, MT 59874 or call (406) 847-2432.

Hikers who like to avoid retracing their steps, but dislike the difficult, two-car logistics that most one-way hikes involve should like the Baree, Bear Lakes hike. The trailheads to the two lakes are less than a mile apart, and the lakes are connected by a trail along the top of the Cabinet Divide.

A quick study of the Cabinet Wilderness Map shows that there are a number of short hikes in the Cabinets. This hike has the advantage of being among the least traveled routes. Also, these trails are generally open a couple of weeks earlier (late June) than most of the Cabinets.

From Kalispell, take U.S. 2 west for 65 miles to the East Fisher River Road. Turn left (south) and proceed up the road for six miles until it forks. Take the right fork, the Silver Butte/Fisher River Road. The Baree Lake trailhead is approximately ten miles up the road.

Trail #489 to Baree Lake goes through a lush forest within earshot of Baree Creek most of the way. The three-mile hike to Baree gains 1,700 feet in elevation.

Baree Lake has fair cutthroat fishing and two abandoned cabins on its shores. Camp at the upper end of the lake.

After Baree Lake, the trail makes an easy climb to the Cabinet Divide, then follows trail #560 along the divide to the north. The viewing from the ridge is excellent, particularly to the west and northwest into Swamp Creek, Wanless and Buck lakes, and the peaks surrounding them. Although grizzlies are uncommon along the Cabinet Divide, making noise along the trail provides extra security.

After a mile of ridgeline hiking, trail #63 to Bear Lakes splits to the right (east). This trail runs just below the top of a spur ridge off the Cabinet Divide. A five-minute detour to the top of the ridge affords a nice view of the upper Trail Creek Basin. Stay on the ridgetop until it intersects the trail a mile to the east where it crosses the ridge and drops down into the Bear Lakes.

Only one of the Bear Lakes (the largest and northernmost) has fish. It has one good campsite.

Trail #531 back to the Silver Butte Road cuts east across the outlet of the southernmost Bear Lake, then generally southeast through forested country. After reaching the powerline corridor that runs parallel to the Silver butte Road, follow it southwest for three-fourths mile to the Baree Lake trailhead and your vehicle.

Most of the trail after Bear Lake, much of the Baree Lake trail, and two

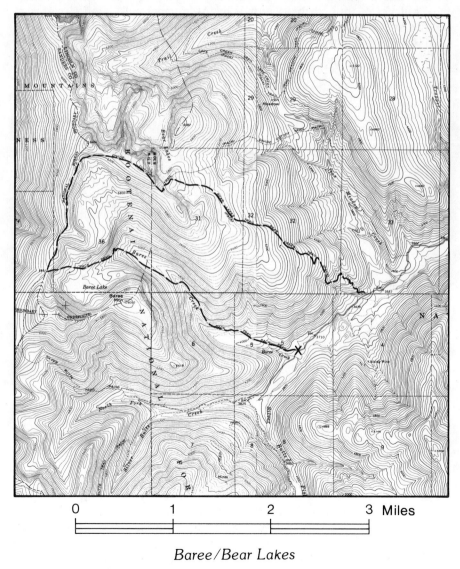

Baree/Bear Lakes

of the three Bear Lakes lie on Burlington Northern land. The Kootenai National Forest land use plan for the upper Fisher River Country recognized that this and other adjacent private land is important to the integrity of the Cabinet Mountains Wilderness and should be bought or traded for public land in other areas. So far, no steps towards acquisition have been made.

The Trail Creek and Iron Meadows areas to the north and east of Bear Lakes offer interesting variations on the Baree, Bear Lakes hike. This variation requires leaving a car at the Trail Creek trailhead, seven miles up the West Fisher River Road. Rather than returning to the Silver Butte Road from Bear Lake, take the Iron Meadow Trail. This takes the hiker through some of the Kooteani Forest's best elk country. From Iron Meadows, take the Trail Creek trail to the waiting car. Although small, Trail Creek is a productive cutthroat stream.

Like the Bear Lakes area, much of the Trail Creek area is owned by Burlington Northern. BN has announced plans to begin logging in this area in the near future, and the Kootenai National Forest plans to log parts of the Trail Creek drainage. Contact the Kootenai National Forest for an update on logging activities, and express your opinion on how they could affect backcountry recreation in the area.—*John Westenberg*

12   *Moran Basin, St. Paul Peak*

General description: An easy day or overnight hike that offers a fairly easy mountain climb as an option.

General location: Twenty-five miles southwest of Libby in the Cabinet Mountains Wilderness.

Maps: Elephant Peak USGS Quad and the Kootenai National Forest Cabinet Mountain Wilderness Map.

For more information: Write the District Ranger, Cabinet Ranger District, Kootenai National Forest, Box 97, Trout Creek, MT 59874 or call (406) 847-2432.

To find the trailhead, take State Highway 200 40 miles west from Thompson Falls to its junction with State Highway 56, known locally as the Bull River Highway (or Highway 202 on older highway maps). Follow State Highway 56 north for about eight miles and turn onto the East Fork Bull River Road. One-and-a-half miles later take the right fork in the road, which crosses the East Fork of the Bull River; this road climbs through heavily logged areas (watch for logging trucks) for nine miles to the trailhead.

The well-maintained trail is only two miles long, but gains 1,700 feet before topping out on the ridge that shelters Moran Lakes. The trail is dry, forested, with occasional small openings. Don't forget to bring drinking water.

Oddly, the area isn't heavily used. Upper Moran Lake has a campsite with plenty of small cutthroats for supper and enough wood for a good fire.

Motorized vehciles aren't allowed on the trail, and all other signs of man disappear upon dropping into the basin.

Black bear are plentiful in the area, and the Cabinet Mountains still hold a

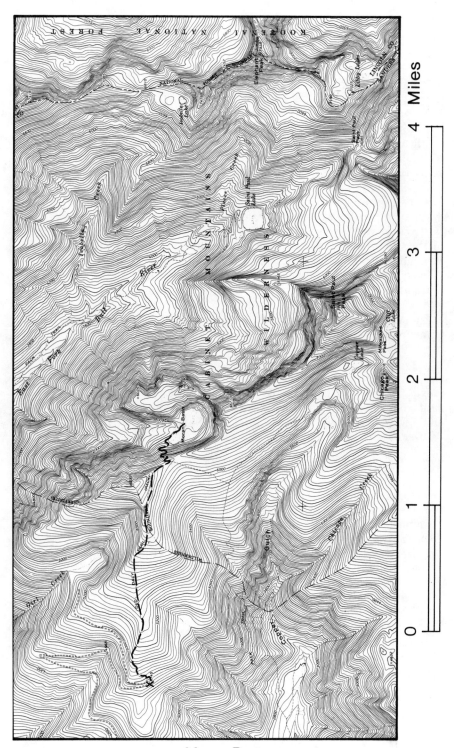

Moran Basin

few grizzlies. However, if bear country common sense is used, the likelihood of trouble is very slight.

Don't forget your mosquito repellent. Moran Basin has its share of these pesky insects.

Families with small children should camp overnight at the lake if they plan to walk up St. Paul Peak, southeast of the lake.

To climb the peak from the lake, retrace the trail that drops into the basin back to the ridge overlooking the lake. Then, follow the ridge southeast for 2.5 miles moderately steep miles to the summit. There is no maintained trail, but the ridge is open, easy walking. Watch for mountain goats on the peak. For amateur botanists, St. Paul Peak has perhaps the best selection of mid-summer, alpine flowers on the Kootenai National Forest—over 60 species identified there.

From St. Paul Peak, hikers can see signs of development in the Clark Fork Valley to the southwest, and some clearcuts to the north. But the views of the Cabinets to the northwest and south, and the Bull River Valley and Scotchman Peaks to the west overshadow these distractions.

Early fall is best for this hike. The larch are turning yellow, and most mosquitoes have died. Northwestern Montana often enjoys pleasant fall weather.

The Cabinet Mountains contain many lakes and peaks that could be termed more beautiful than Upper Moran Lake and St. Paul. However, this trip offers a nice combination of solitude, easy access, and appetite wheting scenery that make a beginning hiker more curious about the rest of the Cabinets, one of Montana's lesser known and most threatened mountain ranges. The major threat to the surrounding area comes from a variety of hard rock mining proposals. If you're interested in the progress of this mining activity, check with the Kootenai National Forest in Libby. —*John Westenberg*

13 Leigh Lake

General description: A fairly rigorous, three-mile round trip for beginners.
Maps: Snowshoe Peak USGS Quad and Kootenai National Forest's Cabinet Wilderness Map.
General location: Twelve miles south of Libby.
Special attractions: A large, deep mountain lake nestled on the east flank of Snowshoe Peak.
For more information: Write the District Ranger, Cabinet Ranger District, Kootenai National Forest, Box 97, Trout Creek, MT 59874 or call (406) 847-2432.

The Cabinet Wilderness is small in size but large in diversity. It contains high peaks, glaciers, rain forests, and numerous lakes. Leigh Lake is the largest lake, nearly a mile across.

Take the Big Cherry Creek turnoff on U.S. 2 about seven miles south of Libby. After three miles, turn right and go seven miles on the Leigh Creek Road to the trailhead at the end of the road. Trail #132 climbs about 3,000 feet in 1.5 miles and ends at the 5,144-foot elevation lake.

At the west end of the lake is a massive, 3,000-foot wall, the high point being 8,712-feet Snowshoe Peak, the highest peak in the Cabinet Range and the highest peak between Glacier National Park and the Cascades.

Hikers can climb this peak from the lake, but it takes most of the day. From the outlet of the lake, head northwest straight up the face of a large east ridge. Once on the ridgetop, follow it southwest to the main ridge, being

Waterfall on the way to Leigh Lake in the Cabinet Mountains Wilderness. U.S. Forest Service photo.

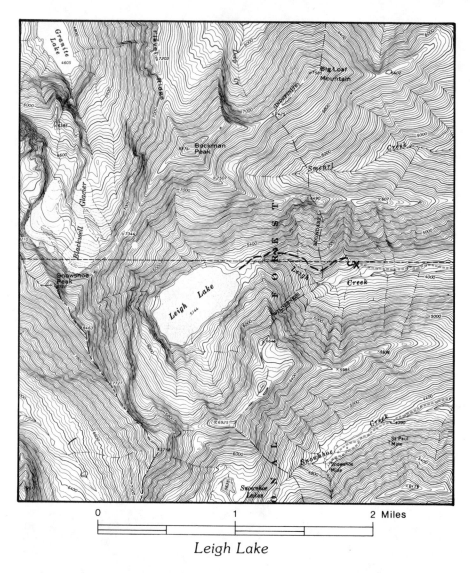

Leigh Lake

careful to notice Blackwell Glacier to your right and also being careful not to fall in that direction. After intersecting the main ridge, work your way up along the west side of this ridge until it levels out at the peak. Don't venture out on the snowfields on the east side of the main ridge unless you're properly trained and equipped for ice work.

Leigh Lake is good fishing. The trout (good-sized rainbows and brookies) are under ice most of the year and get particularly excited over fresh bait. If you're a hardy soul, you can pack a small rubber raft for use on the lake.

This area records phenomenal amounts of snow (20-30 feet). In July, the lake is still full of icebergs. The waves lap them into strange designs, and paddling around them, looking down and seeing the odd shapes down in the deep blue water gives one an errie feeling. Some ice floes are quite large, and one can land (wearing a life vest, of course) and fish from them.

The lake is well within the Cabinet Mountains Wilderness but easy to reach. This makes it popular locally, so hit this one on a weekday if you're seeking solitude. —*Pat Caffrey*

14 *Three Lakes Peak*

General Description: A fairly demanding one-day climb.
General location: Thirty-five miles northwest of Missoula on the Reservation Divide.
Maps: Perma and Tarkio USGS Quads and Lolo National Forest Recreation map. (Note: The quad maps are somewhat outdated and do not show the road to the trailhead. Also, recent Lolo National Forest Recreation Maps fail to show the trail.)
Special attractions: Pleasant hike along a subalpine ridge, with great views of much of Western Montana.
For more information: Write the District Ranger, Ninemile Ranger District, Lolo National Forest, Huson, MT 59846 or call (406) 832-4464.

Squaw Peak, the highest peak on Reservation Divide and a well-known landmark for Missoula residents, is easily and frequently climbed. Three Lakes Peak, a dozen miles northwest of Squaw provides a slightly more demanding, but more interesting, hike.

To find the trailhead, take I-90 west from Missoula to the Nine-mile exit; follow the county road north to the Nine-mile Ranger Station. Turn left at the ranger station and follow the road that heads up the Nine-mile valley. Go 13 miles before crossing a cattle guard and entering the Lolo National Forest. One mile after entering the National Forest, the road forks. Take the right fork, (north) toward the Reservation Divide. Follow this road for five miles to the trailhead.

The trailhead to Three Lakes Peak is not marked, nor is the trail shown on any Forest Service maps. The trailhead is located at the west end of a clearcut on the north side of the road. The trail begins as a winding logging road skirting the edge of the clearcut. The logging road soon becomes a trail and climbs up to the Reservation Divide by the way of the Burnt Fork Pinnacle, the former site of a lookout tower. Some stretches of trail between the trailhead and Burnt Fork Pinnacle show signs of erosion from trailbike abuse.

Soon after Burnt Fork Pinnacle, the trail intersects the Reservation Divide pack trail. Turn right (east) onto this trail. Here, the trail is usually above timberline and offers excellent views of the Nine-mile Valley, Nine-mile Divide, and the higher portion of the Hoodoo roadless area on the Montana/Idaho border to the southwest.

Continue east for 2.5 miles until directly below the south summit of Three Lakes Peak. Scramble up the talus slope to the south summit, then on to the higher summit.

From the summit of Three Lakes Peak you can see the Cabinet Mountains to the northwest, the National Bison Range and Flathead Lake to the north,

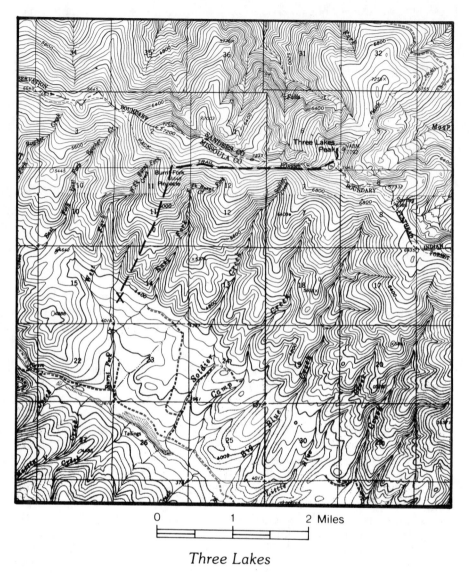

0   1   2 Miles

Three Lakes

the Mission Mountains to the east, and the Bitterroots to the south. Below the summit to the east is a picturesque glacier cirque with, appropriately, three lakes. East along the Reservation Divide is conical-shaped Squaw Peak.

The 10-mile round trip to the peak and back takes a full day. And it's dry, so take plenty of water. Wait until July for the snow to melt and allow this climb.

There are a number of enjoyable hikes along the Reservation Divide. The Three Lakes Peak hike is a good introduction to an area that is rarely used and quite wild.

Oddly, it isn't wild enough to warrent serious wilderness study by the Forest Service. Thus, the future of this *de facto* wilderness is uncertain.

The proposed Northern Tier Pipeline may go through the foothills of the Reservation Divide. Although the exact route has not been established, Lolo National Forest officials have expressed their concern. Call the Lolo Forest office in Missoula for an update on the pipeline and wilderness study situation. —*John Westenberg*

15 *Hub Lake, Ward and Eagle Peaks*

General description: An excellent day or overnight family trip, with a number of short day trips from Hub Lake.

General location: Seventy miles northwest of Missoula in the Bitterroot Mountains.

Maps: Haugan USGS Quad and Lolo National Forest Recreation Map.

Special attractions: Beautiful sub-alpine country on a scale small enough to be easily enjoyed by families with small children.

For more information: Write the District Ranger, Superior Ranger District, Lolo National Forest, Box 457, Superior, MT 59872 or call (406) 822-4233.

The Ward and Eagle Peak area is a "pocket wilderness" that, in spite of its small size, holds many scenic and recreational attractions.

It can be reached by taking I-90 west from Missoula for 57 miles to St. Regis. About eight miles past St. Regis, turn south (left) onto the Ward Creek Road. Follow the Ward Creek Road for about eight miles, until it crosses Ward Creek. The trailhead is on the right side of the road just before it crosses the creek.

The three-mile trail to Hub Lake follows Ward Creek much of the way so don't worry about carrying drinking water. Soon after the trailhead, it enters a beautiful, fern-bottomed, cedar grove with some cedars over six feet across at the base. Soon after leaving the grove, the trail overlooks Dipper Falls, a pleasant spot for a break.

The next mile of walking is steep, consuming most of the 1,500 foot altitude gain in hiking to Hub Lake. Here, the main diversion is picking huckleberries. About 2.5 miles from the trailhead, the trail passes Hazel Lake, which has pan-sized cutthroat, but its shore is too steep and brushy for camping.

Hub Lake is only a half-mile beyond Hazel Lake, not 1.5 miles as indicated on the Forest Service sign at the trailhead. Take this hike anytime after June.

There are two campsites at Hub Lake. The one near the outlet is brushy, but generally dry. The remains of an old prospector's cabin, now almost hidden in brush, lie between the trail and the campsite and an abandoned mine overlooks the upper end of the lake. When dry, the meadows at the upper end of the lake offer good camping. Both campsites have plenty of firewood.

Although Hub Lake only offers fair fishing for cutthroat, it does lie in a picturesque subalpine setting. Hub Lake is also a good jumping-off spot for day hikes to Ward or Eagle peaks (both are within the capabilities of children) or fishing trips to Clear (rainbow), Gold (rainbow) Square (brook),

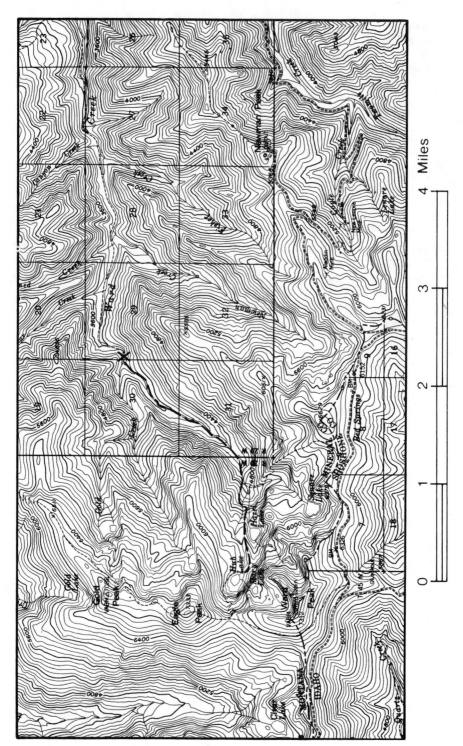

Hub Lake

4 Miles

0   1   2   3   4

and Hazel (cutthroat) lakes. You won't catch anything large, but you will probably add fish to your camp fare. You'll want the Haugan USGS Quad for the cross country hiking needed to reach some of these lakes. Mary Lake, in the cirque below Ward Peak, has no fish, but is a pleasant stop enroute to Ward Peak.

Most of the western Montana's big game species are found in this area, and the alert hiker has a chance of seeing them. Although grizzlies are gone from the Bitterroots, a good population of black bear remains.

The Lolo National Forest has not banned motorcycles from the trail to Hub Lake. However, there is little sign of cycle use and, except for the clearcuts that can be seen from the peaks, there is no significant sign of man. The abandoned mining ruins gradually being reclaimed by nature contribute to the sense of being in the backcountry.

The Ward-Eagle Peak area offers small doses of most of the medicines that give Montana's mountains their healing power—beautiful forests, waterfalls, wildlife, berries, interesting history, and fishing. And they are accessible to all hikers. —*John Westenberg*

16 *Illinois Peak*

General description: An easy day hike.
General location: Forty-five miles west of Missoula in the Bitterroot Mountains.
Maps: Illinois Peak USGS Quad and Lolo National Forest.
Special attraction: A grassy mountaintop with an excellent view of the northern Bitterroot Mountains.
For more information: Write the District Ranger, Superior Ranger District, Lolo National Forest, Superior, MT 59872 or call (406) 822-4233.

Perhaps because the higher portions of the Bitterroot Mountains north of the Lolo Pass aren't visible from a major highway, they remain relatively unknown. On a map they are easily overlooked and underrated; none of the peaks reach 8,000 feet.

Because they're among the westernmost of the mountain ranges in Montana, they receive an abundance of rain and snow. The result is an abundance of alpine scenery at lower elevations than most mountain ranges. At 7,690 feet, Illinois Peak is one of the highest peaks in the northern Bitterroots. The walk to the top goes through pleasant sub-alpine country and offers lots of scenic views, as does the peak itself.

From Missoula, take I-90 west to Superior. After taking the Superior exit, turn left and go under the freeway, then turn left again onto the gravel road on the far side of the underpass. About 1.5 miles down the country road, the Cedar Creek Road takes off into the foothills to the right. Follow this winding road for 20 miles to the Bitterroot (or Stateline) Divide, which is clearly marked.

The trail to Illinois Peak takes off to the left. It, and the pass, are dry, so stock up on water at one of the creeks you'll cross while driving to the trailhead.

The trail is faint in places, but by sticking close to the divide, you'll be sure to find it again. It's about five miles from the trailhead and Illinois Peak—making this a ten-mile round trip.

The Mission and southern Bitterroot Mountains and vast roadless areas in the Idaho Panhandle are frequently in view. Illinois Peak, 1,200 feet higher than the trailhead, offers a good view of much of the proposed Hoodoo Wilderness to the southeast. Illinois Peak's grassy top is a good place to sit back and enjoy lunch.

On this hike, the wind keeps the hiker cool, and the bugs down. This is a good hike from mid-July to mid-October.

The only fly-in-the-ointment is the motorcycle use of the trail. They have

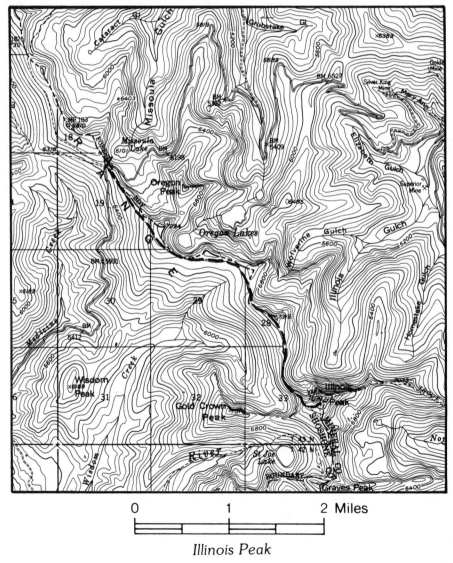

0   1   2 Miles

Illinois Peak

begun to tear up some of the sub-alpine vegetation on the trail traverses. Contact the Lolo National Forest in Missoula, if you're interested in protecting this trail from the noise and erosion. —*John Westenberg*

17 Bonanza Lake, Lost Creek

General description: An easy, overnight or day round trip or if two vehicles are used, a mostly downhill point-to-point hike.

General location: Fifty miles west of Missoula in the Bitterroot Mountains.

Maps: Illinois Peak USGS Quad (outdated on roads and trails) and the Lolo National Forest Recreation Map (important because of the new roads on the way to the trailhead).

Special attractions: An abundance of easily accessible sub-alpine country.

For more information: Write the District Ranger, Superior Ranger District, Lolo National Forest, Box 457, Superior, MT 59872 or call (406) 822-4233.

Most Montanans think of the spectacular eastern front of the Selway-Bitterroot Wilderness when the Bitterroot Mountains are mentioned. However, from Lolo Pass north to Lookout Pass lies a section of the Bitterroots with a slightly different, but equally appealing, character. Although the northern Bitterroots are less craggy than their southern counterparts, they are heavily dotted with lakes. There are over 40 fishable lakes on the Montana side of the Bitterroot Divide, most within an easy walk from a trailhead. Because of the fire which swept through much of the area in 1910, these mountains feature a more open, easily traversable terrain.

The Bonanza Lake trailhead begins where the Cedar Creek Road crosses the Bitterroot (or Stateline) Divide. To get there from Missoula, take I-90 west of Superior. Exit at Superior, and turn left to go under the freeway. Take another left just beyond the underpass onto the paved county road. After 1.5 miles, turn right onto the Cedar Creek Road. Follow it for 20 winding miles to the clearly marked divide and trailhead.

At the trailhead, you have two options. One is to take the signed trail taking off just to the left (Idaho) side of the divide. It quickly splits with the left fork dropping down into Idaho. Take the right fork, which follows a contour along the Idaho side of the ridge.

The trail forks again 1.5 miles beyond the trailhead. Again, take the right fork back across the divide into Montana and through a grassy basin for about one mile to Bonanza Lakes.

The other option to the trailhead is to follow the jeep road that straddles the crest of the divide. The jeep trail soon disappears, and you follow the trailless but open ridge—with good views both ways—until you intersect the trail mentioned in the first option 1.75 miles later. Follow it to the right down into the basin holding Bonanza Lakes.

Both routes are about two miles and have a small elevation loss from trailhead to the lakes, so they are suited for hikers of all ages and ability. Bring drinking water, as both routes are dry.

A pleasant, open campsite with plenty of firewood is located between the two lakes, slightly closer to the larger, upper lake. Both lakes contain small brookies.

By far the best, but more demanding, trip to Bonanza Lakes requires

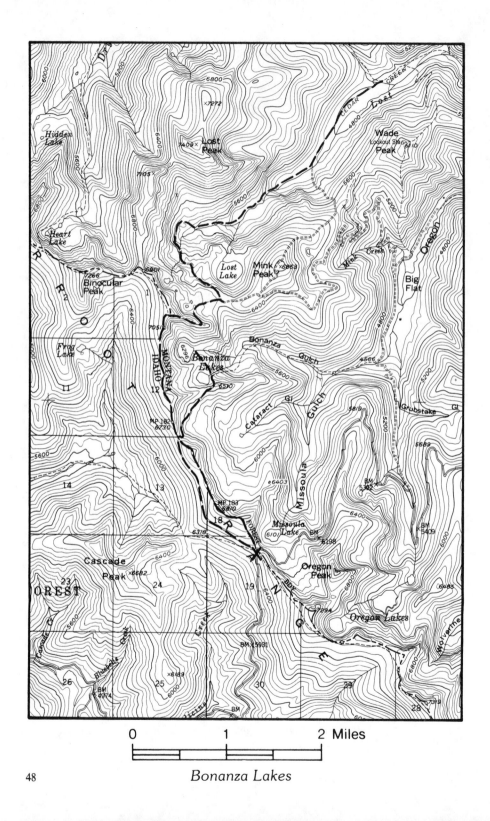

Bonanza Lakes

leaving a second car at the trailhead near Lost Creek Meadows. This trailhead is reached by turning right onto the Oregon Gulch Road about six miles up the Cedar Creek Road and following it eight miles to the marked Lost Creek trailhead on the left side of the road.

Leaving a car at Lost Creek makes it possible to leave Bonanza Lakes by way of the seldom-traveled Lost Creek area. From Bonanza Lakes, return to the divide. Instead of turning southeast (left) back to the stateline trailhead, turn northwest (right) and continue along the crest of the divide. About 1.5 miles later, the trail forks, the right fork going to the Lost Creek area.

The trail follows an open, east-west ridge that looks down on Bonanza Lakes. It soon drops down into the upper Lost Creek Basin, crossing an open sub-alpine flat before intercepting an old jeep road. Turn left on the jeep road and begin the gradual descent into Lost Creek.

Lost Lake soon comes into view on the right. If you have an extra day, there are a couple of campsites between the trail and the lake. Like the Bonanza Lakes, Lost Lake contains pan-sized brookies.

At this point you have come about three miles from Bonanza Lakes and you're four miles from the Lost Creek trailhead. As you continue down into Lost Creek, the old jeep road becomes almost overgrown with alder. Later, it becomes an indistinct foot path that is difficult to follow without the help of the occasional ribbon that has been tied to trees and brush. The country remains quite open, however, so the indistinct trail doesn't present insurmountable problems.

The trail totally disappears about a quarter-mile beyond the end of the old jeep road. Drop straight down the hillside to Lost Creek where you'll soon pick up the ribbon-marked path on the northeast bank of Lost Creek.

Much of the trail from this point on goes through active and abandoned beaver meadows. Although the meadows are spongy in the early summer, that's the best time for spotting the elk, deer, and bear that frequent them. After paralleling Lost Creek for a mile the trail leaves the stream to get around Lost Creek Falls. Upon dropping back down to the valley floor, take the short one-quarter mile spur trail leading back to the falls. From this point, it's only one mile to the Lost Creek trailhead.

The trails in this part of the Bitterroots, particularly in this area, are poorly signed and maintained and the maps are outdated. Fortunately, the area is open enough that close attention to the landscape, topo map, and Forest Service map makes this hike accessible to average hikers.

The Bonanza Lakes/Lost Creek area was rejected for wilderness consideration by the Forest Service, so it's future will probably be decided in the Lolo National Forest's land use planning process. Contact the Lolo National Forest in Missoula to express your interest in the area, and get an update on the planning process. —*John Westenberg*

18 *Blodgett Canyon* ⭒

General description: An easy day or overnight hike.
General location: Five miles northwest of Hamilton in the Bitterroot Mountains.

Maps: Printz Ridge USGS Quad and Bitterroot National Forest's Recreation Map.

For more information: Write the District Ranger, Stevensville Ranger District, Bitterroot National Forest, Stevensville, MT 59870 or call (406) 777-5461.

There is a tendency to think of a hike as something that's done to get somewhere. In Blodgett Canyon, no object is necessary beyond the hike itself. Just a few hundred yards from the car, the hiker is walking along a beautiful stream and looking up at spectacular canyon walls.

These basic scenic ingredients continue throughout the hike. Because there is no need to get to any particular point and there are ample campsites along the way, a hike up Blodgett Canyon is ideal for families and anyone who enjoys unhurried walking with lots of pleasant stops.

To get to Blodgett Canyon trailhead, take U.S. 93 south from Missoula up the Bitterroot Valley. Turn west (right) onto the county road two miles north of Hamilton just before U.S. 93 crosses the Bitterroot River. Follow this road west for .5 mile, south for 1.75 miles, then west again for the last two miles to the trailhead.

Blodgett Canyon is the most spectacular of the many canyons penetrating the east front of the Selway-Bitterroot Wilderness. The vertical relief from the canyon bottom to ridgetops is about 5,000 feet. Blodgett Creek itself, like all of the streams in the Bitterroots, is very clear and cold. It also has good fishing for pan-sized rainbows. The trail, which is never steep for extended

Blodgett Canyon in the Bitterroot National Forest. U.S. Forest Service photo.

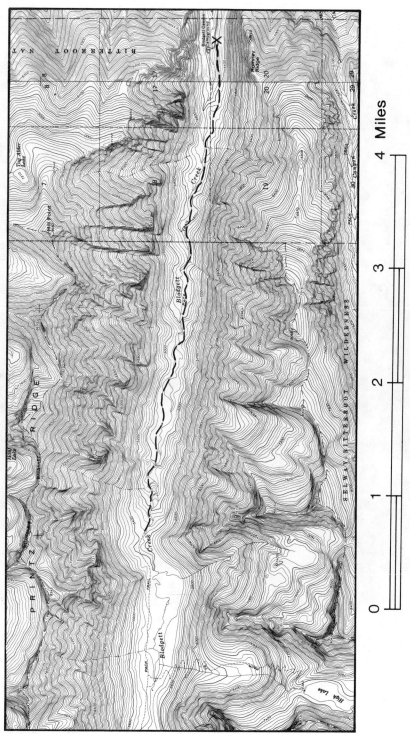

Blodgett Canyon

Scenic delights along Blodgett Creek in the Bitterroot Mountains. U.S. Forest Service photo.

periods, generally goes through pleasant forest environment, sometimes crosses talus slopes and is always close to Blodgett Creek. (So don't worry about drinking water). Sheer granite faces of 500-600 feet are common on the north side of the canyon, and there are several waterfalls between three and six miles into the hike.

Because it stays low, this trail is open earlier than many hikes. Chances of seeing wildlife increase farther up the canyon. Moose, elk, and deer are found in Blodgett, and mountain goats range the ridgetops. Hikers willing to tackle the steep, 1,400 foot climb up to High Lake, on the south rim of the canyon, have a good chance of seeing mountain goats.

Although you can hike a full 20 miles up the canyon, most hikers take shorter day or overnight hikes into the area. Go until you feel like stopping and either pick a campsite (all with plenty of firewood) or turn back to the trailhead.

Though surrounded by the Selway-Bitterroot Wilderness, Blodgett Canyon is not part of it. When the Selway-Bitterroot Wilderness was set aside in 1939, Blodgett Canyon was excluded because it was considered a possible site for a dam and reservoir for Bitterroot Valley water users. Although the Forest Service has recommended Blodgett Canyon for wilderness, there has been some local opposition to the proposal. Contact the Bitterroot National Forest for an update on the issue. —*John Westenberg*

19 *Overwhich Falls*

General description: A moderate, two-day backpack.

General location: Eight miles southwest of Sula or about 80 miles south of Missoula.

Maps: Medicine Hot Springs and Piquett Mountain USGS Quads and Bitterroot National Forest, Sula Ranger District.

For more information: Write the District Ranger, Sula Ranger District. Bitterroot National Forest, Sula, MT 59871 or call (406) 821-3201.

Drive south of Missoula on U.S. 93 and keep going until you're 13 miles past Sula at the Lost Trail Ski Area. From the ski area's parking lot, take the Saddle Mountain Road (signed) and follow it about four miles to where it ends and the trail begins. The Saddle Mountain Road is rough and rocky, so expect a bumpy ride.

Leave a vehicle or have somebody pick you up at the Crazy Creek Campground, 22 miles north by road. To find this campground, drive 4.8 miles north of Sula on U.S. 93 to Warm Springs Road #370. Turn southwest at the Moosehead Museum and follow Road #370 for 4.5 miles to Crazy Creek Campground.

This 15-mile, point-to-point hike has a very unusual characteristic—a loss in elevation. The trail goes from 8400 feet to 4880 feet, a 3520-foot loss.

From the trailhead, take Trail #605 to the junction with Trail #83 at Colter Creek. Take #83 to Overwhich Falls. Then, turn north on Trail #103 and stay on it all the way to Crazy Creek Campground. There are several trail junctions along the way, so keep your map handy. Most junctions are well-marked.

All these trails are well-maintained except for a small relocation just before Overwhich Falls on #605 and a few brushy spots on #103. Although not abundant, drinking water is usually available. Trail #605 has two good springs, and Trail #83 follows Shields Creek. Trail #103 follows streams most of the way, but since the lower portions are grazed with domestic cattle, you should treat water before drinking.

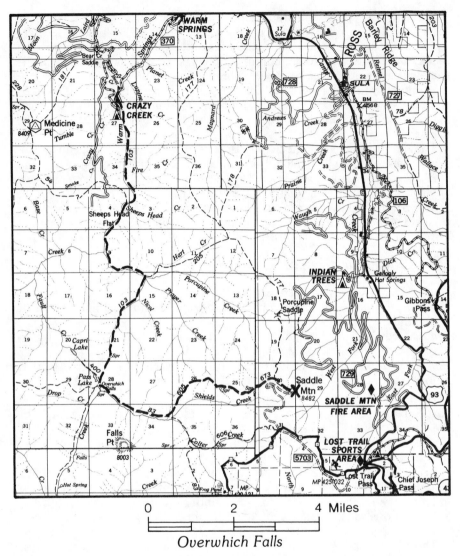

Overwhich Falls

Since there isn't a steep climb—as is the case with most long hikes—the Overwhich Falls trip is suitable for all hikers. Most hikers are interested in a leisurely hike and take at least two days, but ambitious hikers could hike this in one day.

All three trails are open to motorcycle use, and cattle graze the Warm Springs area during summer months. With these exceptions, the signs of civilization are rare. Wait until July for the snow to make the Saddle Mountain Road passable.

The highlight of the trip is, of course, 200-foot Overwhich Falls which can be viewed from the trail. For a closer look, drop your pack and bushwhack a short way to the creek below the falls.

Just past the falls, you can take a short side trip up Trail #400 to Pass and

Capri lakes. Although both lakes have a few cutthroat, fishing is considered marginal, as it is in the streams along the way with the possible exception of Warm Springs Creek which can be good. The area is noted for its large, productive huckleberry patches, so consider substituting berry-picking for fishing.

The hike has several good campsites—Overwhich Falls, Pass or Capri Lakes, Three Forks, or Sheepshead Flat. All have plenty of firewood. Overwhich Falls doesn't have readily available water, but the other sites do.—*Wayne Avants.*

20 *Blue Joint*

General description: A four-day backpack.
General location: Thirty-five miles southwest of Hamilton on the Idaho/ Montana border.
Maps: Painted Rocks Lakes, Blue Joint, and Nezperce Hollow USGS Quads, Bitterroot National Forest, West Fork Ranger District, and special hiking map for this area available from West Fork Ranger Station, Darby, Montana.
Special attractions: Very pristine high country where solitude is easy to find.
For more information: Write the District Ranger, West Fork Ranger District, Bitterroot National Forest, Darby, MT 59829 or call (406) 821-3269.

Getting to the Blue Joint area involves a long drive for most hikers, but it's well worth it, especially if you like long backpacking trips into wild country seldom visited by hikers.

To find this trailhead, drive south from Darby on U.S. 93 for about five miles. Just before you cross the Bitterroot River, turn right up the West Fork of the Bitterroot. There is a sign for Trapper Creek Job Corps Center and West Fork Ranger Station at this junction along with the Peaks & Pines trailer court.

Drive up this road for about 13 miles until you see the Forest Service's West Fork Ranger Station. Go past the ranger station, and after only one-half mile, turn right on the Nezperce Road and drive about 16 miles to Nezperce Pass. At the pass, turn left and park in a parking lot where the trail starts.

This is a 29-mile loop starting and ending at this trailhead. It can be taken in either direction, but it would be easier to take the stateline trail first and then come back to the trailhead by hiking down Blue Joint Creek.

The trail continues on a ridgetop hill all the way to Reynolds Lake—about 13 miles. Be careful not be get on the Castle Rock trail which junctures with the stateline trail about one-fourth mile from the trailhead. The trail down Jack the Ripper Creek takes off to the left about one mile from the trailhead. This is the trail that will bring you back to your vehicle, three days later.

With the exception of Two Buck Springs (about seven miles from the trailhead), there is no drinking water until you reach Reynolds Lake. So leave the vehicle with full water bottles and fill them again at Two Buck Springs which, incidentally, is a good place to spend the first night.

All along this trail, including from Two Buck Springs, the view of the

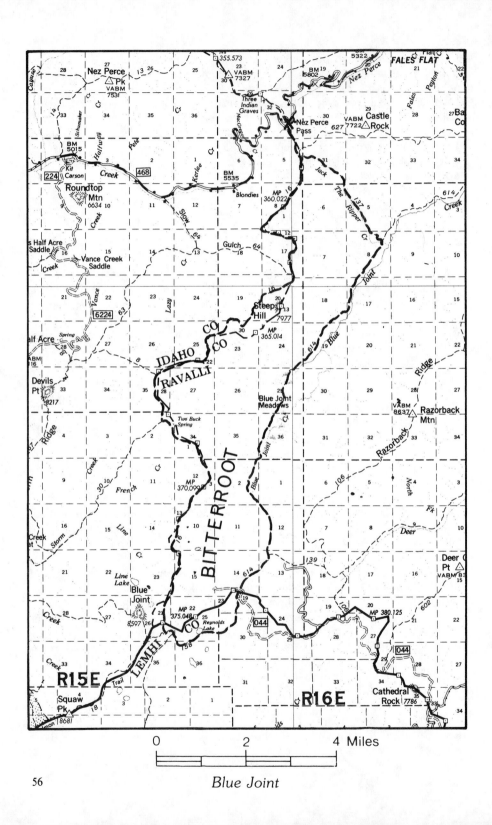

Blue Joint

Selway River country in Idaho is spectacular. This is subalpine country, featuring whitebark pine and lots of standing snags. Although firewood is available, it's often scarce and asthetic. Be sure to bring your backpack stove.

The second day's hike is more ridgetop hiking with scenic vistas on each side. It's about six miles to Reynolds Lake, a good second campsite. Don't miss the trail junction just before Reynolds Lake. It occurs in a small, grassy valley with water. Take the lefthand trail to the lake. Reynolds Lake has fishing for cutthroat to add to the evening's entertainment.

About two miles after leaving Reynolds Lake, you reach the Blue Joint Creek trail junction. There is a primitive road leading to this trail junction, and it's possible to have a vehicle left here to make this a point-to-point hike. However, it would be your big loss to miss Blue Joint Creek. The trail down this drainage is 12 miles and well-maintained with plenty of drinking water. It winds through a wide valley with grassy meadows and a meandering Blue Joint Creek. The stream has good fishing for small cutthroats.

Blue Joint Meadows (six miles from Reynolds Lake) is especially beautiful and a wise choice for your third campsite. This leaves eight miles for the last day.

The trail up Jack the Ripper Creek takes off about five miles from Blue Joint Meadows. Watch carefully for this junction. It juts off to the left just after a creek crossing. It's easy to see, but there is no sign.

The trail gradually climbs up Jack the Ripper for about three miles along a small, troutless stream and through small but gorgeous meadows. The last half-mile is fairly steep as you approach the ridgeline.

Then, retrace your footsteps from three days hence for about one mile to the trailhead and your waiting vehicle, leaving some of Montana's most spectacular, yet gentle, backcountry behind you.

Although you won't see grizzly bears along this hike, black bears are fairly common, so be careful with your food and keep a clean camp. The area also has adequate supplies of most other wildlife associated with western Montana, including mountain lion, mountain goats, elk, deer, and moose. Mosquitoes usually aren't a big problem after June. You'll want to wait until at least July anyway to let the snows free the area.

On the way home, your enthusiasm for the grandeur of this area might be dampened by the fact that it might not be the same for the next generation. Although the area is undergoing a congressionally mandated wilderness study, there is intense pressure to develop the minimal timber resource in the Blue Joint Wilderness Study Area instead of setting it aside. Check with the Bitterroot National Forest for a progress report on this controversy.
—*Bob Oset*

21 Stoney Lake, Dome Shaped Mountain

General description: An overnighter for families with the option—for hikers in good condition—of climbing Dome Shaped Mountain.

General location: Twenty-five miles northeast of Hamilton in the Sapphire Mountains.

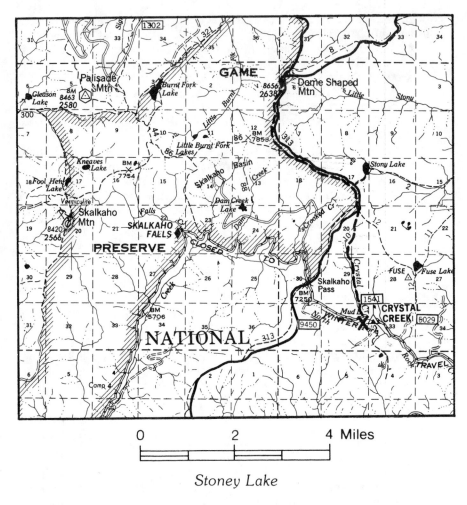

0   2   4 Miles

Stoney Lake

Maps: Deerlodge National Forest, Philipsburg Ranger District. (No USGS Quads for this area.)

For more information: Write the District Ranger, Philipsburg Ranger District, Deerlodge National Forest, Philipsburg, MT 59858 or call (406) 859-3211.

Part of the enjoyment of hiking in the Sapphires is the feeling that you've discovered an area that most hikers would ordinarily drive past without a second glance. The Sapphires (once they've got your attention) prove that there is more to the "wilderness experience" than craggy peaks and snowfields.

Stoney Lake is one place where this point is well made. To find it, take U.S. 93 south from Missoula to its junction with the Skalkaho Road #38, three miles south of Hamilton. Turn east (left) on this winding mountain road going past Skalkaho Falls and over Skalkaho Pass. About two miles over the pass is Crystal Creek Campground, a good place to park.

Ignore the Forest Service maps showing trails to Stoney Lake going by way of Fuse Lake, or Skalkaho Pass and the Sapphire Divide. (Although they're shown on the map, there are no trails.) The real trailhead to Stoney Lake is across the road and several yards up (west) from the Crystal Creek Campground. The trail begins as a logging road with Crystal Creek on the right and a clearcut on the left. The road changes into a hiking trail after a few hundred yards, but continues to follow Crystal Creek for three miles to its beginning at the Sapphire Divide—also called the Bitterroot Divide or Rock Creek Divide on some Forest Service signs.

The trail goes steadily, but gradually, uphill, much of the time through meadows. Upon reaching the divide, the trail heads north for a little over a mile before the trail down to Stoney Lake splits off to the right.

Stoney Lake offers average fishing for cutthroat, a good campsite with firewood near its outlet, and a chance of seeing mountain goats on the cliffs across the lake from camp.

If you have an extra day or you are a strong hiker, it's possible to return to the divide trail and follow it north to Dome Shaped Mountain. With the Burnt Fork Game Preserve on your left (west), you stand a good chance of seeing deer and elk. Although they don't appear to be what is generally considered mountain goat country, the Sapphires are home for a surprisingly large population, particularly around Half Dome Mountain. The occasional open spots along the divide provide views of the Pintlers (southeast), the Flint Creek Range (northeast), the Bitterroots (west) and to the south across Skalkaho Pass, the higher peaks of the Sapphire Wilderness Study Area.

The only possible interruption in a Stoney Lake trip would come from a trail bike. Although they aren't allowed at the lake, they have been there. The failure of the Deerlodge National Forest to correctly map the trail may contribute to this.—*John Westenberg*

22 *Legend and Spud Lakes*

General description: A three-day trip for ambitious hikers who want to explore the Sapphire Mountains.

General location: Thirty miles southeast of Hamilton.

Maps: Bitterroot National Forest's Recreation Map. (No USGS Quads available.)

Special attractions: Solitude, wildlife, and an introduction to a little-known mountain range.

For more information: Write the District Ranger, Sula Ranger District, Bitterroot National Forest, Sula, MT 59871 or call (406) 821-3201.

Facing the rugged Bitterroot Mountains across the Bitterroot Valley, the Sapphire Mountains seem like low, rolling hills. However, they offer first-rate wilderness recreation. This hike takes the hiker into the center of the Sapphire's largest remaining roadless area.

To reach the trailhead from Missoula, take U.S. 93 south 82 miles to Sula. Then, take the road up the East Fork of the Bitterroot for about 20 miles to its junction with the Moose Creek Road just beyond the East Fork Ranger Station. Take the Moose Creek Road north until it ends five miles later at the trailhead.

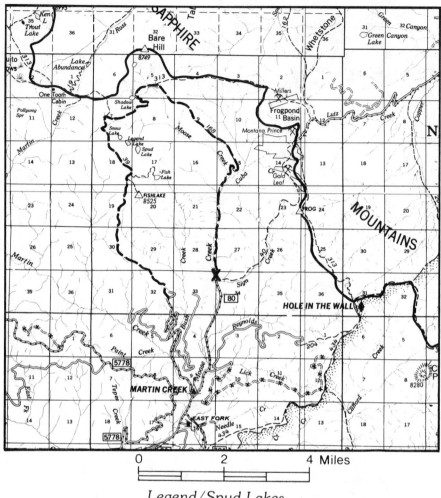

Legend/Spud Lakes

For the first three miles, the trail borders Moose Creek, going up its narrow, talus-filled canyon. The trail then turns east and climbs up the ridge between Moose Creek and Cuba Creek. This one-mile climb marks the beginning of a dry section, so stock up with water before climbing out of Moose Creek.

The trail then heads north along the ridge for 3.5 miles until intersecting with an abandoned jeep road. Although not as pleasant as a trail, the road is gradually going to seed, with little sign of vehicle use. Turn west (left) and follow the abandoned road for approximately three miles, passing Shadow Lake (no fish) and several meadows on the right.

After entering a particularly beautiful meadow, you come upon a second fork in the trail. The right fork takes you into country you'll want to investigate tomorrow. However, by this time you'll probably be more interested in the left fork, leading to Legend and Spud lakes (only one mile farther) and your campsite. A final fork in the trail comes just beyond this

60

point, with the right fork climbing the ridge above the lakes and the easily missed left fork leading directly to the lakes. Missing this fork and finding yourself on top of the ridge is no cause for regret. You can explore the ridge, looking down on the lakes, south and east to the Pintlers and west to the Bitterroots. In the foreground to the west are the scars of the huge Sleeping Child fire of 1953. The easiest place to scramble back down to the trail leading to the lakes is at the north end of the ridge. After passing fishless Snow Lake, you come to Legend and Spud lakes. Although both small lakes, they contain pan-sized cutthroat trout. They're also good vantage points for seeing mountain goat. This is heavily timbered country, so there's no shortage of firewood.

If you have time for a second night at the lakes, you can spend the next day exploring the country to the north. Climb 9,000-foot Kent Peak, exploring the meadows and watching for deer, elk, and goats enroute or drop down into the upper Rock Creek drainage to Lake Abundance, a rarely visited lake with good fishing for cutthroat.

There are two possible variations for the return trip. If you're taking two cars, leave one at the trailhead at the end of the forest road that runs north through the Martin Creek Recreation Area. To find this trailhead, take the road that leaves the Moose Creek Road about one-third mile past the junction of the East Fork and the Moose Creek Roads. This makes it possible for the backpacker to return to the ridge above the lake, and follow the trail seven miles along the ridge and down to the waiting car.

Hikers with one car can return by dropping directly down to Moose Creek from the lakes. This means cross-country hiking and carefully descending some steep slopes while clinging to underbrush—definitely not for novice hikers or families. Once down in the Moose Creek bottom, follow the game trails parallelling Moose Creek for approximately three miles until you intercept the trail you came in on as it crosses Moose Creek. This option gives the hiker an excellent chance of seeing elk or moose, and also takes the hiker through beautiful groves of huge Engelmann spruce.

The third return trip option is, of course, retracing your steps back to your vehicle.

The Forest Service has plans to log and build roads into Moose Creek. For the time being, however, Moose Creek is safe within the boundary of the 90,000-acre Sapphire Mountains Wilderness Study Area, one of nine such areas contained in the late Senator Metcalf's Montana Wilderness Study Act. Watch for developments on the Forest Service plans for Moose Creek.—*John Westenberg*

23 Welcome Creek

General description: A moderate round trip suitable for a day hike or overnighter.

General location: Twenty-five miles east of Missoula in the Sapphire Mountains.

Maps: Cleveland Mountain and Ravenna USGS Quads and Lolo National Forest, Missoula Ranger District.

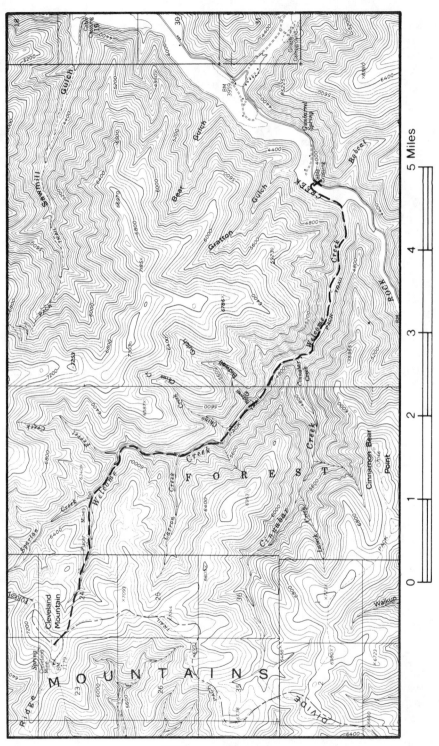

Welcome Creek

Special attractions: A very accessible, pleasant hike in Montana's newest wilderness area, the Welcome Creek Wilderness.

For more information: Write the District Ranger, Missoula Ranger District, Lolo National Forest, 2801 Russell, Missoula, MT or call (406) 329-3111.

Besides offering scenic, timbered hiking trails, the Welcome Creek Wilderness has a rich history. Mined extensively around the turn of the century, the area has many haunting reminders, now abandoned and

The flush of a blue grouse can rudely jolt hikers from their daydreams. Harry Engels photo.

decaying into the landscape to greet the Welcome Creek traveler.

The trail starts about 12 miles up well-known Rock Creek east of Missoula. Drive east from Missoula for 25 miles on I-90 and turn right (south) at the Rock Creek exit. Go up the gravel Rock Creek Road for 12 miles and watch for a sign on your right (west) marking the Welcome Creek trailhead.

After leaving your car, you cross over Rock Creek on a cable bridge. Then, veer left and follow the stream upstream for a half-mile before turning right (west) up Welcome Creek. From here, you gradually climb, following Welcome Creek, until you feel like camping or turning around and returning to your vehicle. The trail goes up about five miles and ends.

It isn't really a canyon, but the valley is steep and narrow. It has a mystery and lonelinesss of its own, as you walk by old mining sites and see how the forest is gradually reclaiming them.

This is a wet area, so wait until July for hiking. If you go earlier, expect a boggy trail and the mosquitoes to be out in force. However, drinking water poses no problem, as clear, clean water is everywhere. Although Welcome Creek has small brookies, the fishing takes a back seat to famous Rock Creek running past the trailhead.

If you're camping, you have a wide selection of sites. Perhaps the best are where Cinnabar and Spartan creeks join Welcome Creek. Both sites have old mining ruins to explore after supper.

Although some protesters of wilderness classification claimed that Welcome Creek has too many signs of civilization to qualify for wilderness, the reverse is true. Man's hold on the area has long faded into history. Now, the ghosts of old timers (such as outlaw Frank Brady who was shot in 1904 in Welcome Creek) only enrich the wilderness experience. It also shows how fast nature heals the wounds of past carelessness.—*Don Berg*.

24 Stuart Peak, Twin Lakes

General description: A two or three-day backpack for hardy hikers.

General location: The upper Rattlesnake Creek drainage—Missoula's municipal watershed—just north of Missoula.

Maps: Northeast Missoula and Stuart Peak USGS Quads and Lolo National Forest, Missoula Ranger District.

Special attraction: Vistas of at least four major mountain ranges from the summit of Stuart Peak.

For more information: Write the District Ranger, Missoula Ranger District, Lolo National Forest, 2801 Russell, Missoula, MT 59801 or call (406) 329-3111.

Drive north on Van Buren Street from the Van Buren I-90 interchange, bearing to the right until you find yourself on Rattlesnake Drive. Turn left onto the unmarked road just beyond Wildcat Road, four miles from the interchange. The parking area and entrance to the Upper Rattlesnake Area are located at the mouth of Sawmill Gulch, just a few yards beyond the bridge.

A large wooden map at the gate provides an overview of the entire drainage. Additional information and a few regulations are contained in a brochure prepared cooperatively by the Montana Power Company and the

The Missoula Valley from Stuart Peak, deep in the Rattlesnake wild area. Joseph A. Mussulman photo.

Missoula District of the Lolo National Forest. Copies of the brochure are available at the gate.

The hike along trail #517 is a popular trip with beginning backpackers, possibly because it appears from the wooden map that Stuart Peak and the enticing lakes to the north are but a short distance from the gate. Also, it would seem that one would be comfortingly close to civilization throughout the trip. (Indeed, from time to time en route, one is within sight—and sometimes even sound—of Missoula.) However, the sign at the entrance to Spring Gulch, less than halfmile north of the gate, reads "Stuart Peak, 9.5 mi.; 7 hrs.," a tip-off that the hike actually is somewhat challenging. And a quality of wildness pervades the atmosphere.

The first three miles up the bottom of Spring Gulch are quite easy regardless of whether you follow the old cow paths to the west of the creek, or the farm lane to the east. Both routes lead past the sites of homesteads

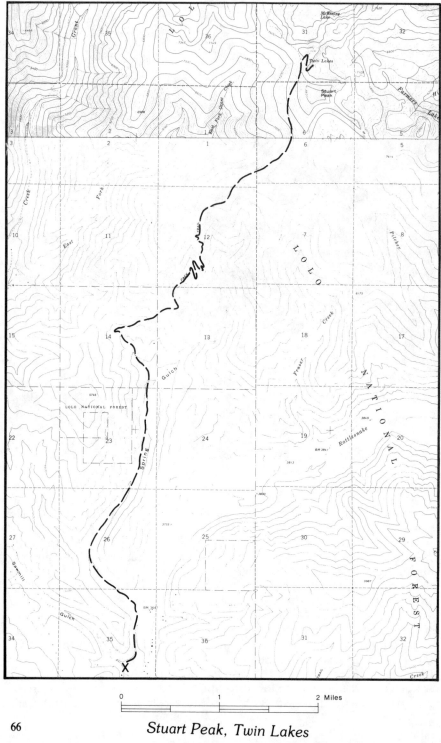

Stuart Peak, Twin Lakes

established a century or more ago, though all that remain are traces of foundations and hearths, a few persistent lilac bushes and apple trees, and two alien Lombardy poplars.

From the head of the Spring Gulch, trail #517 begins winding relentlessly upward, 6.5 miles to Stuart Peak. There is usually water at the 5,800-foot level, but no more until you reach Twin Lakes, which lie in the cirque just north of 7,960-foot Stuart Peak.

The Twin Lakes are barren, but Cliff and Peterson lakes, accessible by poor trails to the southeast, contain fish.

Given the time and the energy, one might prefer to proceed northward along the ridge to the Lake Creek drainage, whose principal lakes (McKinley, Worden, Carter, Big, and Sheridan) also provide some fishing.

If you're primarily out for exercise and scenery (or huckleberries, in season) you might wish to pitch camp one evening at the upper end of Spring Gulch, spend the following day walking to Stuart Peak and back, and pack out on the morning of the third day. There are half a dozen pleasant campsites along the creek on the fringes of Kench Meadow.

Much of the Rattlesnake high country remains untrailed or served by only the faintest tracks. Despite the Rattlesnake's popularity, secluded, almost undiscovered basins and lakes dot the far reaches of this high country. There are those who make a fetish of exploring these untrailed areas, and they report that they frequently travel several days without encountering other hikers.

Proximity to Missoula results in high use over much of the area. This—plus the fragile nature of the high country itself and the area's status as Missoula's municipal watershed with Montana Power a large private land holder—impose unusual constraints on users. Access through the privately held low country depends on retaining good relations with Montana Power. Abuses will pose a threat to continued public access. In particular, you should observe the closure to fishing of Rattlesnake Creek and its tributaries.

Evidence of high country campsites is proliferating. Make every effort to go light on this fragile terrain. Camp well back from the lakes, and don't add to the blight of fire rings.

Spectacular scenery and access from a large metropolitan area make the Rattlesnake a unique area. Local groups are working actively to insure that it remains unspoiled and undeveloped. They may secure wilderness protection for this backyard hiking area, but the success of this effort depends on having responsible users.—*Bill Brown and Joseph A. Mussulman*

25 *Rainbow Lake*

General description: An ideal hike for campers willing to work hard for round trip to a high lake in the heart of the Anaconda-Pintler Wilderness.
General location: Thirty miles southwest of Anaconda.
Maps: Warren Peak USGS Quad and the Forest Service's Anaconda-Pintler Wilderness map.
Special attractions: A secluded wilderness lake ringed with spectacular scenery.

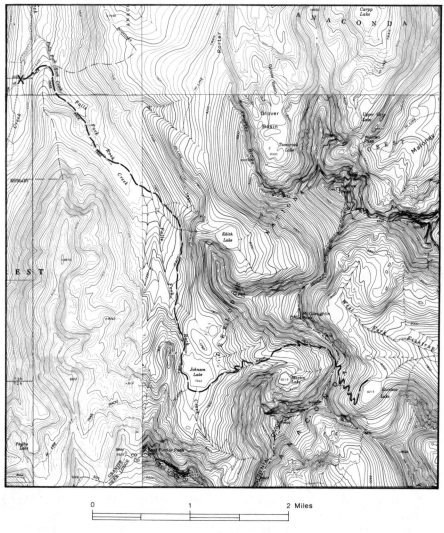

0   1   2 Miles

Rainbow Lake

For more information: Write the District Ranger, Philipsburg Ranger Station, Deerlodge National Forest, Philipsburg, MT 59858 or call (406) 859-3211.

Ever want to set up camp in a secluded apline clearing, away from the mainstream of wilderness traffic, where a diversity of peaks surround a small, deep lake loaded with trout? There are many of these secret spots in Montana, but those who find them usually keep them secret, which is a selfish way to handle any blessing. Rainbow Lake is one of these blessings. Promise not to tell?

To find the trailhead, take State Highway 38 south from Philipsburg, and

11 miles past the Georgetown-Anaconda turnoff, turn south onto the Moose Lake Road. Follow this road for 12 miles until you reach Copper Creek Campground. Then, take the Middle Fork Rock Creek Road and follow it until it dead ends five miles later. Here, take Falls Fork Trail #29.

It's a 4.5-mile uphill grind to Johnson Lake (elevation 7,720). Hike along the west shore of this lake to a trail junction at the south end, and take the left-hand fork to the east (Trail #9). Then, climb a 2.5-mile stretch with moderate switchbacks to 9,040-foot Rainbow Pass.

The snow usually clings to this high land until at least late June, so mid-July or later is best for this hike. There is plenty of water along the trail except for the stretch between Johnson and Rainbow lakes.

This pass is a great place to relax and enjoy the surroundings. To the east is the ominous, broad pyramid of 10,793-foot West Goat Peak, highest in the Pintler Range. To the south are slopes covered with rare alpine larch. And right below you is your destination—Rainbow Lake. You can see the trail switchbacking down to the 8,215-foot lake.

The outlet is the best spot to camp. The rainbow trout are especially active in the morning and evening. Dead trees provide plentiful firewood. Trails-to-explore and peaks-to-climb are in all directions.

The geology is rather striking. The range is mainly the more typical Montana sedimentary rock, but with granitic intrusions, which accounts for all those odd-looking granite boulders strewn about in unexpected places. This phenomenon is especially evident on the trail to Warren Lake.—*Pat Caffrey*

Johnson Lake in the Anaconda-Pintler Wilderness. U.S. Forest Service photo.

26 Pioneer and High-up Lakes

General description: A fairly strenuous overnight round trip (well suited for a three-day trip) to a small lake just below the Montana/Idaho border.

Maps: Goldstone Mountain USGS Quad and Beaverhead National Forest, Wisdom Ranger District.

General location: On the east slope of the Continental Divide in the Beaverhead National Forest, 15 miles southwest of Jackson, 65 miles west of Dillon.

Special attractions: A remote high mountain lake way off the beaten path.

For more information: Write the District Ranger, Wisdom Ranger District, Beaverhead National Forest, Box 236, Wisdom, MT 59761 or call (406) 689-2331.

To get to the trailhead, drive one mile south of Jackson on State Highway 278 and turn right on a gravel road near the top of a hill. Follow this road south and west to Van Houten Lake Campground, crossing many of the upper tributaries of the Big Hole River on narrow bridges. Near the campground at the south end of Van Houten Lake, turn west on a primitive road. Shortly after leaving Van Houten Lake, the road forks. Continue driving west; be sure not to take the left-hand fork which goes to Skinner Meadows.

During wet weather (most of the time in the Big Hole), you will encounter mudholes. So be prepared to walk soon after leaving the campground. In dry weather (or if you have a rugged vehicle), it's possible to drive on.

High-up Lake in the West Big Hole proposed wilderness. Fred Swanson photo.

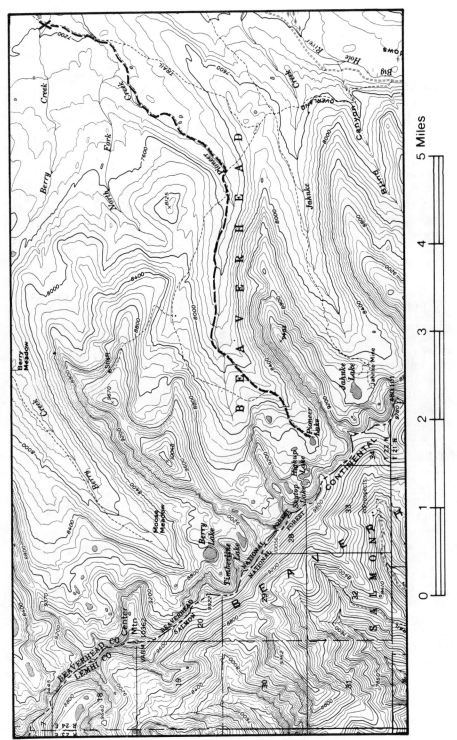

5 Miles

Pioneer Lake

About a mile past Van Houten Lake the road forks in a sagebrush-covered park, which is covered with sego lilies in midsummer. Take the left fork and head southwest less than a mile to where Berry Creek crosses the road. There is no bridge here, so park and start walking. One-half mile farther south, the road crosses Pioneer Creek on the remains of a primitive bridge. People trying to cross the stream with four-wheel drive vehicles have cut ruts into the soft banks.

Shortly after this crossing is the junction with trail #442, which continues along the south side of Pioneer Creek as a primitive vehicle track. It's more pleasant to walk along this track as it winds among parks and groves. Watch for moose in the willow bottoms by the creek.

The trail climbs slowly and crosses the creek again about six miles from Van Houten Lake. Just past this crossing, the trail branches; the shortest route continues along the creek, while the right-hand trail climbs the hill to an old miner's cabin and eventually rejoins the main trail. The trail starts to climb more steeply as you approach the high peaks along the Continental Divide. Even at this high elevation (7-8,000 feet), there are large spruce and fir growing close to the creek.

The route for the last few miles is a regular hiking trail. It crosses the north branch of Pioneer Creek and cuts across a slope to the south branch of the creek. Soon, it comes to a jumble of trees from a recent snow avalanche that started on the steep slopes to the south. This section of the trail away from the stream can be confusing, so consult your map and watch for faint blazes.

Pioneer Lake lies about one mile past the avalanche (about ten miles from Van Houten Campground). It offers some good camping spots and a close-up look at the Continental Divide.

Enterprising hikers may want to try a short climb up the hill west of Pioneer Lake on faint animal paths to High-Up Lake, actually a pair of alpine jewels just below the divide. There is a good campsite on the east end of the lake with a fine view back down the valley you've just labored up. A third lake, Skytop, lies over the next ridge, but its shores are rockier.

Try to catch the sunrise above the Big Hole Valley as it rises over the high peaks of the East Pioneer Mountains. A moonrise is also worth staying up for—ghostly light silhouetting the limbs of the dead whitebark pine surrounding the lake. Pine beetles killed these trees decades ago, but this treeline forest is renewing itself.

Enjoy a small fire from deadfall at one of the fire rings in place at the lake. Chances are you will be the only people at this remote spot; try to leave the lakeshore as undisturbed as it was when you came.

High-Up Lake is a great place to spend an extra day for exploring. The Continental Divide is a short climb on steep talus above the south end of the lake. On top of the divide it's fairly common to see mountain goats among the crags. The west slope of the divide is more gentle than the steep glacier-carved east wall, and it's possible to walk north and south along the crest amid wild scenery. Center Mountain rises three miles north along the ridge and is a moderate, nontechnical climb, but use caution among its loose sliderock. To the west are the rugged Big Horn Crags in the great wild area of central Idaho, the proposed River of No Return Wilderness.

Both Pioneer and High-Up lakes have small cutthroat, but neither are noted for their fishing.

Trail hints: The Big Hole and its surrounding mountains are notorious for their mosquitoes. Plan a late summer hike or bring plenty of repellant. The trail along Pioneer Creek stays close to water most of the distance. Fishermen and less ambitious hikers will enjoy ambling along the willow-bordered stream on the lower portion of the trail.

High-Up Lake and most of the Pioneer Creek valley are within a wilderness area proposed by local sportsmen's groups. The Forest Service has also proposed a smaller wilderness area, but they have plans to cut timber and build roads in the lower slopes of this range. As roads increase along the fringes of the Big Hole, some of the remoteness that makes it special will be lost. —*Fred Swanson*

27 Bobcat Lakes

General description: A moderate, eight-mile day hike or overnight trip in the West Pioneer Mountains.

General location: In an eastern drainage of the West Pioneer Mountains, 20 miles south of Wise River and 60 miles southwest of Butte in the Beaverhead National Forest.

Maps: Odell Lake and Shaw Mountain USGS Quads and Beaverhead National Forest, Wise River Ranger District.

Special attractions: Lower Bobcat Lake is one of several lakes in the West Pioneers that support the rare southern grayling.

For more information: Write the District Ranger, Wise River Ranger District, Beaverhead National Forest, Box 86, Wise River, MT 59762 or call (406) 839-2201.

Bobcat Lakes lie in small glacial cirques in the middle of the gently rolling West Pioneer Mountains. There are two good trails to the lakes, and it is possible to make this a loop trip. Both trails begin from Forest Service Road #90 which follows Lacy Creek, a tributary of the Wise River.

To get there, drive south from the town of Wise River on the Wise River Road about 15 miles. A mile or so after the Wise River road leaves the river canyon and enters a broad meadow, turn right on Road #90 (Lacy Creek Road) and go west. About two miles up the Lacy Creek Road a narrow, not-too-obvious, old wagon road angles steeply uphill to the right, climbs out of Lacy Creek valley, and meets trail #26 in about a mile. There is a gate where the old wagon road leaves Lacy Creek, so you must park and walk up the road.

Trail #26 heads west along a small stream through thick stands of lodgepole, spruce, and fir. After a little over two miles, you come to a pretty meadow near the junction of the trail to the Bobcat Lakes. Turn southwest on this trail and hike for about two more miles to the lakes. The total distance from the Lacy Creek Road is about six miles.

A more direct route to the Bobcat Lakes begins just past the end of road #90, about four miles from the Wise River Road. Park at the primitive campground, cross Lacy Creek, and take trail #50 up the Bobcat Creek canyon about four miles to the lakes. This trail passes through attractive

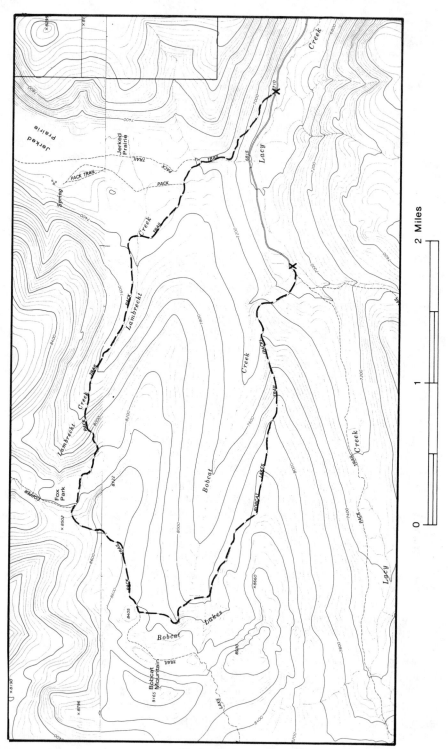

0   1   2 Miles

Bobcat Lakes

stands of lodgepole pine and fir, with occasional vistas across the broad slopes of the West Pioneers.

Lower and Upper Bobcat Lakes lie just below Bobcat Peak. At 9,241 feet, it is one of the higher points in the range. From the upper lake, a steep trail leads west to the ridge separating the Bobcat Creek and the Pattengail Creek drainages, the latter dissecting the heart of the East Pioneers. Elk often frequent the small meadows that dot this high area. Farther west is a long ridge topped by Odell Peak. Several cirque lakes lie at the base of this ridge.

An interesting feature of Lower Bobcat Lake is its grayling population. These native fish are now mostly restricted to the Big Hole River drainage. The grayling have specialized habitat requirements which make it hard for them to compete with other sport fish in lower elevation waters. The remoteness of the Bobcat Lakes helps them survive. Please take care to avoid disturbing the small stream that drains Lower Bobcat Lake—the grayling depend on the fine gravels in the streambed for spawning.

As with any backcountry lake, it's best to avoid camping on the delicate lakeshore. There are, however, several suitable campsites along the margin of the woods surrounding Bobcat Lakes. If you're diligent, you can find enough deadfall for a good fire.

For an enjoyable loop trip, leave your car at the end of road #90, take trail #50 to the lakes, and return via trail #26. Where you rejoin the Lacy Creek Road, stow your pack and walk a mile or so up the road to retrieve your car. There is drinking water near both trailheads, but fill your canteens here, as the rest of the hike may be dry.

To ensure the continued remoteness of the grayling lakes in the West Pioneers, conservation groups have proposed special management protection for the area. The Forest Service is conducting a wilderness study of the West Pioneers; you may want to contact the agency and offer your views. —*Fred Swanson*

28 Hollowtop Lake

General description: A moderate 12-mile, overnight round trip to an attractive lake in a high mountain basin.

General location: On the east side of the Tobacco Root Mountains in the Beaverhead National Forest, 55 miles west of Bozeman or 90 miles south of Helena.

Maps: Harrison USGS Quad and Beaverhead National Forest, Madison Ranger District.

Special attractions: Hollowtop Lake is bordered on three sides by the high peaks of the Tobacco Root Mountains.

For more information: Write the District Ranger, Madison Ranger District, Beaverhead National Forest, Box 366, Ennis, MT 59729 or call (406) 682-4254.

The trailhead is 2.5 miles southwest of Pony, an interesting old mining town in the foothills of the Tobacco Roots six miles southwest of Harrison. Drive west through Pony and proceed up a narrow dirt road 1.5 miles to the fork. Take the lower, left-hand road downhill to the North Fork of Willow

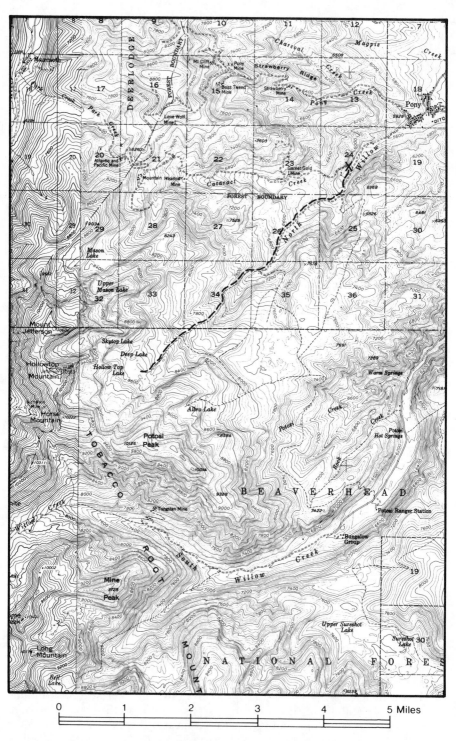

0   1   2   3   4   5 Miles

Hollowtop Lake

Creek. There is a good place to park at a bridge over the creek about two miles from Pony. Beyond the bridge a rocky jeep trail follows the creek, becoming a foot trail after about five miles.

Starting from the parking area at the bridge, walk up a moderate grade one-half mile along the south side of the creek to a primitive bridge. In the spring, watch for fuzzy blue pasqueflowers in the grassy meadows.

Above the primitive bridge, the trail climbs steadily along the north side of the creek, passing a good camping spot. Three miles from the trailhead, the jeep trail forks. The south fork (trail #333) heads over a ridge to Albro Lake; the other fork (trail #301 to Hollowtop Lake) continues along the north side of the creek through groves of spruce and fir and back into open meadows. Above this fork, the trail is closed to vehicles over 40 inches wide.

About 3.5 miles from the trailhead, the trail again crosses the creek. Pause here to fill canteens as the trail heads away from the main creek at this point. This stream crossing can be tricky during early summer runoff, and a stout staff selected from among the deadfall along the trail will help. Later into the summer, you can more easily cross the stream on jammed logs.

Above the crossing, the trail climbs more steeply to the 8,550-foot lake. You will pass some beautiful, sloping meadows with great views east into the Bozeman valley and the Spanish Peaks. Hollowtop Lake (which has pan-sized rainbows) is about six miles from the trailhead and is the source of the stream you have been following.

There is a good campsite near the outlet. Northwest of the lake is Mount Jefferson, at 10,600 feet, the highest point in the Tobacco Roots. Hollowtop Mountain (10,513 feet) lies west of the lake. And to the south is Potosi Peak, named by miners after a fabulous mine in the Andes. All three mountains are technically easy scrambles, but be prepared for rough weather on the windswept alpine slopes. —*Fred Swanson*

29 *Lake Louise*

General description: A short, but steep, overnighter.
General location: Forty miles southeast of Butte in the Tobacco Root Mountains.
Maps: Waterloo USGS Quad and the Deerlodge National Forest, Jefferson Ranger District.
For more information: Write the District Ranger, Jefferson Ranger Station, Deerlodge National Forest, Whitehall, MT 58759 or call (406) 287-3223.

The Tobacco Roots aren't well-known as a hiking area, but the range has much to offer—particularly short hikes suitable for families, such as Lake Louise.

To find the trailhead, take the turn south off I-90 at the Cardwell exit 31 miles east of Butte. Instead of taking U.S. 10 along the Jefferson River, veer south on State Highway 359. After about four miles turn right (southwest) on the South Boulder Road. Stay on this road for about 20 miles, past a small town named Mammoth to the trailhead. The road gets steadily worse as you proceed, but in dry weather late in the summer, a two-wheel drive vehicle can make it. The trail leaves the South Boulder Road to the left about five miles past Mammoth and just before the Bismark Reservoir.

Four-wheelers sometimes travel the first half-mile or so of this trail, but they can't make it to the lake. Motorcycles frequently use the trail, however.

You cross the South Boulder immediately after hoisting your packs on. It's a safe crossing, but there isn't a bridge, so you'll get your feet wet.

Lake Louise in the Tobacco Root Mountains. Bill Schneider photo.

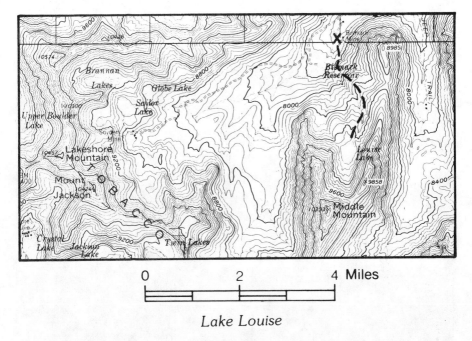

0   2   4 Miles

Lake Louise

After this, the trail (which isn't shown on the topo map) climbs for three long miles to the lake. The elevation gain—about 2800 feet—makes it seem longer. Carry your drinking water, as there are only a few water holes along the way.

The lake sets in a bowl-shaped cirque with massive, 10,353-foot Middle Mountain to the south. The best campsite is to your left when you hit the lake. Although firewood isn't readily available, there's enough for a healthy fire.

The lake has a small population of large cutthroat trout that can be very fussy about which fly they take. If you find the fly that works, only catch enough for supper, returning the rest for the next angler.

Although the trail is steep, the hike is popular with families. With children, plan on at least four hours to reach the lake—and probably more.

Climbers in your party will be tempted to scramble up Middle Mountain, a nontechnical climb.—*Bill Schneider*

30 *Trask Lakes*

General description: A moderate overnighter.
General location: About 12 miles west of Deer Lodge in the Flint Creek
    Range.
Maps: Rock Creek Lake, Pike's Peak, and Pozega Lakes USGS Quads and
    Deerlodge National Forest, Deerlodge Ranger District.
Special attractions: Good fishing for small brookies.
For more information: Write the District Ranger, Deerlodge Ranger District,
    Deerlodge National Forest, Deer Lodge, MT 59722 or call (406) 846-1770.

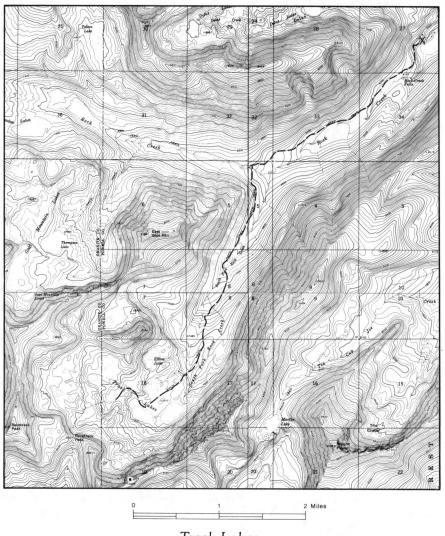

0   1   2 Miles

Trask Lakes

Although this area lies close to Butte, Deer Lodge, and Helena, it remains relatively unknown.

Without doubt, the Flint Creek Range is among the most scenic in the state. Unfortunately, most of it has been extremely roaded. This remaining island of roadless land contains several trout-filled lakes.

To find the trailhead, go down the main street of Deer Lodge and turn west at the corner with the bank. Follow this road for two miles until it splits. The left-hand fork goes to the prison farm. Take the right fork (actually straight ahead) and follow it ten more miles to Rock Creek Lake. Park at the upper end of the lake where the good road turns into a rugged jeep road. (It may be too rugged even for jeeps.) The parking area is private land with limited space for vehicles.

The first three miles of the trip are on this old jeep road (Forest Service Road #168.2) which is—by order of the Deerlodge National Forest's travel plan—closed year-round to all motorized vehicles except snowmobiles. In practice, however, motorized recreationists use the road frequently because the Forest Service has neglected to post signs explaining the travel restrictions. (This would be a good subject for a phone call to the Deerlodge National Forest when you return.)

At the three-mile mark, watch for a trail junction. The road continues on, but you must turn left, crossing Rock Creek and then following the South Fork of the Rock Creek to the lakes. Forest Service Trail #63 continues climbing gradually for four miles to the Lower Trask Lake, one of four lakes (plus several potholes) in this small but gorgeous cirque. Once you're off the jeep road, the signs of civilization fall behind and the hike becomes more of a quality backcountry experience.

The 7,800-foot Trask Lakes offer excellent fishing for small brookies. In fact, fish are so abundant and hungry that even the youngest angler can expect a good catch. (The fishing is also good in the main Rock Creek along the jeep road in the first three miles of the hike.)

The good fishing and moderate, 14-mile round trip (1,900-foot elevation gain) makes Trask Lakes perfect for family backpacking. But don't forget the insect repellent or your kids won't want to leave the tent. Drinking water is available all along this trail.

The basin has many suitable campsites. However, firewood is scarce, so use your stove and avoid fires. Also, take a few minutes to collect and carry out garbage left by thoughtless visitors.

After you're bored with hauling in fish, you might try an interesting side trip to Racetrack Peak. Stay on the trail for three miles past the lakes until it climbs to the top of 8,507-foot Racetrack Pass. Then, turn right (west) and make a one-mile scramble to the summit of 9,524-foot Racetrack Peak for an outstanding view of the entire area.

The low point of the Trask Lakes trip is the knowledge that without increased support for preserving the area, it will probably be developed like the rest of this mountain range.—*Frank Culver*

31 *Humbug Spires*

General description: An easy day hike or overnighter into a unique primitive area.

General location: Twenty-six miles south of Butte in the Humbug Spires Wilderness Study Area.

Maps: Butte South USGS Quad and the Bureau of Land Management's "Humbug Spires Instant Study Area" handout.

Special attractions: Fifty granite spires, towering 300-600 feet above one of Montana's largest designated primitive areas on Bureau of Land Management land.

For more information: Write the District Manager, Bureau of Land Management, 220 N. Alaska, Butte, MT 59701 or call (406) 723-6561.

Of all the roadless country in Montana, the 11,174-acre Humbug Spires area must rank among the most intriguing. Besides the granite protrusions,

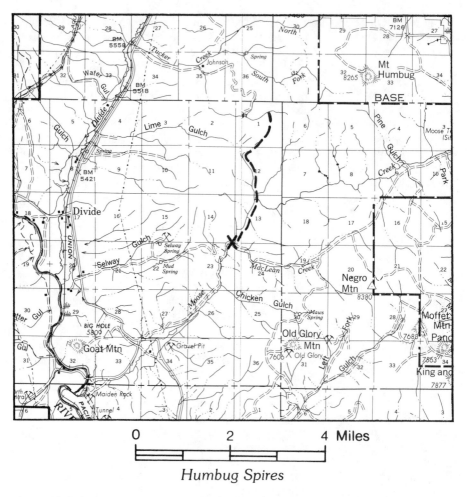

0   2   4 Miles

Humbug Spires

for which it is named, the area has a lovely, trout-laden stream (small cutthroat) and a forest of primeval Douglas fir, somehow overlooked by early timber cutters.

After driving south of Butte for 26 miles, turn left (east) at the Moose Creek Interchange. Drive for three miles up the Moose Creek Road to the BLM parking lot where the trail begins.

Upon leaving the parking area, you cross a culvert to the west side of Moose Creek where there is a BLM sign announcing the primitive area and notifying recreationists that motorized vehicles aren't allowed. In the first 1.3 miles, you pass by numerous ancient trees, possibly 200 years or older, truly noble reminders of what it was like when the pioneers arrived.

At the 1.3 mile mark, the trail forks. Take the left fork and continue up the west side of the stream. Stay on this trail for about two miles until you reach the only private inholding in this vast tract of public domain. At the barn, take a right turn up a small gulch with a small stream (excellent drinking water).

This turns into a deep gulch, steep in a few places and containing the beginnings of the spires. About a mile up this steep gulch, you leave the small stream, climbing off to the left over a short pitch to the ridge where the incredible Humbug Spires unfold before you in all their majesty.

It's four miles to this point, making this an eight-mile round trip. The trail has only a few steep, but short, upgrades. In places, the trail becomes indistinct, but careful scrutiny will reveal its presence.

Although this is usually a day hike, you can camp along the stream just before you climb out of the gulch. You could also camp on the ridge—if you feel the scenery pays for the extra work of hauling water up from the stream.

If you camp, plan on spending the first half of your second day wandering around, possibly awe-struck, among the spires. You'll come home exclaiming about the beauty and uniqueness of the Humbug Spires.—*Herb B. Gloege*

32 *Murr Canyon*

General description: A moderate day trip.
General location: Forty-five miles southwest of Kalispell in the McGregor-Thompson Roadless Area.
Maps: Shroder Creek USGS Quad and Lolo National Forest, Thompson Falls Ranger District.
Special attractions: A hidden canyon filled with white water.
For more information: Write the District Ranger, Plains Ranger District, Lolo National Forest, Box 429, Plains, MT 59859 or call (406) 826-3629.

Even though the McGregor-Thompson Roadless Area is large and lies close to Kalispell, Missoula and other cities, it isn't commonly used by hikers. Consequently, many scenic treasures like the Murr Canyon periodically go undiscovered.

To find the trailhead, drive west from Kalispell on U.S. 2 for 40 miles to the Thompson River Road. Turn left (south) here and go slightly over six miles until you see a trail sign on your left (east) for Murr Creek Trail #145.

The trail gradually climbs through deeply forested country along Murr Creek for about four miles to a junction with trail #118 which juts off to the northeast to Pinehill. About a half-mile past this junction a short spur trail takes off to the right just after crossing a creek in a deep gulley. This spur trail, which goes about a half-mile to a good viewpoint over Murr Canyon, is marked but hasn't been maintained for several years. It's possible to climb down into Murr Canyon, but this requires rugged, cross-country hiking—for the very experienced only.

Murr Canyon is a lovely, steep-walled gorge with a waterfall at the east end where Murr Creek once again becomes a normal stream. On the way up, you can leave the trail and hike along the creek for about a mile to see this waterfall. To see the waterfall, however, you must fight through heavy brush. It's best to try this in the spring.

The well-maintained trail gains only about 300 feet in elevation on the way to this hidden gorge. Although the trail has several places to get water, it also has some dry sections. The nine-mile round trip is easy enough for any hiker.

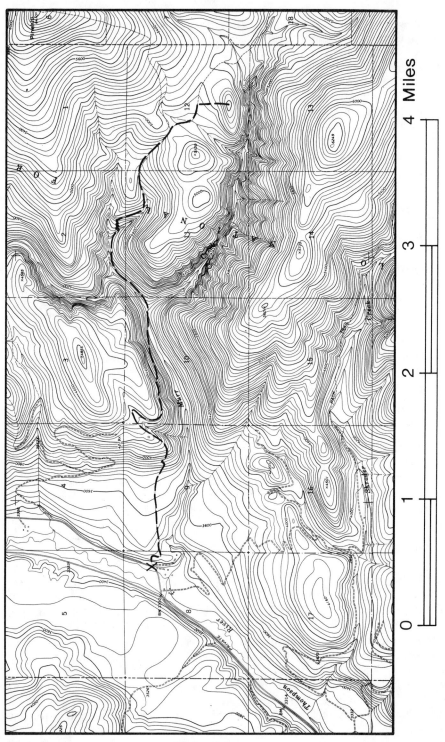

Murr Canyon

Motorized vehicles are allowed, but they aren't commonly seen in the area. Except for a clearcut at the beginning of the hike, the signs of civilization are few.

There are wilderness proposals for the McGregor-Thompson area, but so far they haven't gone far. Perhaps the greatest stumbling block is the "checkerboarding" of private and public land throughout much of the area.—*Elaine Snyder*

33 McDonald Peak

General description: A tough, nontechnical climb for experienced hikers and mountain goats.
General location: Five miles northeast of St. Ignatius.
Maps: Mount Harding and St. Mary's Lake USGS Quads, Flathead National Forest, and Hal Kanzler's Mission Mountain Map.
Special attractions: High mountain scenery and excitement including views of McDonald Glacier and the Mission Range.

McDonald Peak is a 9,868-foot summit, the highest in the Mission Range, and stands nearly 7,000 feet above the Mission Valley.

The route from the west up Ashley Creek is a direct, nontechnical assault generally free of snowfields. Nonetheless, knowledge and preparedness in high mountain terrain and weather is essential. Also, watch for grizzly bears which still survive in these mountains.

The climb can be made in a day— *if* you're in excellent shape and only want to spend a few minutes on top. Most climbers spend the night at Ashley Lakes.

To climb from the west side, drive two miles north of the signal light on U.S. 93 in St. Ignatius and turn right (east) on a county road and go three miles. Then, turn left (north) and go one-fourth mile before turning east again and driving until you cross the irrigation canal and come to a right-hand curve in the road. Park anywhere between here and Ashley Creek which is just up the road.

Head up the creek, keeping to the left-hand side. There is a game trail which starts at the end of an old logging road on the north-south running ridge west of the creek. Three miles up this primitive trail is an ideal campsite at Lower Ashley Lake. Both Ashley lakes are good fishing for cutthroat.

The rock wall at the east end of Upper Ashley Lake blocks all further progress. This appears difficult, but once you find the hidden trail, it's easy.

Bypass the lake on the north side and look for a prominent talus slope that extends all the way up into a line of cliffs. Climb up this talus slope to within about 15 feet of where it comes out of the cliffs, and then look to your right and find a goat trail starting on ledges into the rock wall. Follow this intriguing trail up through the gullies and ledges of the rock wall until you reach the top.

From there, it's an easy walk up along the creek. Get water while you can; there isn't any above this point.

Within two miles the drainage makes a dog leg to the left, opening out into small meadows with clumps of scrawny trees. A large draw comes in

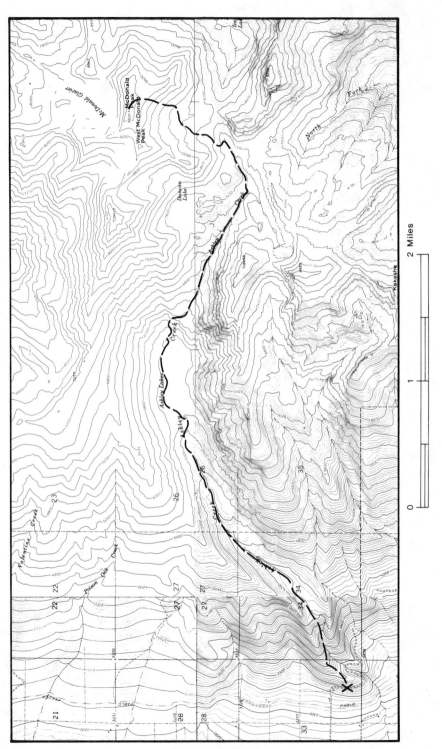

McDonald Peak

from the right (south), but stay out of it and continue up the main draw.

Soon, the massive south buttress of McDonald Peak comes into view. Head towards the pass near the south end of this buttress, and when almost there (within one-fourth mile), find an easy way north up out of the draw and into a large, broken cirque. Work across this area, heading towards the junction of the south buttress and the main summit ridge. Once there, claw your way up loose scree slopes until you hit the summit ridge and, you will quickly realize, the top of the world.

Carefully, retrace your steps to your vehicle. —*Pat Caffrey*

34   *Summit Lake*

General description: A day trip or overnight loop for wilderness enthusiasts in good shape.

Maps: Mount Harding USGS Quad, Flathead National Forest, and Hal Kanzler's Mission Mountain Map.

General location: Ten miles southeast of Ronan in the Mission Mountains.

Special attractions: Post Creek chain of lakes, Eagle Summit Pass, Mount Harding—very rugged mountain country.

The Mission Mountains have been nicknamed "The Alps of America" and can rival Glacier National Park for sheer grandeur. Post Creek is the only trail to go completely through the steep valleys and lofty peaks of the southern portion of this range.

This can be an overnight loop trip starting from either trailhead or an out-and-back day trip from either trailhead.

To get to the Eagle Pass Creek trailhead, go 5.5 miles south of Ronan on U.S. 93 and take the county road to the left (east) at Ninepipes Reservoir and just north of the Allentown Motel. Go east exactly four miles on this county road. Then, just across an irrigation canal, turn left (north). In about one-eighth mile, there's a road taking off uphill to the right (east). Drive this old logging road as far as you can. Then, start walking, as the road gradually becomes a trail. (Parking is very limited at this trailhead.)

To get to McDonald Lake, go 7.5 miles south of Ronan on U.S. 93 and turn east on the county road (two miles south of the Allentown Motel or one mile north of the Post Creek Store). Drive four miles, cross the irrigation canal, and hang a sharp left. In 1.5 miles, you'll reach the lake. Drive across the dam to the end of the road on the north shore where you'll find a picnic table and the trailhead. Looking east, McDonald Peak looms 6,200 feet above the lake.

Assuming you begin your hike at McDonald Lake, the trail stays along the lake and through stands of large cedar and hemlock for three miles. After this, you're completely swallowed up by the mountains. The next two miles are a steep, steady climb. This is a very exciting section of the hike, as the roar of waterfalls fills the whole valley. Steep mountain buttresses rise on all sides. The trail, built in the CCC days, climbs up a cliff through a series of switchbacks that are an engineering marvel, not to mention a thrill to climb.

After that, the trail runs three miles past a chain of lakes (Moon Lake, Long Lake, and Frog Lake) to Summit Lake, which sits in the middle of a

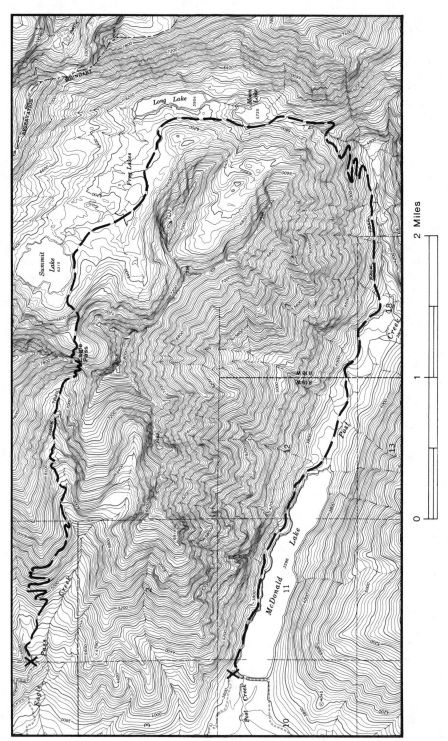

Summit Lake

circular valley at 6,300 feet. All these lakes are worth fishing (rainbow). All told, it's about eight miles to Summit Lake from McDonald Lake with a 2,700-foot elevation gain.

From Summit Lake, you can see the back of vulture-shaped Mount Harding (9,061 feet). To the south lies 7,500-foot Eagle Summit Pass, complete with its unique rock monolith. But don't try this pass until August, as the east side is quite steep and choked with snow earlier in the summer. The trail is easy to lose when under snow, and the steep snow is very dangerous. If you go out through Eagle Summit Pass, it's five miles from Summit Lake to the trailhead, making a 13-mile loop.

This hike usually has plenty of water with the possible exception of the trip over Eagle Summit Pass. Be wary, lest you have an unpleasant meeting with one of the Mission Mountain grizzly bears.

If you want to climb Mount Harding as a side trip, cross over to the west side of Eagle Summit Pass. Then, work north up through steep meadows to the southwest ridge and on up to the south peak. From here, you can enjoy the scenery and decide whether or not you want to tackle the more difficult and slightly higher central peak.

If you're staying overnight, there is a variety of good campsites near Summit Lake. You also have a good selection of hikes from Summit Lake.

The entire western half of the Mission Range is part of the Flathead Indian Reservation, so secure a Tribal Recreation Permit before you leave on this hike. —*Pat Caffrey*

35 *St. Mary's Peaks*

General description: A demanding, cross country day hike for experienced hikers.
General location: Thirty miles north of Missoula in the Mission Mountains.
Maps: St. Mary's Lake USGS Quad.
Special attractions: A spectacular view of the rugged southern Mission Mountains and much of northwestern Montana.

The hike to the top of St. Mary's peaks is physically demanding, but requires no special climbing skills. Along the way expect a view of some of the most spectacular mountain terrain in western Montana.

It's only a short drive from Missoula. Take U.S. 93 north, past Ravalli, to the blacktop road that takes off to the east (right) from U.S. 93 one mile south of St. Ignatius. After one mile turn right onto the road that skirts the south side of St. Ignatius and follow it for about 12 miles as it heads southeast to St. Mary's Reservoir.

Park at the northwest end of the reservoir, and strike out cross country north-by-northeast up the mountain.

Although not a must, your compass and topographic map will help you find and follow the ridge that eventually becomes the east shoulder of the peaks. It's a steep, dry walk, not an idyllic stroll through the woods. Although the 9400-foot peaks are only four horizontal miles (eight miles round trip) from the trailhead, they're a vertical mile higher.

Since you are on the Flathead Indian reservation, be sure to get a tribal

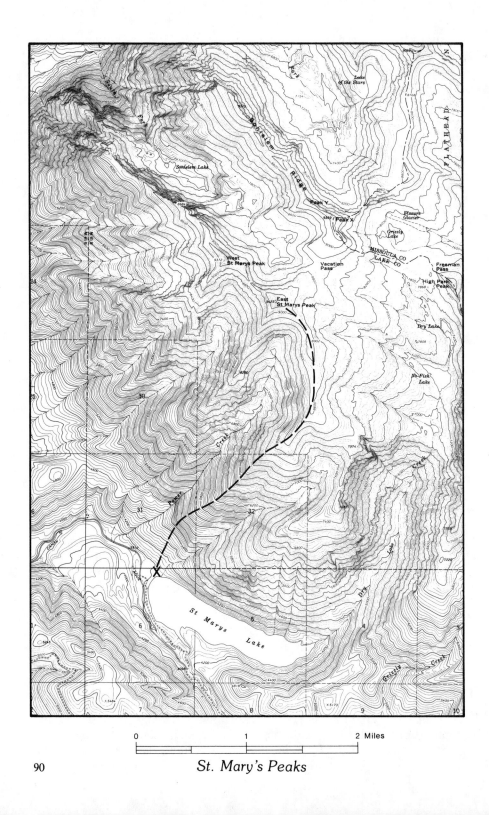

0   1   2 Miles

St. Mary's Peaks

recreation permit. They are available at many sporting goods stores on or near the reservation.

The alpine area to the northeast of the peaks is very enticing. If you have the time or have taken overnight gear, it is well worth investigating. Although this area does not have the highest concentration of grizzlies in the Missions it supports a few big bruins, so exercise standard precautions.

The view of the other Mission Mountain peaks from the St. Mary's peaks is outstanding. Although anyone seeing the Missions from the Flathead Valley floor can recognize that the Missions are rugged, the view from St. Mary's peaks gives their rugged character a new dimension. Also, on clear days the more distant viewing is incredible, particularly in late fall when the larch begin to color in the Rattlesnake Mountains, which lie just across the Jocko Valley from St. Mary's peaks. Fall often means hazy days, due to the slash burning that takes place across western Montana, so try to hike close on the heels of an air-scouring front.

The Flathead tribe is in the process of making critical decisions about how to manage its magnificent half of the Mission Mountains. There have been proposals to log dangerously high on the flanks of these classic peaks. Meanwhile, the tribe has not yet fully explored the benefits of emphasizing the recreation potential of the Missions in their current undeveloped state. Like many other wild places in Montana, greater recreation use may be essential to recognize the full value of the wild character of the Mission Mountains.—*John Westenberg*

36 *Morrell Falls*

General description: A fairly easy, five-mile round trip for any hiker.
General location: Ten miles north of Seeley Lake.
Maps: Morrell Lake USGS Quad and Lolo National Forest, Seeley Lake Ranger District.
Special attractions: Large waterfalls, small lakes.
For more information: Write the District Ranger, Seeley Lake Ranger District, Lolo National Forest, Seeley Lake, MT 59868 or call (406) 677-2444.

The Morrell Falls is a series of large cascades which drop about 100 feet. In winter, it qualifies as one of Montana's larger icicles.

To find the trailhead, turn east onto the Morrell Creek Road one-fourth mile north of the Seeley Lake Post Office. Go for slightly more than a mile and take a left on the West Morrell Road and drive seven miles. Then, hang a right, cross the bridge over Morrell Creek and take a left at the next junction. From here, it's one mile to the trailhead.

The trail is mostly flat and wanders 2.5 miles through open, lodgepole stands. There's only one short steep stretch and a few streams to cross (most of which are bridged). About one-fourth mile from the falls, you'll pass Morrell Lake, a handy place to camp and swim.

The main trail goes to the lower falls. But there's a steep goat trail (which leaves the main trail just before it reaches the falls) that offers more viewpoints of the falls and climbs up to the upper falls. It's a tough hike, but it only lasts a few hundred yards.

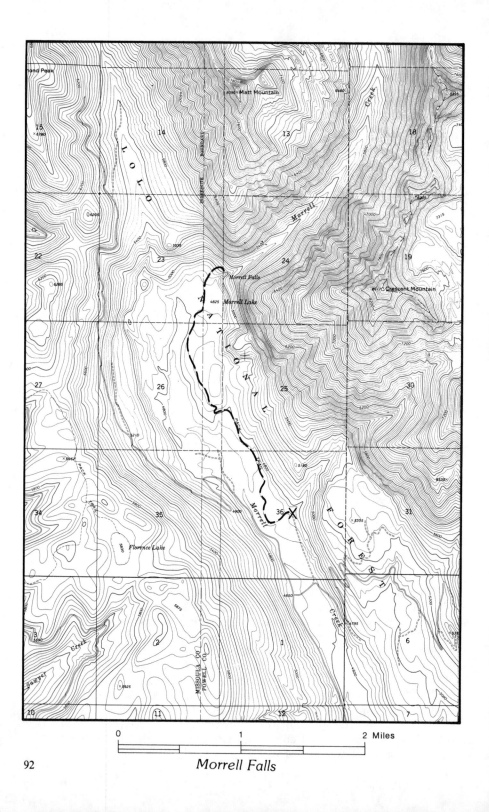

Morrell Falls

The trail is generally free of snow mid-May through October, and there's enough drinking water. June is the best time to feed the mosquitoes, or you can shoot them for sport. They are as overwhelming as the volume of water coming over the falls, so don't forget your repellent.—*Pat Caffrey*

37   Crater Lake

General description: An overnight hike through subalpine terrain to a good fishing lake.

General location: Twenty miles north of Swan Lake in Swan Range.

Maps: Jewel Basin and Crater Lake USGS Quads and Flathead Forest, Swan Ranger District.

Special attraction: A level hike through western forestland similar to Glacier National Park.

For more information: Write the District Ranger, Swan Ranger Station, Flathead National Forest, Bigfork, MT 59911 or call (406) 837-5081.

To reach high elevation lakes, hikers usually expect a healthy climb. Crater Lake is the exception. The trail starts high, so it's seven, easy miles to this scenic fishing lake, a 14-mile round trip. This is commonly known as Alpine Trail #7.

To reach this trailhead, go north on Highway 209 from Swan Lake. After 13 miles, 209 turns left, but keep going straight (north) on Highway #326. After about three miles, turn right at the Echo Lake Store on the Noisy Creek Road. Follow this road with the help of the signs for about seven miles to a parking lot. Beyond this parking lot, the road is not maintained for public use; but can be driven to a smaller parking lot at a microwave station on the Mount Aeneas Ridge.

From the smaller parking lot, the trail heads north along the west face of Mount Aeneas. A quarter-mile later, it splits. You take the trail to Birch Lake. Then, it cuts through a lush forest sprinkled with wet meadows for six miles before making a slight drop into Crater Lake. There are several trail junctions along the way, but they're unusually well-marked, so simply follow the signs to Crater Lake.

At two miles, you reach Birch Lake, and at three miles Squaw Lake can be seen a few hundred yards east of the trail.

The Forest Service adequately maintains this trail all summer. And there's no need to carry drinking water, as it's available all along the trail. The area is remote, and motorized vehicles are banned. This trail is very popular, so expect to see other hikers.

Sharp-eyed hikers often spot a mountain goat on the crags above the trail or a deer or elk in one of the many open parks. Wildflowers abound, especially at the beginning of the hike along the face of Mount Aeneas.

An occasional grizzly is reported in this area, and black bears are fairly common. However, reports of bear trouble are almost nonexistent.

Crater Lake can be nearly perfect for a family overnighter. The hike is easy, about the right distance, cool, and can be taken anytime from July through October. Be sure to bring mosquito repellent, however, as Crater Lake always seems to have its share of these pesky insects.

Most campers stay at Crater Lake where the fishing for brook trout is

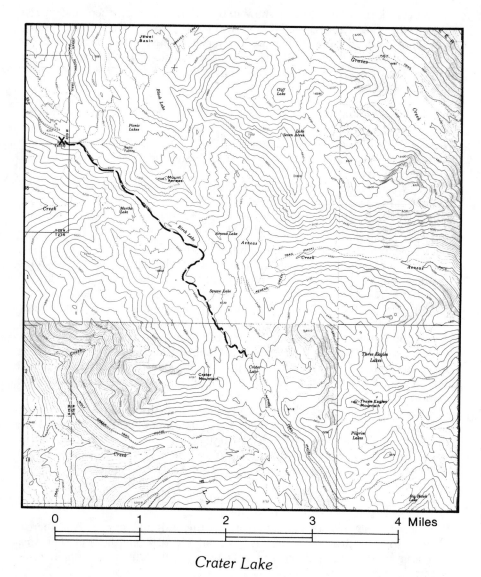

0   1   2   3   4 Miles

Crater Lake

excellent. However, a few stay at Squaw or Birch Lakes which are along the trail to Crater Lake and have equally good fishing. All three lakes have several Forest Service campsites. At Crater Lake, firewood is scarce, but it's everywhere at the other lakes.

Perhaps the highlight of this trip is the rocky, glacier-scoured basin around Crater Lake. There seems to be more rock than vegetation in this basin. Except for the Crater Lake basin, the entire trail goes through a series of moist mountain glades similar to those of Glacier Park.

The Crater Lake hike has a wide selection of possible side trips. Perhaps the most popular is to continue north on the same trail for two more miles to Big Hawk Lake which is slightly larger than Crater Lake, but not quite as scenic.

Another common side trip is a loop around the east face of Mount Aeneas through part of the Jewel Basin. Leave Alpine Trail #7 at Birch Lake and drop abruptly down to Jewel Basin and then climb sharply around the south side of Mount Aeneas back to the lookout.—*Larry Thompson*

38 Jewel Basin

General description: A collection of easy-to-moderate hikes.

General location: Ten miles northeast of Bigfork, on the northern tip of the Swan Range.

Maps: Jewel Basin, Crater Lake and Big Hawk Mountain USGS Quads and a special Forest Service handout and map on the Jewel Basin Hiking Area.

Special attractions: A beautiful chunk of backcountry set aside for hikers only.

For more information: Write the District Ranger, Hungry Horse Ranger District, Flathead National Forest, Hungry Horse, MT 59919 or call (406) 387-5243.

The Forest Service has designated Jewel Basin, with its 28 lakes and 35 miles of trail, as a special hiking area, prohibiting pack stock and motorized vehicles. The 15,349-acre area is aptly named.

To find it, drive two miles north of Bigfork and turn east off State Highway 35 onto State Highway 83. Drive about 2.7 miles and turn north on the Echo Lake Road. After 2.5 miles, take the Noisy Creek Road to the east and follow it until it ends at a parking area where several trails into Jewel Basin begin. A pick-up or similar vehicle with high clearance is best for the last few miles of the Noisy Creek Road.

Instead of detailing a single hike, choose from the wide selection of scenic trips leaving from this trailhead. Five trails leave from the end of Noisy Creek Road, all of which will get you into Jewel Basin in two miles or less. Get a map and plan a trip that suits you.

Jewel Basin is perfect for beginning hikers wanting to see what backpacking is all about—or for families ready to introduce their children to the wilderness without working too hard the first time. The area is also just right for a leisurely day hike—perhaps with a brief sampling of the area's good fishing.

You can take a short hop into tranquil Picnic Lakes, or a longer hike covering most of the basin, stopping to fish and camp at several lakes. Almost all lakes have suitable campsites, but plan on using your backpack stove to keep the sites from showing the wear-and-tear of heavy use.

The Jewel Basin even has something for those who have irresistible urges to climb to the top of something. From the end of Noisy Creek Road, they can take a short hike on a trail along Aeneas Ridge to the top of 7,530-foot Mount Aeneas, which offers super views of Flathead Lake and the southern portion of Glacier National Park. —*Pat Caffrey and Loren Kreck*

Because the above description describes a general area instead of a specific hike, there is no map.—Editor

39 Columbia Divide

General description: A long, three-day hike for experienced hikers.

General location: Just southeast of Columbia Falls.

Maps: Doris Mountain, Jewel Basin, and Hash Mountain USGS Quads, Forest Service's Jewel Basin Hiking Area map, and Flathead National Forest Swan Lake Ranger District.

Special attractions: Outstanding panoramic views of northwestern Montana and Flathead Lake from a delightful, ridgeline trail.

For more information: Write the District Ranger, Swan Lake Ranger District, Flathead National Forest, Bigfork, Montana 59911 or call (406) 837-5081.

This 27-mile hike isn't for beginners or small children. It usually requires three days with a full pack and involves a 3,500-foot elevation gain.

To reach the trailhead, turn south off U.S. 2 about 1.3 miles east of the U.S. 2/State Highway 40 junction. This turn is marked with a "Columbia Mountain Trail" sign. Follow this road .8 mile to the trail marked "Columbia Mountain Trail #51."

Trail #51 climbs steadily up the slopes of Columbia Mountain where it intersects with Trail #7. Take #7 south all the way to Strawberry Lake and then turn west on Trail #5 for a short drop down to Krause Road and the end of your three-day ridgeline excursion.

This is a point-to-point hike, so it's best to leave a vehicle at the end of the hike (Strawberry Lake trailhead) or have somebody pick you up there. To find the Strawberry Lake trailhead, turn east from U.S. 2 (four miles north of Creston) on the Lake Blaine Road. Just after passing Lake Blaine, turn south on the Mountain View Road and go about eight miles. Then, turn left (east) up the Krause Creek Road to Strawberry Lake Trailhead.

Although there is water at many places along the trail, there are some stretches in the northern half of this hike where hikers must carry it. Mosquitoes can be a problem early in the season, but they seem less severe than many areas. Shelter from wind and drinking water can often be found by dropping over the ridge to the east into the high meadows.

Black bears and grizzlies inhabit this area, so there is a chance of a bear/man confrontation. The likelihood of such an encounter might be higher here than on many trails in Montana's national forests, but the probability of bear trouble is still much lower than in nearby Glacier National Park. Proper bear country manners will further lower the probability of bear trouble.

Except the trail below Strawberry Lake, few motorized vehicles are encountered on this trail because of its remoteness. The signs of civilization—clearcuts, cities, etc.—can be seen in the distance, but the terrain is relatively untouched along the trail.

The 27 miles can be made in two days, but to really enjoy the scenery on this high-altitude hike, allow three days. Although the trail is remote and primitive, it's still well-maintained—good enough to follow easily. There is a fair chance of spotting elk or deer, and a great variety of wildflowers greet summer hikers, particularly in mid-July. Snow may block this trail until early July.

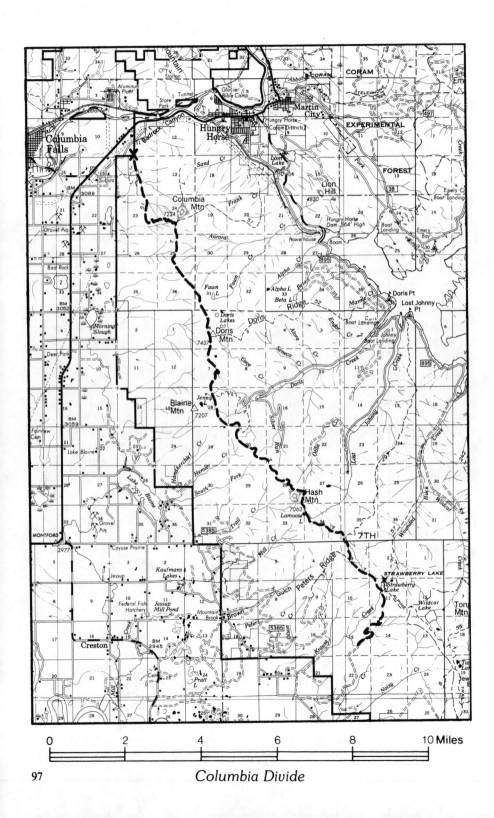

Columbia Divide

The best campsites are Lamoose and Strawberry lakes, but there is a good selection from which to choose. Both of these lakes have fish and easily available water, but firewood is scarce, so bring your backpack stove.

Although there is some fishing in Strawberry and Lamoose lakes, this hike isn't known for its fishing. The main attraction is vistas inherent to crest trails.

There are many variations of this hike because of the extensive trail system in the area. For instance, hikers could easily be lured into extending into the nearby Jewel Basin. —*Loren Kreck*

40 *Logan Creek*

General description: A steep, day hike for experienced hikers.
General location: Just east of Hungry Horse Reservoir.
Maps: Felix Peak and Nimrod USGS Quads, Flathead National Forest's Great Bear Wilderness map, and Flathead National Forest, Hungry Horse Ranger District.
Special attractions: Scenery—especially rock cliffs and one very high waterfall.
For more information: Write the District Ranger, Hungry Horse Ranger Station, Flathead National Forest, Hungry Horse, MT 59919 or call (406) 387-5243.

Although the trip up and back Logan Creek usually makes a nice day hike for good hikers, a few decide to spend the night near where the trail ends—on the divide between the South Fork and Middle Fork of the Flathead River.

To find the trailhead, turn south off U.S. 2 at Martin City and go along the east shore of Hungry Horse Reservoir for 35 miles until you reach Logan Creek. There should be a sign marking the turn off onto a smaller dirt road up Logan Creek. Follow this road for about one mile to the trailhead which is also marked with a sign. Be alert for logging trucks.

For the first two miles, the trail follows Logan Creek through deep spruce forests. Then, the trail leaves the creek and heads into alders and other brush. The mid-section of this hike can try a hiker's patience, as the brush gets jungle-like in a few places.

Be sure to look up as you're fighting the brush. You will be treated to the sight of sheer cliffs at your left and a cascading waterfall on your right.

Just about the time you're cursing about the poorly maintained trail, you break out into a luscious subalpine meadow, and the hard work all seems worth it.

Through the meadow flows a babbling brook lined with buttercups and other wildflowers. It also has a small pond, elk wallow, and a crescendoing waterfall just below you. Actually, you're in a hanging valley above the big waterfall. The last mile of the hike gradually climbs through subalpine meadows and large spruces and larch snags to the divide where you get an unsurpassed view into Dirtyface Creek and the Middle Fork of the Flathead River.

It's six miles from trailhead to divide with an elevation gain of 2,300 feet which will take at least six hours for the round trip. Water is available all

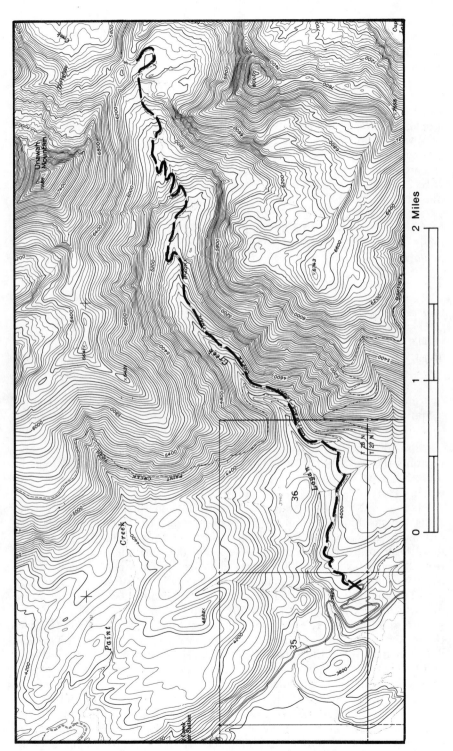

Logan Creek

2 Miles

along the trail. In a few places, you have to sort of feel your way through the brush, but the only possible hazards are two crossings of Logan Creek which could be tricky at high water. Mosquitoes exist in tolerable densities, especially in July, August, and September which is the best time for this hike.

If you prefer to make this an overnighter, the best campsite is in the meadow just as you break out of the brush and just below the divide. It has a delicious stream and carpets of wildflowers. Bring your backpacker stove, however, as firewood is scarce, unless you want to carry it from the edge of the meadow.

This trail continues down Dirtyface Creek through old clearcuts and hits U.S. 2 3.5 miles west of Essex. However, most hikers prefer to make it an out-and-back hike.

Apparently, part of this area was left out of the Great Bear Wilderness because of numerous mining claims. This means that this beautiful hike might someday be a paved road to an open pit mine.—*Elaine and Art Sedlack*

41   Ousel Peak

General description: A long, day hike for experienced hikers.

General location: Just southwest of West Glacier and just west of the Great Bear Wilderness.

Maps: West Glacier and Nyack USGS Quads, Flathead National Forest's Great Bear Wilderness map, and Flathead National Forest, Hungry Horse Ranger District.

For more information: Write the District Ranger, Hungry Horse Ranger Station, Flathead National Forest, Hungry Horse, MT 59919 or call (406) 387-5243.

Although the trailhead may be difficult to locate, the Ousel Peak hike warrants the extra time. To make sure you don't have trouble finding the trailhead, however, check with Hungry Horse Ranger Station on U.S. 2 in Hungry Horse.

Take U.S. 2 and turn south at Martin City on the Forest Service road along the east shore of Hungry Horse Reservoir. Go seven miles and turn east on the Emery Creek Road. Follow this road up onto the Highline Loop Road. The trail begins about 7.5 miles from the reservoir road or 2.5 miles from the only big bend (180 degrees) in the road. The first 200 yards of the trail was eliminated by a clearcut in 1978, so until the Forest Service puts up new signs the trail will be hard to find. Now, the trail starts 20 feet up a skid trail which was cut through the logging debris.

This is a rugged, 12-mile, point-to-point hike that goes from Hungry Horse Reservoir on the South Fork of the Flathead River over the Flathead Range and through the Great Bear Wilderness down to U.S. 2 on the Middle Fork of the Flathead. After finding the trail, you move through an open forest of large tamaracks. Then, the trail enters a rocky drainage before breaking out on open, rocky ridges with views of Deerlick Creek, Nyack Creek, the Middle Fork of the Flathead, Harrison Lake in Glacier National Park, and many of the highest peaks in the park. The trail follows the rocky ridges for about three miles before ducking around the back of

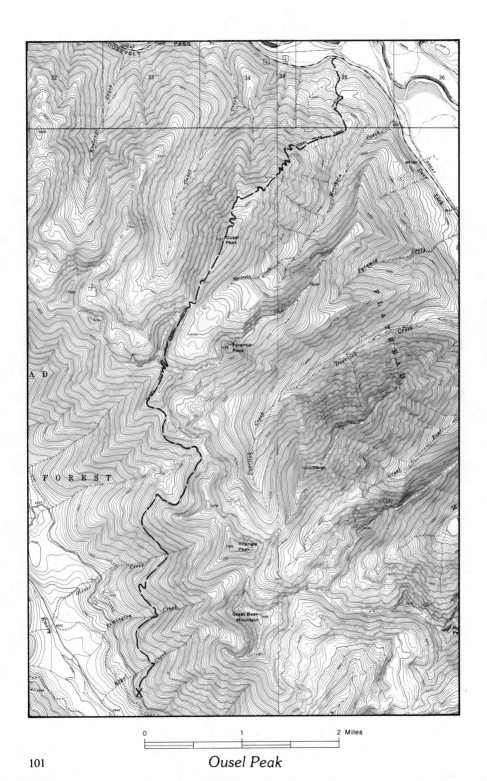

Ousel Peak

0   1   2 Miles

Ousel Peak. Then, it drops abruptly down to U.S. 2, five miles east of West Glacier.

This point-to-point hike is actually two trails—trail #388 up from Hungry Horse Reservoir and trail #331 down to U.S. 2. They meet at Ousel Peak, but this junction is poorly marked and difficult to find. Plan on spending some extra time looking around and referring to the topo map.

The trail is sometimes hard to find as it comes off Ousel Peak, so watch your topo map closely. The last three-mile drop to the highway cuts through alder thickets that can be bothersome.

This isn't a trip for beginners. It rises 2,700 feet (4,400 to 7,100), and the trail can be hard to follow on the rocky ridges. In addition, you have to bring drinking water for the entire trip, as the trail is quite dry. There are also a few blowdowns on the South Fork side to slow progress. On the plus side, mosquitoes are rarely a problem.

It takes a good hiker eight hours to make this hike. Unless you want to hike through snow, wait until mid-July to try it.

Most hikers leave a vehicle where the trail meets U.S. 2 or have somebody pick them up there. Hitchhiking back to the trailhead would be most difficult.

Wild animals—elk, deer, black bear, and others—are fairly common. Even an occasional grizzly bear is spotted. And watch for glacier lillies, lupine, and other wildflowers. Later in the year, expect to find some excellent huckleberry patches.

Few—if any—hikers make this an overnighter. And there aren't any good campsites.—*Elaine and Art Sedlack*

42   Great Northern

General description: A mountain ascent through timbered undergrowth and up scree slopes for scramblers with good stamina.

General location: Thirty miles east of Kalispell, between Hungry Horse Reservoir and Glacier National Park.

Maps: Mount Grant USGS Quad, Flathead National Forest, and "Climbing Great Northern," a Forest Service handout.

Special attractions: Goat trails, fine scenery, Stanton Glacier, and spectacular views of seldom-seen southern Glacier National Park.

For more information: Write the District Ranger, Hungry Horse Ranger Station, Flathead National Forest, Hungry Horse, MT 59919 or call (406) 387-5243.

Although named for a former railroad, the mountain's name suggests exactly what it is. It's graceful curves and broad faces are irresistible to the individual who has acquired a taste for the high places. With the incomparable peaks of Glacier Park close at hand, this mountain attracts many individuals solely on the merits of its own beauty.

Two popular routes are described on a Forest Service flyer available at the Hungry Horse Ranger Station. The following is a shorter variation of the western approach described in the flyer.

Take the East Side Road of Hungry Horse Reservoir, which leaves U.S. 2 as the main street of Martin City. About 8.5 miles past the Emery Creek

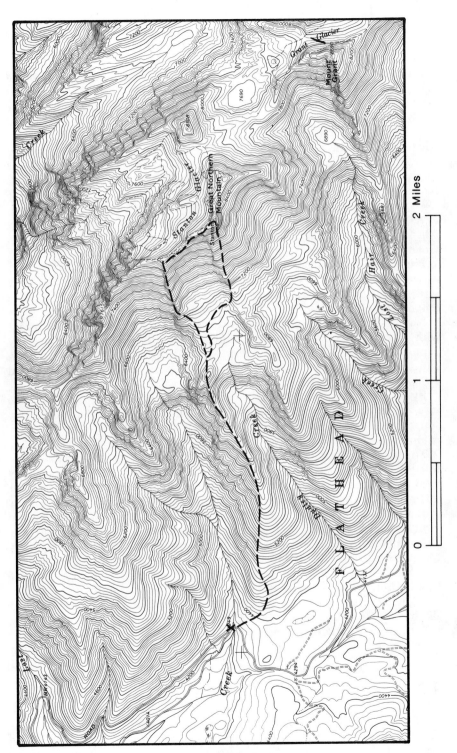

Great Northern

boat landing area, hang a left (uphill) and go one-half mile to the Highline Loop Road junction, where you will find a small bridge. Park at this bridge (elevation 4,249), fill your canteen, and start climbing.

Look south of the bridge and notice the impenetrable thickets of brush and small trees. After briefly considering whether the whole idea is worthwhile, charge into these thickets. They don't last long and are the hardest part of the climb. Find a game trail to help escape this jungle.

Climb the ascending ridge on the south side of Hungry Horse Creek, where you just filled your canteen. Initially, work to the south, climbing and contouring to get out of the brush and windfalls on the north side of the ridge. In early August, be careful not to delay too long in these massive huckleberry patches.

Within one-half mile, a definite ridgetop, complete with a definite trail, develops. Follow this ridge for one mile to where it peaks out at timberline. Ahead of you is a small timbered saddle, on the other side of which is the Great Northern.

From here, you have a choice of two routes. Note the rocky, open spur ascending directly to the peak. Save this route for the descent. It's loose scree, and with great care and concentration, you can run down its slopes in ten minutes.

Now, note another ascending spur to the left (north) of the main peak, with clumps of gnarled trees reaching almost to the summit ridge. Try climbing this way; the rock is firmer. Once on the summit ridge, after a few gasps at the scenery, follow intriguing little goat trails along ledges and around rock knobs to the 8,720-foot summit.

By now, you've noticed the 120-acre Stanton Glacier which reaches all the way to the summit ridge on the east side. This is a "real" glacier of hard, slippery ice and deep crevasses, so stay off it unless you're properly equipped.

To the east is the Middle Fork of the Flathead River and across it the usually unseen array of peaks of southern Glacier Park. One unusually monstrous-looking peak sticks up above the others. The south portion of this peak is pyramid-shaped, with a chopped-off ridge to the north. This is Mount Stimson, at 10,142-feet elevation, the second highest peak and the most exhausting climb in the park. North of it is 10,052-foot Mount Jackson, with huge Harrison Glacier flung across the entire south face. A few miles to the south of Mount Stimson, you can pick out 9,376-foot St. Nicholas, the most difficult technical climb in the park. It's just north of Church Butte, a flat-topped rectangle. St. Nicholas is easy to spot because, quite literally, it sticks out like a sore thumb. And it appears impossible to climb.

Perhaps this briefly explains the magic lure of the Great Northern. Notwithstanding, it's a true mountain, and it's never mistaken for anything less. —*Pat Caffrey*

43 *Stanton Lake*

General description: A short hike suitable for any hiker.

General location: Thirteen miles southeast of West Glacier on the edge of

the Great Bear Wilderness and just southwest of Glacier National Park.
Maps: Mount Grant, Pinnacle and Stanton Lake USGS Quads, Flathead
National Forest's Great Bear Wilderness maps, and Flathead National
Forest, Hungry Horse Ranger District.

Wild trout add to the backcountry vacation. Bill Schneider photo.

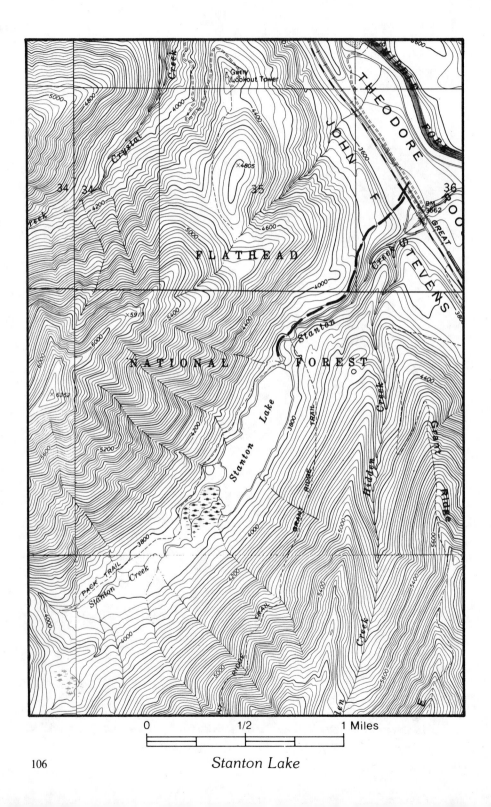

Stanton Lake

Special attractions: An easy way to get a choice view of the mountains of Glacier Park and of Great Northern Mountain in the Great Bear Wilderness.

For more information: Write the District Ranger, Hungry Horse Ranger Station, Flathead National Forest, Hungry Horse, MT 59919 or call **(406) 387-5243.**

The Stanton Lake trail begins right on U.S. 2 just east of Stanton Lake Lodge about 13 miles east of West Glacier. So, for once, the trailhead is easy to find.

Except for some motorcycle traffic on the first part of the trail, this hike is remote. The trail is well-maintained with a gradual incline, rising 500 feet in two miles. There isn't any drinking water until you reach the lake.

This trail receives fairly heavy use, and it's easy to see why. It's an easy hike, open from June through October. (Bring your insect repellent in June and July.) The fishing is good, and the likelihood of bear trouble is minimal.

Hikers often get a glimpse of a moose at the head of the lake or a beaver in the beaver ponds as the stream leaves the lake. Wildflowers are fairly common—beargrass, wild hollyhocks, cow parsnip, and others.

Some hikers carry in small rubber rafts for float fishing. Usually, this is worth the effort, as it increases the size of the catch of the lake's supply of rainbow and cutthroat trout. However, anglers can usually catch at least some smaller cutthroat from shore.

Although it's only two miles into the lake, the lake still receives substantial overnight use. Most backpackers use the campsite at the head of the lake where water and firewood are easy to find.

Perhaps the highlight of this hike is the vista of the mountains of Glacier National Park to the north and the massive Great Northern Mountain to the south.

Since this popular lake has an above average number of visitors, be extra careful not to leave signs of your passing. And do whatever you can to pick up or cover up the signs of others who weren't so careful.—*Elaine and Art Sedlack*

44 *Marion Lake*

General description: A leisurely day hike or overnighter into one of the many high altitude lakes in the Great Bear Wilderness.

General location: Just south of Glacier National Park.

Maps: Pinnacle USGS Quad, Flathead National Forests Great Bear Wilderness map, and Flathead National Forest, Hungry Horse Ranger District.

Special attractions: An easily accessible wilderness lake.

For more information: Write the District Ranger, Hungry Horse Ranger Station, Flathead National Forest, Hungry Horse, MT 59919 or call **(406) 387-5243.**

Marion Lake is easily accessible and has good fishing. Thus, it probably receives above-average use compared with other mountain lakes in designated wilderness areas.

The trailhead is also easy to find. Turn west on the Essex Creek Road

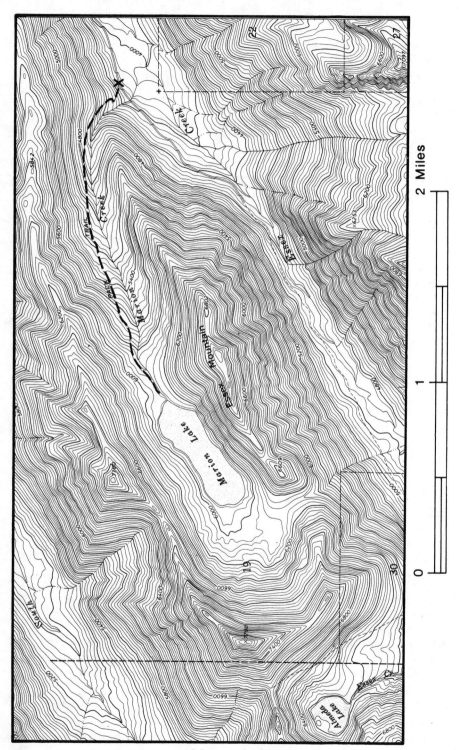

2 Miles

Marion Lake

which turns off from U.S. 2 one mile north of Essex or 24 miles south of West Glacier. Watch for a sign marking the trailhead about 1.5 miles from the highway.

The way to Marion Lake is a steady, uphill pull. The trail gains about 2,000 feet in three miles. This should take a family less than three hours into the lake and two hours or less out.

The hike has a well-maintained trail, plenty of drinking water, and a tolerable number of mosquitoes—except some years in June and July. Since this lake lies within the Great Bear Wilderness, the hike has a remote feeling, and of course, motorized vehicles are banned.

Bear problems are minimal even though black bears are numerous and an occasional grizzly frequents this area. Skip this hike in June unless you want to risk hiking through snowbanks.

At the head of the lake lies a gorgeous, grassy swale blanketed with wildflowers—beargrass, fireweed, wild hollyhocks, dogwood, bunchberry and others.

The trail comes to the foot of the lake. But there is a faint trail around to the head of the lake—about one-half mile.

For an excellent side trip, work your way through the swale to the pass on the horizon. It's only about one-half mile from where the trail hits the lake. At the top of the swale, you can look down over 1,000-foot cliffs into the headwaters of Essex Creek.

Backpackers almost always camp at the head of the lake where scenery is abundant and firewood scarce.

The lake has good fishing, particularly in June when the ice breaks up. Each winter, a few avid anglers ski or snowshoe in for ice fishing, and they usually have good success from the lake's healthy population of cutthroat and rainbow trout.

Fortunately, Montana has such choice spots within reach of everybody. Unfortunately, Marion Lake shows a little wear-and-tear as the result of this accessibility and popularity. Take a bag along and carry out any garbage a thoughtless hiker might have left behind.—*Elaine and Art Sedlack*

45 Nyack *Loop*

General description: A long backpacking expedition for experienced hikers.
General location: Fifteen miles southeast of West Glacier in the Middle Fork region of Glacier National park.
Maps: Nyack, Mount Jackson, Mount Stimson, and Mount Saint Nicholas USGS Quads and the large USGS topo map of the entire park.
Special attractions: A rare opportunity to get intimately close to the wilderness and totally away from everything else.
For more information: Write the District Ranger, Walton Ranger Station, Glacier National Park, West Glacier, MT 59936 or call (406) 888-5628.

Many trails in Glacier Park are heavily used. But others receive surprisingly little use—even though they host as many backcountry rewards. The Nyack Loop is an excellent case-in-point.

It follows Nyack Creek as it flows over a gorgeous falls and colorful bedrock. Mount Stimson, an incredible hulk of a mountain, dominates the

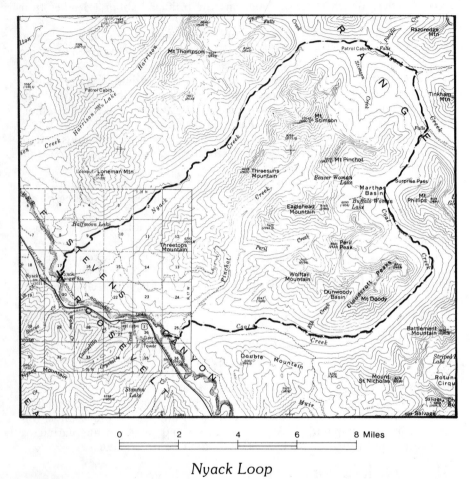

0	2	4	6	8 Miles

Nyack Loop

landscape for much of the hike. And wildlife—including the grizzly—is as abundant as any section of the park.

So what keeps the trail from heavy use or overuse? It's a long hike, 35 miles or more depending on how many side trips you take. There is no fishing. And it starts and ends by fording the Middle Fork of the Flathead River.

But if you aren't a fanatic angler, can tolerate getting your feet wet, and don't mind long walks, this could turn out to be the backpacking vacation of your life. Plan on at least three days, but you can easily spend a week without regretting it.

Another limiting factor for the Nyack Loop route is the difficulty in finding the trailheads and fords over the Middle Fork. The easiest way to avoid confusion is to stop or call the Walton Ranger Station for detailed and updated directions and a special hand-drawn map to both the Nyack Creek and Coal Creek trailheads.

To start this hike, drive west from Walton Ranger Station until you cross the railroad tracks. After this crossing, take the first gravel road to your right. Follow it for a short distance and turn right where it dead ends just before the tracks. Drive about another one-fourth mile and park. Walk down the road a hundred yards or so, cross the tracks, follow a trail through a cottonwood stand, and then wade the river, keeping your eyes peeled for trail markers on trees on the opposite riverbank.

The mighty grizzly, king of the wilderness, Doug O'looney photo.

Leave a vehicle or have somebody pick you up at the Coal Creek trailhead which is about five miles southeast of Nyack Creek on U.S. 2. Drive from Walton to a small parking area which is a short drive up a gravel road to your left. The trail takes off from the highway and crosses the tracks before merging into an old logging road. Ford the Middle Fork about 75 yards south of where the old logging road hits the river.

The trail starts at the abandoned Nyack Ranger Station and crosses Nyack Creek about one mile from the river. This is a large stream and the bridge has been washed out, so be prepared for wet feet again. No, this isn't the last time; there are other streams to cross in the next few days.

The trail gradually climbs along Nyack Creek all the way to Surprise Pass. The trail dips down to the stream occassionally, but stays high much of the way. Although there are a few dry stretches, you can usually find enough drinking water. Although the scenery leaves little to be desired all the way, the scenic highlight may be Nyack Falls with massive Mount Stimson forming the backdrop. On the way up Surprise Pass, spend a few hours gorging yourself on huckleberries. Keep very close watch for grizzlies, however, as this entire hike traverses some of the best grizzly habitat left in Montana.

Soon after dropping over Surprise Pass into Coal Creek, a trail to Buffalo Woman and Beaver Woman lakes juts off to the right. Even if you don't camp here, don't miss these "beautiful women." After the lakes, it's a long, scenic haul down Coal Creek to the Middle Fork.

On such a long hike, you may not be looking for side trips, but if you have extra time, you have several super possibilities. You can take the Dawson Pass or Pitamakan Pass trails for good views of much of southern Glacier Park. Perhaps the most popular side trip is a climb up Mount Stimson. Although one of the—if not the—most rigorous climbs in the park, it's still nontechnical and within the reach of most well-conditioned, experienced hikers.

Leave your fishing pole home, as Nyack Creek, Coal Creek, Buffalo Woman Lake, and Beaver Woman Lake are all closed to fishing by the National Park Service. You'll need the extra room in your pack for food, anyway.

Before taking the hike, be sure to obtain a backcountry camping permit from any park ranger station. You can camp anywhere, and there are numerous excellent campsites. The NPS discourages camping at the patrol cabins along this hike. Also before leaving, check the current park regulations of campfires, as they are often prohibited during dry weather.

As a special precaution, carefully read "Hiking Bear Country" (page 7) to reduce to almost nothing your chance of encountering a grizzly on unpleasant terms. Remember, this is the big bear's home, and you are the visitor, so behave accordingly.—*Bill Schneider*

46   *Akokala Lake*

General description: A moderate day hike or easy overnighter.
General location: Thirty-five miles north of West Glacier in the North Fork region of Glacier National Park.

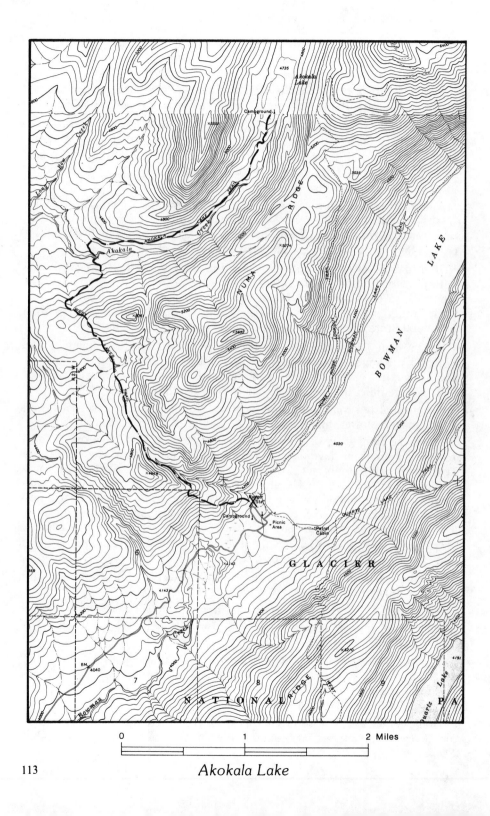

Akokala Lake

Maps: Quartz Ridge and Kintla Peak USGS Quads, the large topographic map of Glacier Park available at retail stores in the area, and the National Park Service brochure/map given to every park visitor.

For more information: Write the District Ranger, Polebridge Ranger Station, Glacier National Park, Polebridge, MT 59928 or call (406) 888-5416.

The North Fork of the Flathead River forms the west boundary of Glacier National Park. Inside the park, there are several lakes that drain into the river with Akokala being one of the smallest. This hike extends through fairly typical North Fork country with lodgepole forests and rolling ridges without snow-capped crags found elsewhere in the park.

The trail leaves from the Bowman Lake Campground which can be found by driving into the park from West Glacier. Shortly after entering the park, turn north on the Camas Creek Road and stay on this paved highway until it crosses the North Fork of the Flathead and leaves the park.

Immediately after crossing the river, the Camas Creek Road dead ends with the North Fork Road, a partly paved Forest Service road going all the way to the Canadian border. Turn north on the North Fork Road and stay on it for about 25 miles until you reach Polebridge, which is little more than a General Store, the Northern Lights Saloon, and a few cabins.

Go through Polebridge and across the river into the park again at the Polebridge Ranger Station. Also drive through the ranger station and go about a quarter-mile north until you see a right-hand turn to Bowman Lake. It's six more miles up this gravel road to Bowman Lake Campground.

(There is also a road following the North Fork within the park. However, this is longer, slower, and dustier.)

From the campground, it's about 5.6 miles to Akokala Lake on an easy-to-follow trail. You have one big hill near the beginning of the hike and a few more small climbs later on, but it's generally easy all the way, only gaining about 600 feet in elevation. When you reach Akokala Creek, you might see a trail junction with a trail following the creek. You turn right and follow Akokala Creek upstream to the lake. The left-hand fork has more-or-less been abandoned by the park and doesn't appear on current hiking maps.

The first half of the hike can be dry in late summer or early fall, but the last half has plenty of drinking water. Be sure to bring your insect repellent—especially in June—as the Bowman Lake is almost infamous for its fierce mosquitoes.

Akokala Lake has a good population of cutthroat and Dolly Varden trout. The fishing is best halfway around the left-hand (west) side where the water deepens close to shore.

The best campsite is near the outlet where the trail hits the lake. However, be sure to check with the rangers at Polebridge or Bowman Lake for a back-country camping permit and updated regulations before leaving on the hike. Fires are often prohibited in this area.

Don't forget that you're in Glacier Park grizzly country. So be religious about every possible bear country precaution and sanitary rule.—*Bill Schneider*

47 Pitamakan and Dawson Passes

General description: A two or three-day hike to two mountain lakes and over two spectacular mountain passes.

General location: On the east side of Glacier National Park about 12 miles northwest of East Glacier.

Maps: Cut Bank Pass and Mount Rockwell USGS Quads (Kiowa and Squaw Mountain cover the first two miles). The USGS also publishes a large contour map of the entire Glacier Park. Of additional help is the Backcountry Map and Trail Guide available at no charge from the National Park Service at all ranger stations.

Special attractions: Crossing the Continental Divide twice, this trail offers at least five separate panoramic views.

For more information: Write the District Ranger, Two Medicine Ranger Station, Glacier National Park, East Glacier, MT 59434 or call (406) 226-4301.

The trailhead is at the outlet of Two Medicine Lake. From the town of East Glacier, drive north on Highway 49 about four miles to a well-marked turnoff on the Two Medicine Road. Drive to the end of the Two Medicine Road and park in the lot near the ranger station.

Note these two points: 1) In order to camp at Oldman and/or No Name Lakes, you must have a backcountry camping permit, which can be secured the day before or the day of your hike at any park ranger station and 2) this is a loop trail and can be taken in the reverse direction from the way it is described below.

Oldman Lake in Glacier National Park. Mike Sample photo.

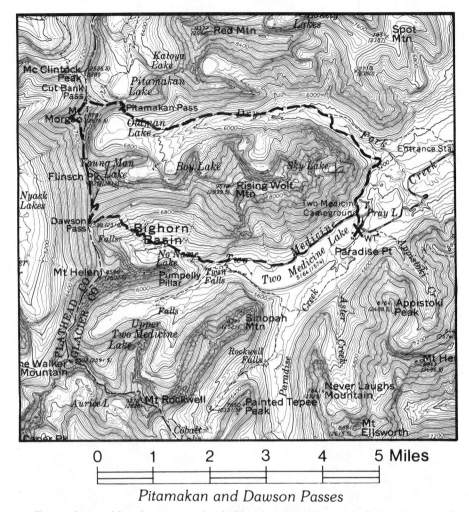

Pitamakan and Dawson Passes

From the parking lot, cross the bridge between Two Medicine Lake and tiny Pray Lake and turn right at the marked trail junction. The first segment of the trail stretches a little less than six miles to Oldman Lake. In the first two miles, the hiker moves around the base of towering Rising Wolf Mountain and across Dry Creek to a marked trail junction where you turn left (west). From here, you face a steady climb up an open valley. Very wet Dry Creek cascades the length of the valley while several smaller streams drop out of hidden criques to add to the volume. Paintbrush and lupine add splashes of color to the scene.

At the head of the valley, you enter a thick forest which is prone to blowdowns. The trail splits shortly before Oldman Lake. The right fork heads directly for Pitamakan Pass while the left leads to the campsites on the lake.

The National Park Service (NPS) has designated five campsites with fire grates in the timber by the lake. An outhouse stands nearby. Campers are required to use the designated sites to minimize man's impact on this beautiful spot.

Flinsch Peak dominates the western skyline. You may see a family of beavers at the far end of the lake in the twilight hours. Twenty-inch cutthroats cruise the shorelines. And on the northern slopes above the lake, a white cloud of beargrass stands as thick as anywhere in the park in late July.

The area around Oldman Lake seems to be natural habitat for grizzlies. Chances are slim of seeing one of the great bruins, let alone having any trouble, but play it safe: it's really their turf. Read over the "Hiking Bear Country" (page 7) before taking this hike.

From Oldman Lake to No Name Lake is a distance of about 7.5 miles, almost all of it is dry by early August, so carry water. Some hikers elect to bypass the camp at No Name Lake and hike all the way out on the second day. This makes for a long day, partly because this segment of the hike begins with an elevation gain of 1,400 feet.

To reach Pitamakan Pass from Oldman Lake, take the short cutoff trail almost straight north from the outhouse instead of going back to the trail junction. The climb to Pitamaken is short and steep—1,000 feet up in about a mile. You will find the pass is actually a saddle in a ridge. Before turning left (west) to follow the trail up the ridge, pause for a look down at Pitamakan Lake 800 feet below you.

Very quickly after leaving the saddle, the hiker encounters two well-marked junctions in the trail; in each case take the trail to the left. Less than a mile from Pitamakan Pass, you cross the Continental Divide. Due west stands mighty Mount Stimson rising 6,000 feet above the Nyack Creek valley.

From here, the trail goes in a southerly direction paralleling the Continental Divide along the shoulders of Mount Morgan and Flinsch Peak to Dawson Pass, where you cross the Divide again. While nearly level through this section, the trail traverses steep slopes of "roller bearing" scree which is dangerous when wet. Because dangerous snow banks lie across these slopes until late June or Early July, the NPS opens this trail later than most. Check with the Two Medicine Ranger Station before planning an early trip.

Dawson Pass is a favorite hangout for mountain goats, which are quite tame in this region. Dawson is also a favorite jump-off spot for people who wish to make the steep walk up the south face of Flinsch Peak.

From Dawson Pass, the trail drops very rapidly through Bighorn Basin to No Name Lake. The lake deserves a more descriptive "no-name," for it lies at the base of sheer Pumpelly Pillar. It is an evocative pool, especially in the first moments of sunlight on a quiet morning.

Again, there is a cluster of five campsites with grates and a nearby outhouse. The campsites are near the creek just before it empties into the lake. Like Oldman Lake, this area is quite "buggy" in July—bring some bug dope.

A fishing rod isn't of much use here. For some reason, the tiny trout which dimple the surface of the lake haven't made it big in recent years.

Leaving No Name Lake, the hiker moves down the valley about two miles to a trail junction. The left fork goes along the north shore of Two Medicine

Lake three miles to the trailhead. The right fork goes only a short distance to another junction, where the hiker can either turn west a short distance to Twin East Falls or east to the head of the lake, where a boat picks up paying customers from the dock to return to the foot of the lake. If interested in the boat ride (which cuts about two miles off the last leg of this trip) inquire about the schedule at the boat concession stand near the trailhead before beginning the hike.—*Mike Sample*

48   *Iceberg Lake*

General description: A 10-mile round trip day hike to a beautiful lake in a spectacular setting.

Backcountry visitor meets backcountry resident. Mike Sample photo.

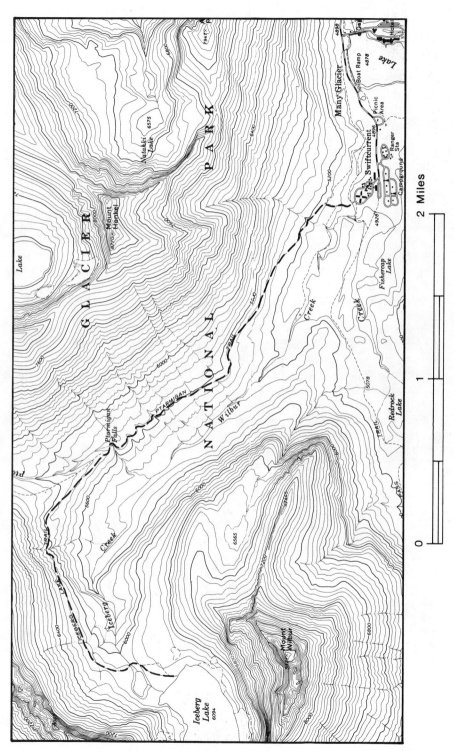

Iceberg Lake

General location: On the east side of Glacier National Park eight miles west of Babb.

Maps: Many Glacier USGS Quad or the USGS contour map for Glacier National Park.

Special attractions: High probability of seeing mountain goats and other wildlife.

Special caution: Of all the hikes in this book, this one is probably the most dangerous in terms of possible close encounters with grizzlies.

For more information: Write the District Ranger, Many Glacier Ranger Station, Glacier National Park, Box 46, Babb, MT 59411 or call (406) 732-5641.

Technically, Iceberg Lake doesn't have icebergs, but it comes as close as any place in Montana. Chunks of ice float around in the lake—usually until September. However, the "icebergs" are larger and more scenic in July and August.

Find the trailhead by driving along the eastern boundary of Glacier National Park eight miles north from St. Mary to Babb and then eight miles west into the park to Many Glacier. The trail starts from a parking lot behind Swiftcurrent Motel. Or you can join the trail at the north side of the bridge over the outlet of Swiftcurrent Lake.

Except for a short section at the very beginning, this trail climbs only 200 feet per mile, a rate most people find comfortable. Wide and relatively smooth, the trail leads through fields of wildflowers. Large flickers with pronounced reddish coloring and swooping flight patterns nest in the ghost trees along the trail.

At the 2.5-mile mark, the hiker passes by lovely Ptarmigan Falls as it plunges over rock layers to a deep emerald pool. Shortly thereafter, a clearly marked trail junction indicates a right turn for those wishing to see Ptarmigan Lake and Tunnel—and willing to take the stiff, 2.5-mile climb to get there. The Iceberg Lake trail goes straight for another 2.5 miles to the lake, making this a 10-mile round trip.

During the summer months, the National Park Service installs a bridge over Iceberg Creek just before the lake. However, this bridge is removed each fall to prevent it from washing out in the spring. So hikers who take this trip after mid-September can plan on getting their feet wet here.

On this last segment of this hike, mountain goats and bighorn sheep are commonly seen on the grassy slopes above and to the right. Like the rest of the Swiftcurrent Valley, this is a prime grizzly habitat. Be alert and make noise. You may sacrifice solitude, but it would be safer to take this trip with a group, possibly the ranger-conducted walks, scheduled almost every morning in July and August.—*Mike Sample*

49 *Gateway Pass, Gateway Gorge*

General description: A three-day hike for experienced hikers.

General location: Twenty miles west of Dupuyer in the Bob Marshall Wilderness.

Maps: Swift Reservoir, Gateway Pass, Gooseberry Park, and Morningstar

Mountain USGS Quads and Lewis & Clark National Forest, Teton Ranger District.

Special attraction: Spectacular scenery—and lots of it.

For more information: Write the District Ranger, Teton Ranger District, Lewis & Clark National Forest, Box 340, Choteau, MT 59422 or call (406) 466-5771.

An experienced hiker can make this 32-mile trip in three days, but the scenery is so spectacular that you may stay longer.

The trailhead is easily located by turning west off U.S. 89 at Dupuyer onto a gravel Forest Service Road. Follow this road for 18 miles until you reach Swift Dam. Then, take the road to the right that passes in front of the dam and goes along the north side of the reservoir. The trail starts at the end of this road. After a heavy rain, the road along the reservoir may be impassable, and you'll have to add an extra two miles to your trip by walking to the trailhead.

After climbing onto a small knob, the trail follows the South Fork of Birch Creek, gradually climbing through thick forests of Douglas fir with a few meadows rich in wildflowers. You reach Gateway Pass at the 11-mile mark. The trail stays high, and in another two miles, you reach Big River Meadows, a great campsite surrounded by open hillsides and mountain panoramas.

From here the trail drops gradually along Gateway Creek and through the awe-inspiring Gateway Gorge. It's about four miles from Big River Meadows to the Strawberry Creek Trail. After leaving the gorge, take the Strawberry Creek Trail north to the East Fork Trail which puts you about 20 miles into the hike and at a good second campsite.

From the Strawberry Creek/East Fork trail junction, the trail climbs easily through forests and meadows for about six miles along the creek to Badger Pass, where the scenery is hard to equal. From that high point, the trail climbs another 600 feet before dropping into the North Fork of Birch Creek. The trail then follows this stream which has very interesting rock formations and little waterfalls. One side drainage has a sheer rock wall similar to those found in the Canyonlands of southern Utah. After eight miles of easy hiking, you come out on the north shore of Swift Reservoir where you started.

The trail is well-used and easy to follow. It has several rocky sections and the stream crossings can be tricky especially after a good rain or early in the summer of a heavy snow year. The trail along Strawberry Creek has a few boggy sections.

The overall elevation gain is 1600 feet. Water is available throughout the trip, and mosquitoes usually aren't a problem after June. It's best to wait until July anyway, so the passes will be free of snow.

Although grizzly bears inhabit this area, hunting pressure keeps them very wary of man. So the chance of an incident is as remote as this trail.

This hike has dozens of possible campsites, but Big River Meadows and a site at the Strawberry Creek/East Fork trail junction are two top choices. Both have good water supplies. Big River Meadows has the edge on scenery but hikers must haul firewood from the edge of the meadow. Strawberry Creek has plenty of firewood.

Gateway

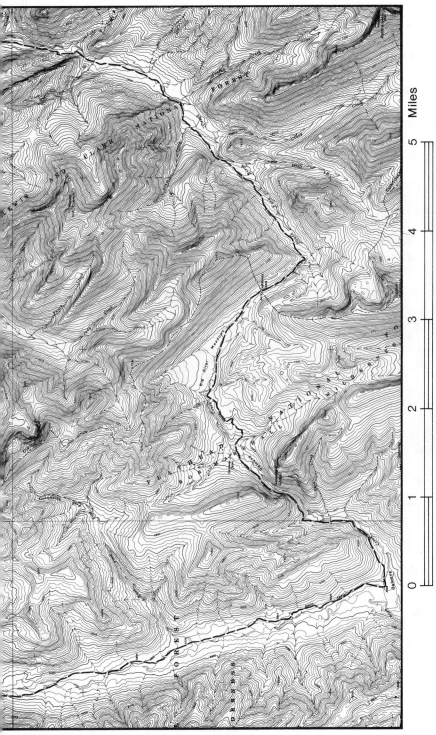

Miles

0 1 2 3 4 5

Although Gateway Gorge is probably the highlight of the trip, you won't be disappointed at the rest of the hike which is probably one of the most beautiful in Montana.—*Art and Elaine Sedlack*

50   Our Lake

General description: A seven-mile round trip suitable for a day or overnight hike.

General location: Twenty-nine miles west of Choteau in the Rocky Mountain Front.

Maps: Our Lake USGS Quad and Lewis & Clark National Forest, Teton Ranger District.

Special attractions: A very pristine mountain lake with good fishing and mountain goats inhabiting the slopes above the lake.

For more information: Write the District Ranger, Teton Ranger District, Lewis & Clark National Forest, Box 340, Choteau, MT 59422 or call (406) 466-3711.

This is a popular overnight or day hike with a well-maintained trail, outstanding scenery, good fishing, and excellent opportunities to view wildlife.

To find the trailhead, drive north from Choteau on U.S. 89, for five miles before turning west on County Road #144, which follows the Teton River. Follow this paved road, which doesn't cross the river, for about 15 miles until you see the sign for Ear Mountain Ranger Station. Here, turn south on County Road #109 (South Fork Road). Cross the Teton River and follow the South Fork of the Teton River for nine miles until the road ends. Take trail #184 which begins where the road ends.

Although it's only 3.5 miles to Our Lake (sometimes called Hidden Lake), expect a fair climb, as the trail climbs 1500 feet to the lake.

The last half-mile to the lake switchbacks up a steep slope which can be hazardous if tried before the snowbanks disappear. Thus, it's best to wait until July or August to try this hike.

Motorized vehicles are banned on this trail and other signs of man are uncommon. Mosquitoes aren't much of a problem except some years in June. Bears aren't common in the area. There is a good source of water at about the three-mile mark, but the rest of the trail is dry, especially in late August and September.

Hikers can almost always spot mountain goats on the alpine slopes behind Our Lake. If they're lucky, they can also see bighorn sheep near Rocky Mountain, the highest peak in the Bob Marshall Wilderness (9392 feet). In addition, expect to see marmots and pikas. Asters, daisies, and lupine seem to prevail among the abundant supply of wildflowers along this trail. Skunkflower is common on the alpine slopes above the lake.

The lake has four campsites which are the only signs of man on this trip. In addition, some hikers camp below the waterfall about one-half mile before the lake. Others stay at one of several good campsites in the basin beyond the lake.

Although there is a good selection of campsites, all of them are high

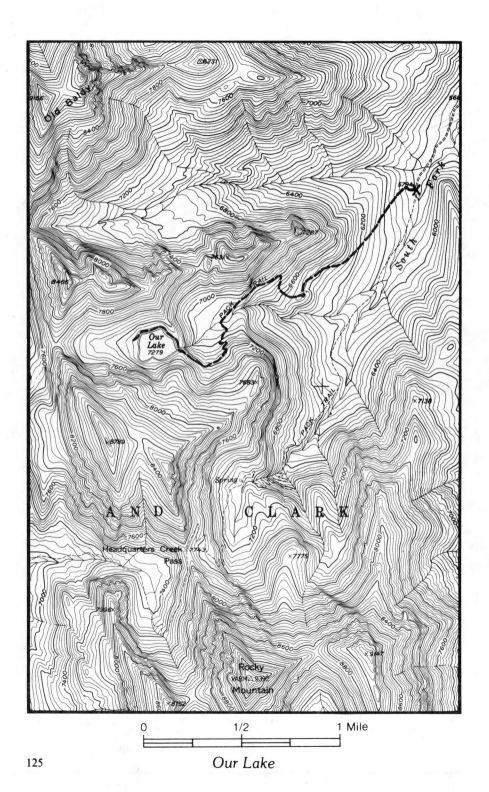

Our Lake

altitude and thus wood is in short supply. A backpacking stove for cooking is necessary.

Since access is easy, the lake is heavily used at times. Still, the fishing remains good. Ten-inch rainbows make up most of the catch. The lake also has cutthroat trout, but they're harder to catch.

For moderate hikers, there is a good side trip to the saddle west of the lake above the basin. From this saddle, hikers can view the Chinese Wall, the backbone of the Bob Marshall Wilderness. The distance to the saddle is approximately three-fourths of a mile.

For experienced hikers only, there is a strenuous side trip up Rocky Mountain. Proceed west over the ridge to the top of Headquarters Pass for this nonhazardous but long scramble. From the top of Rocky Mountain, hikers get a fantastic view of the Bob Marshall Wilderness and the surrounding country. The view of the Great Plains is also exceptional.

The Our Lake area is part of the Rocky Mountain Front which is presently proposed for wilderness designation. However, resource developers, especially energy companies, strongly oppose protective status for this pristine region.—*Dave Orndoff*

51 *South Chinese Wall*

General description: A long, rugged hike to the Continental Divide in the Bob Marshall Wilderness.
General location: Twenty miles west of Augusta.
Maps: Amphitheater Mountain, Slategoat Mountain, Glenn Creek and Patrick's Basin USGS Quads and the Forest Service's Bob Marshall Wilderness map.
Special attractions: Spectacular scenery in the midst of one of America's largest wild areas.
For more information: Write the District Ranger, Sun River Ranger District, Lewis & Clark National Forest, Box 365, Augusta, MT 59410 or call (406) 562-3301.

Hiking into the South Chinese Wall is more than a hike. It's a major vacation.

The trailhead is easy to find. Drive west from Augusta on County Road #208 for about 20 miles until you reach Gibson Dam. At the dam, turn northwest to Mortimer Gulch. The trail begins right at Mortimer Gulch Campground.

From this campground, take trail #201 along Gibson Reservoir and the North Fork of the Sun river. Then, take trail #131 at Two Shacks Flat up Moose Creek to the Chinese Wall.

This is a 60-mile round trip, not including any side trips. So even very experienced and ambitious hikers take at least four days. Most take a week or more to thoroughly enjoy this trip.

The trail rises about 2000 feet in elevation. And hikers must carry water with them on most of the trip, as there are several dry sections. The trail is very distinct because of the heavy horse and pack animal traffic, especially during the hunting season.

This hike goes to the backbone of the Bob Marshall Wilderness. So

The Chinese Wall, the backbone of the Bob Marshall Wilderness. U.S. Forest Service photo.

motorized vehicles are prohibited. The only signs of man are a dude ranch at the head of Gibson Reservoir and some heavily used campsites.

Mosquitoes aren't particularly bad, but during the peak of their season (June), they can take the edge off this magnificent hike. Also beware of the vicious horse flies along the North Fork of the Sun River.

Because of the mosquitoes and snowbanks that often cling in the area

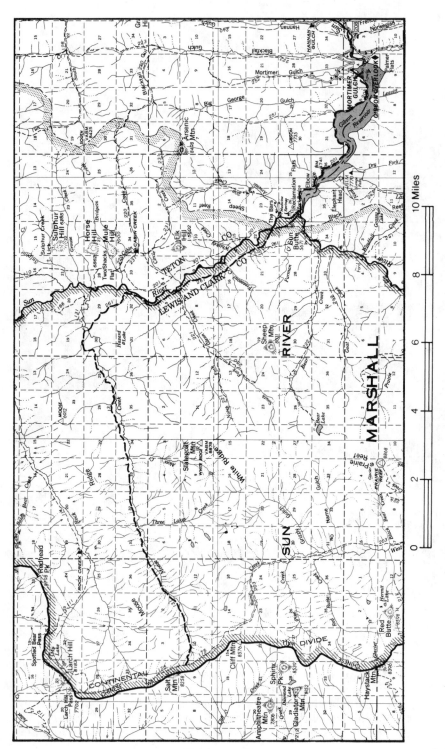

Chinese Wall

through June, early July to late September are best for this hike.

Both grizzlies and black bears range here. Although the chance of bear trouble definitely exists, it's statistically slim.

Alert hikers can often spot bighorn sheep on the cliffs of Sheep Reef north of the stock gate near Arsenic Creek. Elk are numerous, particularly in the North Fork of Sun River area.

Along Gibson Reservoir, watch for owl clover, a wildflower particularly abundant in this area. Alpine buttercups carpet some of the lush meadows below the Chinese Wall.

Fishing along the North Fork of the Sun River is excellent. It seems to hit its peak around Labor Day.

This hike has plenty of attractions—good fishing, abundant wildlife, lush mats of wildflowers. But the presence of the majestic Chinese Wall overshadows everything else. It's 14 miles of arduous cliffs and obvious glaciation. Sitting on top of this formation makes you feel insignificant, as it so dominates the landscape.

Hikers can camp in many places along this trail. However, two of the best camping areas are in the North Fork of the Sun River basin and at the head of Moose Creek. The North Fork camping area has excellent fishing and plenty of firewood. The Moose Creek site is open with no fishing and a shortage of firewood. The Forest Service has closed the area right under the Chinese Wall (within one mile) to camping.

As with campsites, there are many possibilities for side trips. One of the most rewarding, however, is Sphinx Mountain. Look for a route to the top of the Chinese Wall. There is only one obvious one, and it's known as "Trick Pass." After reaching the top, head cross country south for about four miles to the summit of Sphinx Mountain. From the summit, you get a good view of Diamond Lake, which is rarely visited by hikers.—*Dave Orndoff*

52 Halfmoon Park

General description: A three-day hike for experienced hikers.

General location: Sixteen miles southwest of Augusta in the Scapegoat Wilderness.

Maps: Scapegoat Mountain and Jakie Creek USGS Quad and Lewis & Clark National Forest, Sun River Ranger District.

Special attractions: Good views of Scapegoat Mountain, perhaps the highlight of the Scapegoat Wilderness.

For more information: Write the District Ranger, Sun River Ranger District, Lewis & Clark National Forest, Box 365, Augusta, MT 59410 or call (406) 562-3301.

Although this is a fairly rugged, three-day hike, it penetrates the heart of the spectacular Scapegoat Wilderness.

Find the trailhead by taking State Highway #434 south from Augusta for about four miles to the Smith Creek Road. Then, turn west and drive about 12 miles to the end of this gravel road. Trail #214 takes off right at the end of the road and follows Smith Creek. The first two miles are actually a rugged jeep road—too rugged, in fact, even for most jeeps.

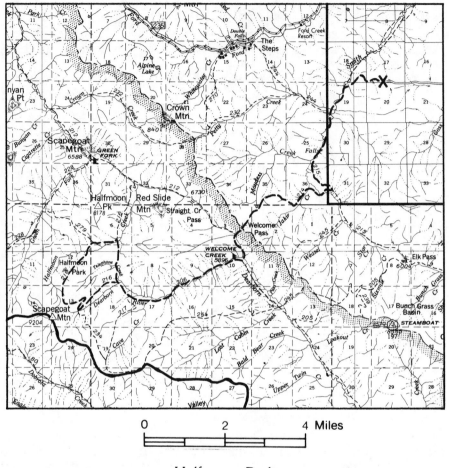

Halfmoon Park

The hike to Halfmoon Park is a 28-mile round trip that climbs 1500 feet to get over Welcome Pass. The trip is more suited for experienced hikers.

Follow trail #214 along Smith Creek and then along Jakie Creek up and over Welcome Pass before turning up the Dearborn River on trail #206. Then, turn up Telephone Creek on trail #254 and finally take #216 into Halfmoon Park.

You can retrace your steps back to the Dearborn River via Telephone Creek or you can make a small loop and see new country. Instead of returning on the same trail east from Halfmoon Park go south on trail #216 until you reach the Dearborn River where the trail turns east and goes back to the Telephone Creek junction.

The hike has well-maintained trails with plenty of water except for a three-mile stretch from Smith Creek over Welcome Pass down to the Dearborn River. Since this hike extends into the Scapegoat Wilderness, no motorized vehicles are allowed. Take this hike anytime between late July and late September.

Halfmoon Creek runs right by Scapegoat Mountain, the highest peak (9204 feet) in the Scapegoat Wilderness. The mountain's slopes offer very visible examples of glaciation.

This hike isn't for fanatic fisherman. There are fish in the lower stretches of the Dearborn River, southeast of Welcome Creek Ranger Station, but they're small and scarce.

However, elk and deer are quite common, especially along Halfmoon Creek and on the slopes of Scapegoat Mountain. Bears—black and grizzly—are also common. But these are wild bears, so if hikers keep a clean camp, the chances of a bear/man confrontation are remote.

Wildflowers, particularly lupine, are present, but not unusually abundant for western Montana. However, the Dearborn River drainage grows some super huckleberry and elderberry crops.

There are many good campsites along this trip, perhaps the choicest being Welcome Creek (halfway point), Halfmoon Creek, and Green Fork Creek. All have ample firewood, easily accessible water, and spectacular scenery.

Many hikers who go to Halfmoon Park allow an extra day to climb mighty Scapegoat Mountain. There is a trail from Halfmoon Creek over the ridge to Green Fork Creek. Then, go southwest up Green Fork Creek to the end of the glaciated valley. From here, find a goat trail that takes you out of this cirque onto the ridge. Walk east along this ridge to the summit. The view from the top is totally impressive.—*Dave Orndoff*

53   Gates of the Mountains

General description: An overnighter through one of Montana's smaller wilderness areas.

General location: Twenty miles northeast of Helena.

Maps: Upper Holter Lake, Candle Mountain, and Hogback Mountain USGS Quads and Helena National Forest, Helena/Canyon Ferry Ranger District.

Special attractions: Several historic points from the Lewis and Clark Expedition.

For more information: Write the District Ranger, Helena/Canyon Ferry Ranger District, Helena National Forest Federal Building, Helena, MT 59601 or call (406) 449-5201.

The 28,560-acre Gates of the Mountains Wilderness has the variety representative of most wildlands—open parks, deep canyons, craggy peaks, etc.,—with one exception: no lakes. More than compensating for this void, however, is a rich history.

The trail starts at Refrigerator Canyon. To get there, drive northeast from Helena on County Highway 280 for about 15 miles until you cross the Missouri on the newly constructed York Bridge. After crossing the bridge, drive for about four miles to the tiny community of York.

Here, turn north on road #224 and drive the well-maintained gravel road until it junctures with the Beaver Creek Road #138. Turn east (right) on the Beaver Creek Road and drive for about five miles until you see a well-

Hikers looking into the Meriwether Canyon from the Gates of the Mountains Wilderness. U.S. Forest Service photo.

marked trailhead for Refrigerator Canyon. The last five miles on the Beaver Creek Road can be dangerous because of sharp, blind corners and logging truck traffic. So if you're driving, don't be caught gawking around at the scenery. Let the passengers take in the steep-walled Beaver Creek Canyon with its whitish, limestone cliffs and beautiful stream.

(As this book goes to press, vehicles can't drive over the historic York Bridge, as county engineers have declared it unsafe. However, a new bridge is under construction at the same site and should be completed in 1981. Until then, you can reach York by driving east from Helena for 10 miles on U.S. 12 and turning north (left) on State Highway 284 and staying on that road for about nine miles until they cross Canyon Ferry Dam. Just after the dam, road #224 heads turns off to the north (left) and reaches York in six miles.)

This hike requires more logistics than usual. It's an 18-mile, point-to-point hike that ends on at Meriwether Campground on the Missouri River. You must leave a vehicle or have somebody pick you up at Gates of the Mountains Boat Club.

The Gates of the Mountains, Inc. (458-5241) offers tours of this scenic

Refrigerator Canyon, on the edge of the Gates of the Mountains Wilderness, is usually 12-20 degrees cooler than the surrounding country. U.S. Forest Service photo.

river canyon several times daily; these tours stop at Meriwether Campground on the way up and back. When you reach Meriwether Campground, you have to wait for the next boat. However, check the schedule before you leave, so you don't miss the last one. Also, bring a few dollars to pay for the ride.

To get to the Gates of the Mountains boat dock, take I-15 north from Helena for about 16 miles and turn right at the Gates of the Mountains exit. Follow the paved road two miles to the boat dock.

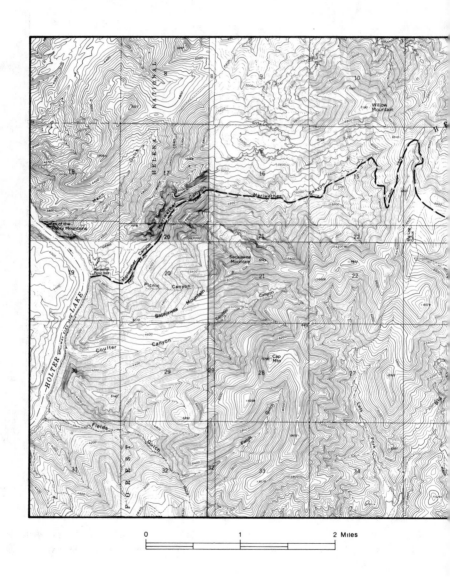

This trail can, of course, be taken in reverse, but most hikers find the boat ride a refreshing conclusion.

From the trailhead, trail #260 gradually climbs for about one-half mile to Refrigerator Canyon. Even on the hottest summer day, it's cool in this extremely steep, narrow canyon.

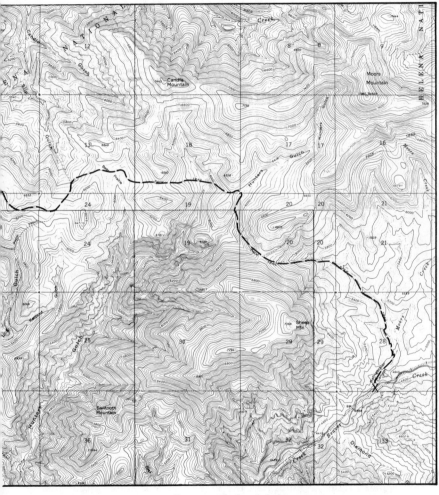

Gates of the Mountains

After Refrigerator Canyon, the trail gradually switchbacks about three miles to the Moors Mountain junction. Trail #260 continues on to the right to Moors Mountain. You turn left on trail #259 to Bear Prairie.

About five miles later, you reach the wildflower-carpeted Bear Prairie, one of the largest and most gorgeous mountain meadows in the Helena area. You can camp here or hike another mile to Kennedy Springs, which sets in a similar but slightly less impressive meadow. Kennedy Springs has the edge on Bear Prairie as a campsite since it has good drinking water.

From the Moors Mountain junction through Kennedy Springs (about seven miles), the trail is fairly level and well-maintained. The only confusing spot occurs just after Kennedy Springs in a large meadow where the trail swings to the right to the top of a ridge and then starts its descent to Meriwether Campground, where the Lewis and Clark Expedition camped almost two centuries earlier. The last five miles switchback steeply downhill—another good reason why hikers rarely take this trip in reverse.

After June, this trail is devoid of water with the exception of Kennedy Springs and a short section of Meriwether Creek for the last mile or so of the hike. On the plus side, the dry climate holds down the mosquitoes. This area has the advantage over many other wildlands because the snow usually frees the area early in the year, even as early as the Memorial Day weekend.—*Bill Schneider*

54 Red Mountain

General description: An easy, cross-country mountain climb.
General location: Eighteen miles southwest of Helena.
Maps: Jefferson City USGS Quad and Helena National Forest, Helena-Canyon Ferry Ranger District.
Special attractions: A short climb with a super view on the outskirts of one of Montana's largest cities.
For more information: Write the District Ranger, Helena-Canyon Ferry Ranger District, Helena National Forest, P.O. Drawer 10015, Federal Building, Helena, MT 59601 or call (406) 449-5201.

Montana has many mountains to climb, but not many are so close to a city nor are so easily climbed. Red Mountain is one of these wonderful exceptions.

To start this hike, drive west from Helena on U.S. 12 for nine miles to the Rimini turnoff. Turn left (south) and drive seven miles to the ghost town of Rimini. (Don't fret—Helena commuters have moved in and driven out the ghosts.) Drive south through Rimini and go another 3.6 miles. Park where the road takes a sharp right, .3 miles past the City of Helena water ditch and cabin. The trail takes off to the left just before this sharp bend in the road.

This trailhead isn't signed and can easily be missed. Watch for an abandoned miner's cabin in the brush on your left and 50 yards before the trailhead. Also watch for a blaze on a ponderosa pine on the left edge of the road at the trailhead. If you come to a major fork in the road, you've driven about a half-mile past the trailhead.

The trail—which is actually an abandoned mining road—starts out

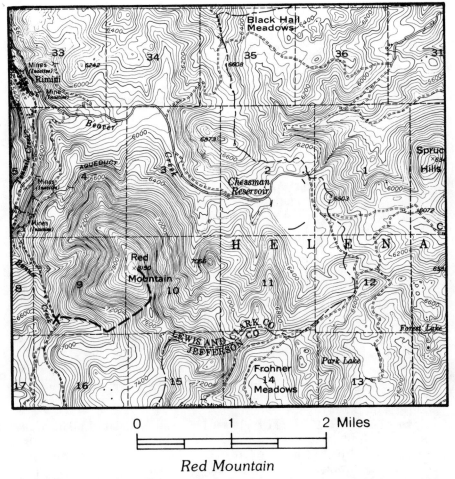

Red Mountain

following a small, unnamed stream and goes past some mining ruins. Follow the stream about a half-mile until it turns off to the right. Here, strike off straight uphill on a cross-country course. Head for a small pass which you'll see ahead and slightly to your left.

Although it's uphill all the way, there is only one really steep pitch in the three-mile trek to the summit of Red Mountain. After climbing this rock slide, you emerge on a saddle at the south side of Red Mountain. From this saddle, enjoy an easy walk to the summit.

The first part of the trail has good supplies of wild strawberries and huckleberries, plus plenty of wildflowers. The trip from the saddle to the summit goes through a forest of veterans of a war against the long, cruel winters at this 8,150-foot altitude. Some of the trees are more ghostly than the ghost town below.

The view from the summit of Red Mountain is one of Montana's grandest. On a clear day, you can see ten Montana counties. Mountain ranges in the view include the Big Belt, Bridger, Gallatin, Madison, Ruby, Tabacco Root, Highlands, Pintlers, and Flint Creek. Also, you can see Peerless Jenny, Sally Bell, Linda, Julia, Crescent, and other abandoned mines whose names have been lost in time.

Drinking water is available from the small stream at the start, but the rest of the trip is dry. Snowbanks usually cling to the summit until early July.

Although only a six-mile round trip which any hiker can make in a day, you can camp on the summit. Be sure to check the weather forecast for a clear night, preferably at the full moon, so you can get all the benefits of sleeping so close to the stars.—*Herb B. Gleoge*

55 *Mount Helena Ridge*

General description: A fairly rigorous day hike.
General location: On the south edge of Helena.
Maps: Helena USGS Quad and Helena National Forest. (Neither map shows the trail.)
Special attractions: Superb east-of-the-divide scenery from a trail starting on the city limits of Helena.
For more information: Write the District Ranger, Helena-Canyon Ferry Ranger District, Helena National Forest, Federal Building, Helena, MT 59601 or call (406) 449-5201.

Although this seven-mile, point-to-point trail was recently declared a National Recreational Trail by the Forest Service, it receives very little use. This is even more amazing when one considers how scenic and accessible it is.

This is probably the easiest trailhead in the state to find. Simply drive up Adams Street (in southwest Helena) until it dead ends at the Mount Helena parking lot on the city limits.

Mount Helena is a 620-acre city park with about 20 miles of hiking trails. There are at least three ways to hike the first three miles, but the easiest route goes west from the parking lot. Follow this well-maintained trail for a half-mile until it forks. Take the right-hand fork and stay on it for 1.5 miles until you reach a trail junction with a picnic table on top of a small saddle (just past a series of switchbacks).

At the picnic table, take the right-hand trail that goes west along a ridge. Stay on this trail all the way—about five miles from this point—to Park City. Since the trail past this point isn't heavily used, it can be hard to follow at times. It's marked with rock cairns and silver, rectangular trail markers on trees.

About one-fourth mile past the picnic table, the trail runs through an open, grassy saddle and temporarily disappears in the ungrazed grass. Watch for a faint trail that leaves the saddle (about 10 o'clock) heading west and slightly south. Once you're on it, it's easy to follow.

In another one-fourth mile, the trail takes a sharp right. Be careful not to follow the trail going straight (south).

After these two confusing spots, the trail is easy to follow for two miles or so. Then, the ridge becomes a series of small hills where the trail hasn't been marked well. You can usually find it through this one-mile section by staying close to the top of the ridge. The most confusing section begins after crossing a fence on a Forest Service "stairs." (You'll have to take the hike to see what that means.) Stay alert, and you won't get lost.

At about the five-mile mark, the trail intersects with a jeep road coming up from the left (east) from Grizzly Gulch.

The Grizzly Gulch Road parallels the ridge (out of sight). It can be found by driving south from Helena down South Park. About one-half mile south of town, South Park forks. Take the right-hand fork and you're on the Grizzly Gulch Road.

The jeep road appears to follow the ridge. But stay off it. The trail turns left (east) a few feet after you step on the jeep road.

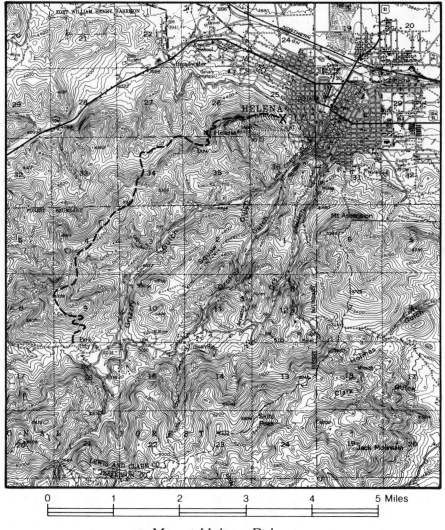

Mount Helena Ridge

At this point, you can see an interesting "tree house" that some ambitious folks have constructed in the lodgepole pine. The trail takes a sharp left (east) about 20 feet before the tree house.

From here to Park City, the trail is well-marked. This is probably the most scenic part of the hike, as you can often look back and see the Mount Helena Ridge and Mount Helena itself, which is several hundred feet elevation below you. The City of Helena also appears frequently in the distance.

The last half-mile of the trail switchbacks down a south-facing, grassy slope just above Park City and a small cluster of rural ranchettes. When you reach a jeep road, walk down it to a well-maintained gravel road where your vehicle should be waiting for you. Once you reach this gravel road, it's only one-half mile to the left to the Grizzly Gulch Road. So to properly place your vehicle, drive a short ways up this road from Grizzly Gulch and park.

Unfortunately, the trailhead at this end hasn't been marked, so it's almost impossible to find the first time. If there is any question, leave your vehicle at the head of Grizzly Gulch and walk the extra one-half mile.

Since this is a ridgetop trail in a rather dry part of the state, there is no water.

Contrary to other suggestions in this book, you might want to give the Forest Service a call and thank them for developing such a fine hiking trail so close to an urban area. —*Bill Schneider*

56 *Crow Creek Falls*

General description: An easy, six-mile, out-and-back hike nicely suited for families.
General location: On the east side of the Elkhorn Mountains in the Helena National Forest 35 miles southeast of Helena.
Maps: Clancy USGS Quad and Helena National Forest.
For more information: Write the District Ranger, Townsend Ranger District, Helena National Forest, Box 29, Townsend, MT 59644 or call (406) 266-3425.

As a general rule, it's rare to find outstanding day hikes close to major urban areas. Crow Creek Falls is a welcome exception.

To find the trailhead, drive 11 miles south from Townsend on U.S. 287. Then, take a right and drive nine miles west on a paved road to Radersburg. Go through town and follow the only major gravel road (locally known as the Hall Creek Road) heading northwest from Radersburg. Follow this road 15 miles to the trailhead which is on the right in a sagebrush park about three miles past the Jenkins Gulch junction. (The recently constructed Hall Creek Road isn't shown on the Clancy USGS Quad.)

The trail immediately crosses Crow Creek. Off to the left, there is a large fallen cottonwood that makes a suitable bridge. The trail then closely follows the stream for about 1¾ miles before making a short climb to a bench above the creek. Set aside a few minutes for eating wild strawberries and raspberries, particularly common along Crow Creek. The last mile or so

Crow Creek Falls—an easy day hike for any hiker. Bill Schneider photo.

is slightly uphill with a short, but steep, dip into Crow Creek Falls. Take a good drink before leaving Crow Creek, as the last mile is without water.

The main trail keeps going into the heart of the Elkhorn Mountains, so be careful not to miss the left turn to the falls. If the trail comes back to the

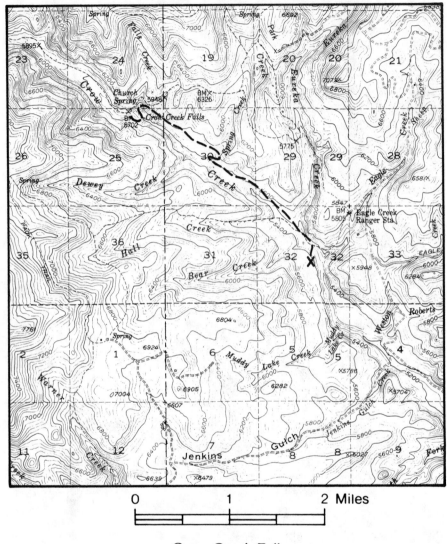

Crow Creek Falls

stream (not crossing it, but back next to it), you've just missed the falls. In fact, you can hear the roar of crescendoing water from that point. Backtrack 200 yards to the turnoff.

Unfortunately, Crow Creek Falls is on a small, private inholding within the Helena National Forest. This may be why the junction to the falls is poorly marked. Forest Service officials have taken some steps to acquire this natural wonder as part of the Helena National Forest, but they could use some encouragement to speed up the acquisition process.

Crow Creek Falls is a picture-perfect picnic site. Most hikers carry in a lunch and eat it here. If you packed a fishing rod in, a few pan-sized rainbows and brookies can be caught below the falls.

All told, the elevation gain for the entire three miles is only 400 feet. And the trail is well-pronounced all the way. This makes it just right for a family day hike. Families take preschool children into the falls with no problems.

If you want an overnight camping trip, there is a nice campsite along Crow Creek about 200 yards above the falls. Few people camp right at the falls.

Some hikers stay overnight in an undeveloped vehicle campground on Crow Creek near the junction of the Jenkins Gulch and Hall Creek roads about three miles before you reach the trailhead. Here, you can camp right on Crow Creek in a scenic campsite and catch a few fish in the stream. However, this vehicle campsite hasn't been improved or maintained, so be extra careful not to abuse it.

Although mosquitoes or other biting insects are rarely serious, it's always best to be prepared for these pests. The trail is hazard-free with the possible exception of two short steep sections at about the one-mile mark.

Motorized vehicles are allowed on the trail, but few of them take the route along Crow Creek. Jeep and motorcycle enthusiasts can ride within a mile of the falls by a different route, so you might see some as you get closer to the falls.

June or July are best for this hike. The wild berries, mushrooms and flowers are out in force during these two months—especially along Crow Creek. Later, this area gets quite hot and dry. During an early season hike, there's also a better chance of getting a glimpse of a bear, elk or deer—all fairly common in the area. —*Bill Schneider*

57 Manley Park

General description: An overnight hike into the heart of the Elkhorn Mountains.

General location: Twenty miles southeast of Helena.

Maps: Clancy USGS Quad and Helena National Forest.

Special attractions: Gorgeous high elevation meadows and large waterfall.

For more information: Write the District Ranger, Townsend Ranger District, Helena National Forest, Box 29, Townsend, MT 59644 or call (406) 266-3425.

When Forest Service planners rate wilderness quality, they often give areas of high, craggy peaks the highest score. The Elkhorns has a limited supply of such geology, but the scenery still rivals that of any Montana mountain range.

Instead of snow-capped peaks, the Elkhorns have lush, high elevation meadows surrounded by gently rolling forests. Poe and Manley parks offer excellent examples.

Refer to the Crow Creek Falls hike (page 140) for most of the route to the trailhead. If you have two vehicles, leave one at the Crow Creek Falls trailhead, as this is where you'll finish this overnight loop.

The Poe Park trailhead is about three miles past the Crow Creek Falls trailhead on the Hall Creek Road. Watch for a FS sign on your right marked "Poe Park." (Recently constructed Hall Creek Road may not be shown on the maps.)

Bull elk in a September battle. Harry Engels photo.

From the trailhead, it's a two-mile stroll into Poe Park. Although you gain about 800 feet in this two miles, most of the climb comes in the first half-mile.

The view from Poe Park is something to behold, especially with the carpets of wildflowers. However, don't be looking around so much that you miss a trail marker. The trail temporarily disappears in the lush grass, but you can stay on it if you keep your eyes peeled for FS trail markers and blazes on trees. If you lose the trail, head for the west edge of the park where the trail enters the timber and again becomes easy to follow.

After Poe Park, the trail switchbacks down to Little Tizer Creek. Just after leaving Poe Park, the trail forks. The right-hand fork is an outfitter's trail and goes to a hunting camp. Take the lefthand fork to Little Tizer Creek.

At the stream, you hit a trail junction. You can get to Crow Creek with either fork, but if you go right, you miss Manley Park which is as gorgeous (if not more than) Poe Park, and the view is even better. So bear left.

Watch carefully for another junction less than a mile after Little Tizer Creek. You must take a sharp right and head up a steep, but short, trail to Manley Park.

Most hikers prefer Manley Park for a campsite. The disadvantage is absence of water. Either you must camp at Little Tizer Creek or haul enough water up to Manley Park. Hauling water might be work, but the view from Manley Park rewards your extra effort.

The trail in Manley Park is easy to follow for about halfway through; then, it gradually disappears, as you approach the timber on the north side. With some care, you can find where it leaves the big meadow.

After a short, steep drop down to Crow Creek, you hit the Crow Creek trail on the north side of the stream. You come out by the abandoned Wildcat Mine and a private cabin—the only signs of civilization along the otherwise remote hike.

From here, the trail follows Crow Creek for about eight miles back to the

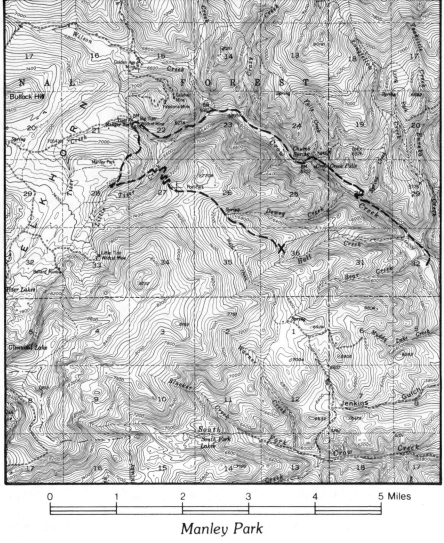

Manley Park

Hall Creek Road. If you don't have a vehicle there, you'll have to hike or jog up the road to the Poe Park trailhead.

Be sure to stop to see Crow Creek Falls which is about three miles from the end of your hike. See page 140 for more details on the falls.

Although there isn't water in either of the parks, there is usually enough along the rest of the hike—primarily in Little Tizer and Crow creeks. Motorized vehicles aren't allowed except for a short section of the trail up Crow Creek. They are supposed to stop before they reach the falls.

If you stay overnight in Poe or Manley parks, you stand a good chance of seeing elk in the early morning or late evening. Crow Creek has a good supply of pan-sized brookies and rainbows for anglers who like to fish smaller streams.

The Elkhorn Mountains have a wilderness quality unlike other ranges—a quiet, gentle, easy beauty. Technical mountain climbers might frown on the Elkhorns, but for the rest of us, it's difficult to surpass. And it's so accessible—close to Bozeman, Butte, and Helena.

The Forest Service, however, doesn't see it that way. The agency has plans to extend the Hall Creek Road into the heart of the Elkhorns to join with the Prickly Pear Road coming up from the west side. This would, of course, limit any possibility of a large wilderness area in the Elkhorns.

Although this land use plan was temporarily stalled by a congressionally mandated wilderness study, it may soon come to the forefront. What the public wants—wilderness or development—may mean the difference for the Elkhorns, so pass your comments along to the Forest Service and your elected representatives. —*Bill Schneider*

58 *Elkhorn and Crow Peaks*

General description: A strenuous day hike.

General location: Fifteen miles southeast of Helena.

Maps: Clancy USGS Quad and Deerlodge National Forest, Jefferson Ranger District.

Special attractions: Views of the entire Elkhorn Mountains from two of the highest peaks in the range.

For more information: Write the District Ranger, Jefferson Ranger District, Deerlodge National Forest, Whitehall, MT 59759 or call (406) 287-3223.

Hikers who have become experienced to the point where they can consider cross country hiking or rock climbing might use this hike to break-the-ice. Although more than half of the hike is trailless and it goes to the summit of the highest peaks in the Helena area, it's reasonably safe with little chance of getting lost.

The trail begins at Elkhorn, a historic mining camp on the southern end of the Elkhorn Mountains. To get there from Helena, drive 28 miles south on I-15 to Boulder. Take the Boulder exit from the Interstate and go five miles south of town on State Highway 281. Here turn left onto a gravel road. There is a large sign for Elkhorn marking this corner.

The gravel road immediately crosses the Boulder River and then dead ends. Turn right and follow the same gravel road for about 13 miles to Elkhorn, bearing left on two junctions along the way. Go through Elkhorn

Mountain goats, a favorite of wilderness visitors. Harry Engels photo.

and park at the northeast corner of town just before the road turns south to the cemetary. The trail—actually a jeep road—heads north out of town.

Most hikers start walking here, but if you have a four-wheeler you can drive another mile on a jeep road until you see the road jut off to the right and up a steep grade. Park here even though there's a sign saying "Four-wheel Drive Vehicles Only." In reality, the road to the Iron Mine is too

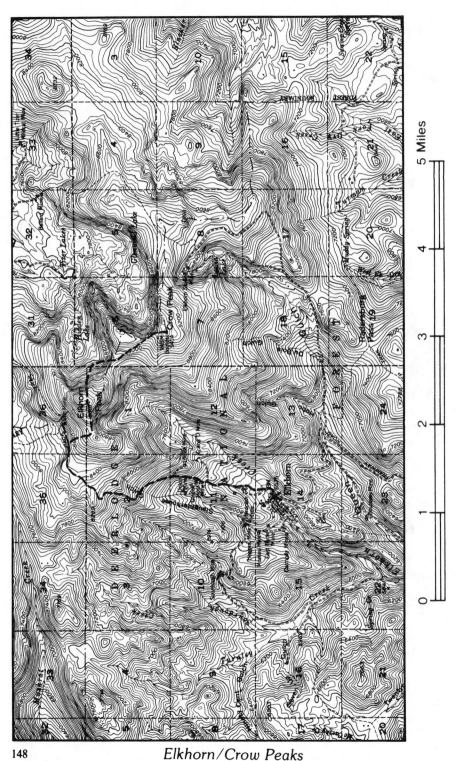

5 Miles

rough for any vehicle. On the Forest Service map, it's marked as Trail #72, so it must be more suited to Vibram soles than steel-belted radials.

From Elkhorn, it's about three tough miles to the Iron Mine, an abandoned mining camp on the west slope of Elkhorn Peak. After exploring this old mine, backtrack down the trail less than a quarter-mile. Here, leave the trail and head straight up for about a half-mile until you reach the top of the ridge. Follow the ridge north for about another mile to the top of Elkhorn Peak. After leaving the Iron Mine Trail, it's cross-country hiking.

Here, you're 2,800 feet above Elkhorn, and the view is something to behold, especially to the north where you can see the entire Tizer Basin, the heart of the Elkhorn Mountains. To the southeast lies 9,414-foot Crow Peak, slightly higher than Elkhorn Peak, 9,381 feet.

Pick your way to Crow Peak along the saddle between the two mountains. Be sure to bear slightly to the north so you can look down steep cliffs into Hidden Lake and, a little farther, Glenwood Lake. Both lakes are nestled in steep, glacier-scoured cirques with sheer cliffs on three sides, opening only to the north. Glenwood Lake, with no trail to it, is perhaps the most difficult spot to reach in the entire Elkhorn Mountains.

From the Iron Mine to Crow Peak, watch for mountain goats, a favorite of hikers in this area. The Elkhorn/Crow complex supports fair numbers of these white-clad mountaineers. Also prepare your heart for the surprise flush of a blue grouse from the weather-beaten whitebark pines between the two peaks.

Unless you spend too much time taking in the vistas, you can easily make it to Crow Peak and back (about 10 miles total distance) in one full day. It is, however, a rugged, cross-country hike that may be too tough for small children or poorly conditioned hikers.

Bring drinking water, as there's only one small stream (about halfway to the Iron Mine), and even that one may dry up by late summer. Snow clings to the area into June and even into July on heavy-snow years, so plan a late summer or early fall conquest. Mosquitoes rarely bother hikers on this high-elevation hike.

The Elkhorn/Crow complex straddles the southern edge of the Elkhorn Wilderness Study Area. After being ordered to do so by Congress, the Forest Service is presently pondering the fate of this 80,000-acre wildland. You might want to pass your comments onto the FS planners to help them in their difficult and controversial task. —*Bill Schneider*

59 *Edith-Baldy Basin*

General Description: A moderate, overnight round trip for beginners or rugged loop for experienced hikers.

General location: Thirty miles southeast of Helena in the Big Belt Mountains.

Maps: Mount Edith and Duck Creek Pass USGS Quads and the Helena National Forest, Townsend Ranger District.

Special Attractions: A lake-filled basin in a small mountain range.

For more information: Write the District Ranger, Townsend Ranger Station, Helena National Forest, Box 29, Townsend, Montana 59644 or call (406) 266-3425.

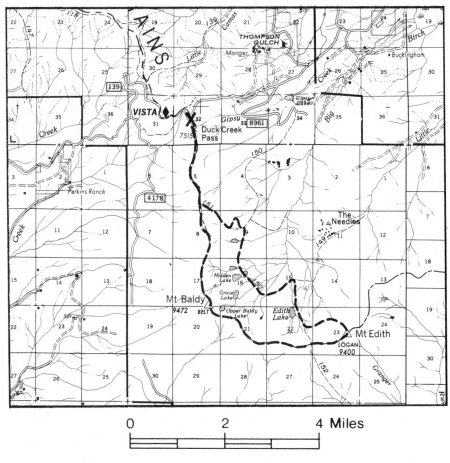

Edith-Baldy Basin

Driving along the highway and seeing Mount Edith and Mount Baldy in the distance, you would never guess that a spectacular, lake-filled basin, accessible to all hikers, lies nestled in their northeastern shadow.

To begin the hike, drive east of Townsend on U.S. 12 for about three miles and turn left (north) on the major paved road skirting the east side of Canyon Ferry Reservoir. Drive north for about five miles and turn right (east) on a well-marked Duck Creek Pass Road. Follow this road for about 12 miles to the top of Duck Creek Pass where the trail begins on the right (south) side of the road.

The first three miles are actually a rough jeep road which bumps its way to a Mountain Bell microwave tower on Baldy Ridge, about one mile before the summit of 9472-foot Mount Baldy. Be sure to bring water along because there isn't any for the first one-half of the hike.

At the microwave tower, there is a trail that drops off the ridge to the east into Hidden Lake. If you aren't an experienced hiker in good condition, take

150

this trail into the basin. However, if you're in good shape and knowledgeable on cross-country hiking, you can make a spectacular loop out of this hike.

Hikers who opt for a shorter, easier trip can camp at Hidden Lake or continue on to any of the other lakes, set up a base camp, and stay for several days, visiting new lakes every day. Then, they can retrace their steps to Duck Creek Pass.

More amibitious hikers can head cross country toward the summit of Mount Baldy. All along this ridge, the vistas are incredible, with the Smith River drainage to the east and Canyon Ferry Reservoir to the west. Expect to see mountain goats around the summits of Baldy and Edith.

After leaving the top of Baldy, you drop rapidly for one-fourth mile into the saddle between the two peaks. Then, you gradually work your way over several false summits to the top of 9384-foot Mount Edith, with Upper Baldy Lake on your left most of the way. It's four miles between the two summits, but it will be four miles of the most scenic hiking you've experienced. Although it's cross country, the terrain is fairly easy to traverse. In addition to mountain goats, this area seems to attract unusually large numbers of golden eagles.

From the top of Edith, you can see a penetrating limestone formation known as the "needles" to the north and Edith Lake to the northwest. Follow a series of rock cairns toward the gorgeous, high-altitude lake.

About one mile before Edith Lake, you intersect the main trail through the Edith-Baldy Basin. Turn right on this trail (which you crossed on the way to the summit of Edith) and work your way back through the basin to Hidden Lake and then up to a series of tough switchbacks to the jeep road leading back to your vehicle.

Although Edith and Baldy are rock and talus, the basin is heavily timbered. Most lakes have suitable campsites. However, some lakes don't have trails to them. You'll want to spend at least one night in the basin before heading home.

The loop is 20-25 miles, depending on how many lakes you visit, about one-third of it cross country. The shorter hike into Hidden Lake and out is only eight miles round trip.

Although the ridge is devoid of water, the basin has plenty. This area accumulates a surprising amount of snow, so wait until at least late June; August if you want to escape the mosquitoes.

Many of the lakes have good fishing for cutthroat or rainbows. Only one, Hidden Lake, seriously shows the hand of man, as motorcyclists have severely scarred the terrain around the lake.

Although this may come as a surprise after a pleasant backpack in this scenic, alpine basin, the 20,000-acre roadless area has been recommended for "nonwilderness" through the Forest Service planning process. If you disagree, write or call the Helena National Forest in Helena.—*Bill Cunningham*

60 *Bear Trap Canyon*

General description: A long but easy hike along a trout-filled river.
General location: Thirty miles west of Bozeman along the Madison River.

151

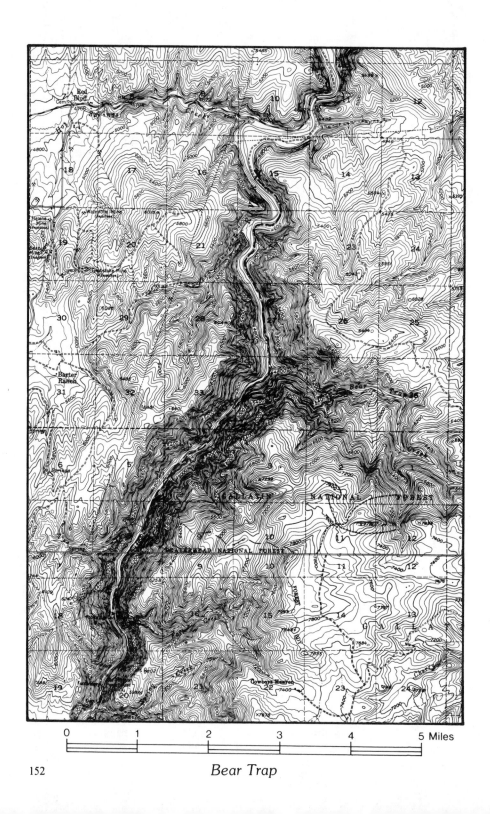

Bear Trap

Maps: Norris USGS Quad and Bureau of Land Management's National Resource Lands map—Madison No. 33.

Special attractions: A rare hike with a primitive flare along a major river with nationally famous trout fishing.

For more information: Write the District Manager, Bureau of Land Management, 220 N. Alaska, Butte, MT 59701 or call (406) 723-6561.

If you're a trout fisherman, you've undoubtedly heard of the Madison River, one of the most highly acclaimed streams in the United States. However, you probably haven't heard of a special hiking trail developed by the Bureau of Land Management (BLM) along the Madison in rugged Bear Trap Canyon. For hikers who fancy large trout, this is a seven-mile slice of heaven.

To find the trailhead, drive west from Bozeman on U.S. 289 for about 30 miles. Immediately before you cross the Madison River, watch for a dirt road turning left from the highway and a sign for the Bear Trap Primitive Area.

After driving four miles on this dirt road, you come to a small parking lot and the boundary of the primitive area. The well-marked trail starts at the parking area.

The trail winds along the river for seven miles, gaining a mere 500 feet in elevation. In past years, hikers could leave a vehicle at Montana Power's Ennis Dam Power House at the end of the hike. For safety reasons, however, Montana Power has closed access to this area, making this, in fact, a 14-mile round trip.

Since the trail follows the river, there's plenty of water. However, most hikers bring their own water as they fear the river water might not be suitable for drinking. Also, bring plenty of insect repellent, as the mosquitoes can be bad, especially in early summer. Many hikers (especially families) choose to stay overnight to take advantage of the early morning and late evening fishing.

There are several campsites, the first at the point where Bear Trap Creek joins the river. Bring your backpack stove, as firewood can be scarce along the narrow canyon.

Also, bring a garbage bag—not only for your own trash, but to carry out junk left by thoughtless hikers. The trail and campsites receive fairly heavy use. With that much traffic, there's often a few who haven't gotten the word about packing out what they carry in.

The area is closed to motorized recreation, so the signs of civilization (except some litter at the campsites) are scarce. Since it remains free of snow most of the year, you can take the hike anytime between April and November. The heaviest use occurs when the fishing is good, especially during the salmon fly hatch in mid-June to early July.

The major drawing card is, of course, fishing. Rainbows and browns two to four pounds and larger are common.

However, the hike would still be attractive without a fishing pole. The trail wanders through a spectacular canyon with sheer rock cliffs and abundant wildlife. This includes rattlesnakes, so be alert and don't forget your snake bite kit.

This represents one of the best hiking trails on BLM land in Montana. Next time you run into somebody from that federal land-managing agency suggest that Montana could use a few more such trails.—*Mike Comola*

61   *Spanish Peaks*

General description: A long, multi-day loop.

General location: Forty miles southwest of Bozeman on the western edge of the Spanish Peaks Primitive Area on the northern tip of the Madison Range.

The moose, largest of the deer family and commonly observed from backcountry trails. Harry Engels photo.

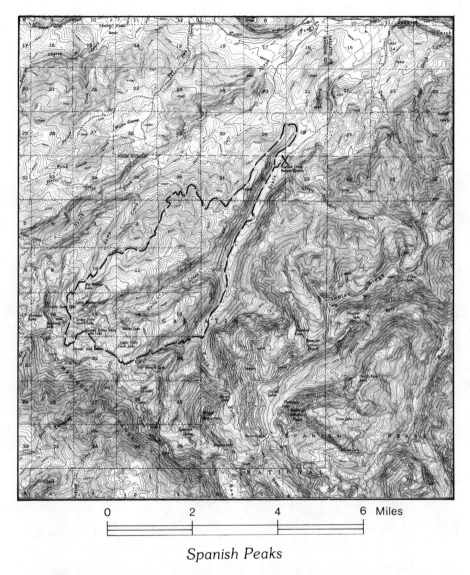

Spanish Peaks

Maps: Spanish Peaks USGS Quad and Gallatin National Forest, Gallatin Ranger District.

Special attractions: Spectacular, high mountain scenery.

For more information: Write the District Ranger, Gallatin Ranger District, Gallatin National Forest, Gallatin Gateway, MT 59730 or call (406) 763-4434.

The Spanish Peaks rank among the most popular hiking areas in Montana. Although this hike traverses the fringe of the primitive area, it doesn't venture into the most heavily used portions. It does, however, provide the same incredible scenery that made the Spanish Peaks Primitive Area nationally famous.

155

To find the trailhead, drive south from Bozeman down U.S. 191. About 10 miles south of Gallatin Gateway and just before entering the Gallatin Canyon take a right (west) up Spanish Creek at a marked turn-off. After five miles, turn left (south) up the South Fork of Spanish Creek. Drive about eight miles along the South Fork until you reach a campground by the Spanish Creek Guard Station where the trail begins.

This is a 26-mile loop going up the South Fork and coming back to the same trailhead through the headwaters of Camp and Cuff creeks. Take at least three days to fully enjoy the scenery.

The hike starts with a gentle, eight-mile hike up the South Fork on trail #407. Stay on the same trail as it leaves the South Fork and climbs to the west through a large group of small, subalpine lakes until you veer right on trail #446 down Camp Creek. You could shorten the hike by taking trail #410 down Falls Creek, but you retrace your steps down the South Fork and miss some outstanding vistas.

The trail has more water than most, so don't worry about carrying any. The trail is well-maintained and easy to follow all the way with the minor exception of a few meadows towards the end of the hike.

You can camp at several excellent sites along the South Fork or depending on how early in the day you hit the trail, you might make it to the high lakes where the scenery popularizes the campsites. Camp at any of the lakes in this subalpine plateau. Plan on using your stove to cook, however, as firewood is scarce.

Most of the lakes have pan-sized cutthroat or rainbow. And the South Fork has good fishing for small brookies.

This trip is loaded with side trip possibilities—Spanish Lakes, the upper reaches of Falls Creek, several excellent climbs to scenic summits—to name a few. You might decide to spend an extra day to get acquainted with this land of rock and thunder.

This area is part of a currently popular wilderness proposal. If designated wilderness by Congress, this area would be the northernmost corner of a tremendous, 280,000-acre wilderness ranging south to the Taylor-Hilgard region and including much of the wild country in the Madison Range. If you have a chance, lend your support to this proposal.—*Art Foran*

62 The Helmet

General description: A long day hike or moderate overnighter including a healthy climb.
General location: Eighteen miles southeast of Ennis in the Madison Range.
Maps: Cameron and Sphinx Mountain USGS Quads and Beaverhead National Forest, Madison Ranger District.
Special attractions: The Sphinx and the Helmet, truly unique geological formations.
For more information: Write the District Ranger, Madison Ranger District, Beaverhead National Forest, Box 366, Ennis, MT 59729 or call (406) 682-4254.

The Madison Range undoubtedly has some of Montana's finest hiking.

Climbing towards the saddle separating the Helmet and in the background, the Sphinx. Bill Schneider photo.

Oddly, only the northern section, the Spanish Peaks, has ever become popular with hikers.

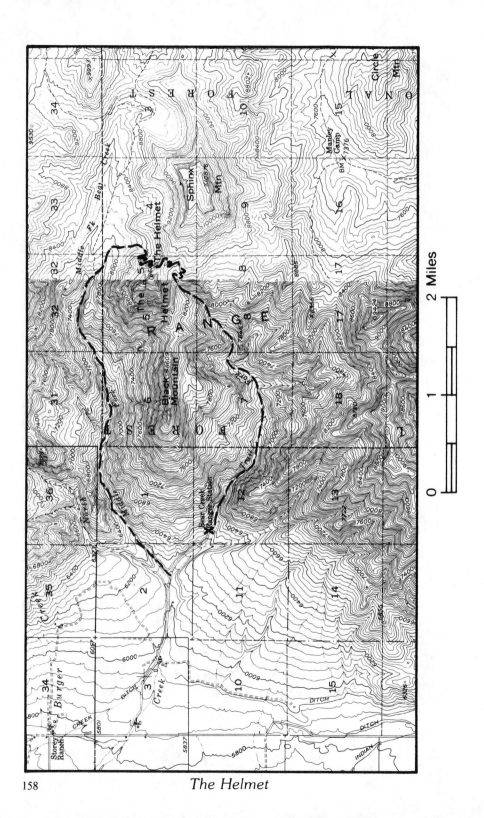

The Helmet

The area south of the Spanish Peaks all the way to the Hilgard Basin (page 162) on the southern tip of the range offers as much or more than the Spanish Peaks. The loop trail between the Sphinx and the Helmet nicely illustrates this fact.

The trail starts at Bear Creek Ranger Station which can be found by turning east off U.S. 287 at Cameron and following a gravel road for three miles before it turns right (south). Continue south on the good gravel road for 1.5 miles until it turns left (east) and goes another mile to Storey Ranch (as indicated on the Cameron Quad). Here, turn south again for less than a mile before angling off to the southeast along Bear Creek to the Bear Creek Ranger Station. Park your car here.

Trail #326 follows the Trail Fork of Bear Creek to the northeast for about two miles before it joins trail #325. (The first mile or so is actually a rough jeep road, but it's best to hike it.) Trail #326 (not shown on the topo maps) heads east to Manley Camp; you take trail #325 to the saddle between the Helmet and the Sphinx—which is another three miles where you experience most of the 2,300-foot elevation gain.

From this saddle, you have two logical side trips—climbs to the summits of the Helmet and the Sphinx which, incidentally, do resemble a helmet and a sphinx. The Helmet takes less than two hours and the Sphinx slightly more. They're both easy, nontechnical scrambles and well worth the effort.

The Sphinx has the edge on the vistas with much of the Madison Range visible from the 10,876-foot summit including the Yellow Mules country to the northeast (which still has grizzly bears) and Koch Peak, Shedhorn Ridge, No Man Ridge, and the Taylor Peaks to the south. At the summit, stay clear of the edge, lest you fall over an incredibly steep cliff into the Indian Creek valley.

After the climbs are behind you and you're back in the saddle, continue down the north side on trail #325 into the Middle Fork of Bear Creek. Near the bottom, you will intersect a trail following the creek back to a point just west of the Bear Creek Ranger Station—a trailhead you drove past on the way up.

It's about five miles out to the road, making this a tough, 10-mile hike, not including the mountain climbs. The Middle Fork and one stream on the climb up to the saddle are the only reliable water sources, so plan on carrying water with you.

When you hit the road, you must walk less than a mile up the Bear Creek Road to your vehicle. Or you can leave the trail just before it ends and heads south cross country to the Bear Creek Ranger Station and your vehicle.

If you're camping, pick one of several good sites along the Middle Fork. There's plenty of firewood, and you can spend some time after supper trying to spot a member of the area's large moose population.

Although there is a current proposal to designate much of the Madison Range as a unified wilderness extending from the Spanish Peaks to the Hilgard Basin, it has run into several obstacles. One of the most serious is the checkerboard land ownership in the area with private and public sections intermingled. For example, the Helmet and part of the Sphinx belong to Burlington Northern. Take a minute to pass your feelings for the area onto the Forest Service or your elected representative.—*Bill Schneider*

63   *Lizard Lakes*

General description: An easy hike for strollers who appreciate gentle, alpine scenery.

Maps: Sphinx Mountain USGS Quad and Gallatin National Forest, Hebgen Lake Ranger District.

The majestic bighorn sheep, a rare sight along hiking trails. Harry Engels photo.

General location: Forty-five miles south of Bozeman; twelve miles south of the Big Sky Resort.

Special attractions: Alpine forests, meadows, and lakes.

For more information: Write the District Ranger, Hebgen Lake Ranger District, Gallatin National Forest, Box 520, West Yellowstone, MT 59758 or call (406) 646-7308.

There's a special scenic quality about the Gallatin and Madison ranges. Strange-shaped buttes and fortresses rest atop plateaus of timber and meadows. Small lakes are tucked away in unexpected places. Every turn in the trail brings a fresh surprise.

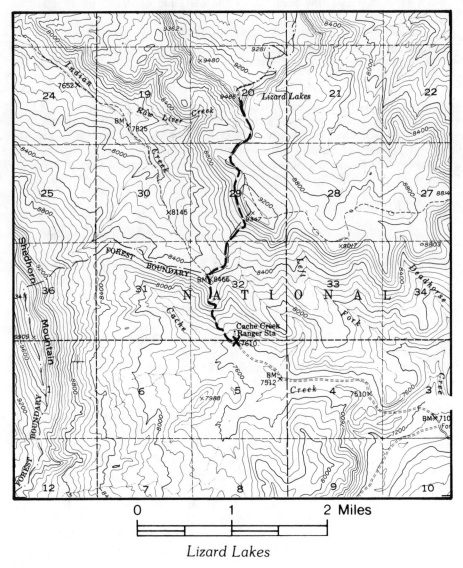

0   1   2 Miles

Lizard Lakes

To find the trailhead, take U.S. 191 south from Bozeman. About 16 miles past Big Sky, look for the Taylor Fork Road heading west. About eight miles up this road, take the fork to the right (Cache Creek Road) and follow it about three miles to the trailhead (Trail #173).

Go north on this trail for one mile to the Taylor Fork/Indian Creek divide, an uphill walk (about 1,000 feet elevation gain) through aspen thickets and open meadows interspersed with sagebrush and wildflowers. The pass is at 8,500 feet. The large mountain off to the northwest is Sphinx Mountain. From this location it actually looks like a Sphinx.

From this pass, the trail follows the east ridge, wandering through mosaics of timber and open grass. Stay on this ridge as it turns north. About three miles from the pass, the trail favors the east side of the ridge as it angles down to Lizard Lakes.

One lake is near the trail. Another is one-half mile downstream from the outlet. Sometimes the higher lake is dry, producing interesting contours of color from the aquatic vegetation. The lower lake has fair fishing for pan-sized cutthroat.

Altogether, it's about a nine-mile round trip. Wait until July for the snows to leave. Bring drinking water; it's dry all the way to Lizard Lakes.

This land is in checkerboard ownership with the Forest Service and Burlington Northern, Inc. BN would like to exchange their lands here with the Forest Service for land in northwestern Montana. Such an exchange could ensure an undisturbed future for the land around Lizard Lakes and similar nearby areas.—*Pat Caffrey*

64 Hilgard Basin

General description: A moderate backpack into a lake-filled, high-altitude basin.

General location: Forty miles south of Ennis or 22 miles northwest of West Yellowstone on the southern end of the Madison Range.

Maps: Hebgen Dam USGS Quad and Gallatin National Forest, Hebgen Lake Ranger District. (The area straddles the boundary of the Beaverhead and Gallatin national forests, but either map will do.)

Special attractions: Open, subalpine scenery in a basin with more than its share of lakes.

For more information: Write the District Ranger, Hebgen Lake Ranger District, Gallatin National Forest, Box 520, West Yellowstone, MT 59758 or call (406) 646-7308.

Of all the Madison Range's natural wonders—the Spanish Peaks, the Sphinx/Helmet complex, Taylor Peaks, and all the rest—the Hilgard Basin might top the list for hiking enjoyment.

To find the trailhead, turn north on the Beaver Creek Road off U.S. 287 two miles west of Hebgen Reservoir or 28 miles southwest of Ennis along Quake Lake. Follow the Beaver Creek Road for about six miles until it ends at Polomageton Park where the trail begins. Two trails start from this trailhead; take the one marked "Hilgard Basin."

The trail gradually climbs along Sentinel Creek at first, then the incline steepens as the trail and creek get closer to Expedition Pass, making the total

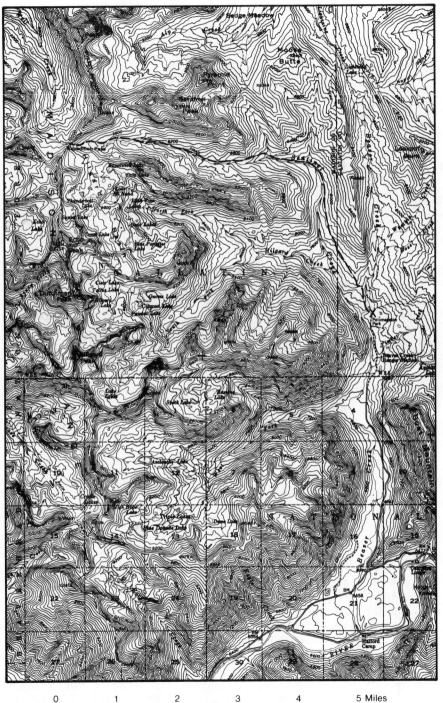

Hilgard Basin

0   1   2   3   4   5 Miles

Expedition Lake in the Hilgard Basin, Echo Peak in the background. Mike Sample photo.

elevation gain 2,720 feet. It's seven miles to the pass, all on well-maintained, easy-to-follow, and hazard-free trail with ample drinking water.

At Expedition Pass, the splendor of the Hilgard Basin unfolds before you with Expedition Lake and several others in the foreground and Echo Peak creating a perfect backdrop. Spend a few minutes taking in the views, then drop into the basin and pick one of many campsites along Expedition, Sunset, Ha Hand, Blue Paradise, Crag, or one of the other lakes.

This is high country with only a limited supply of wood. So plan on using your backpack stove, leaving the area's scarce wood supply to add to the aesthetics.

You can usually plan on fish for supper in the Hilgard Basin. Most of the lakes have pan-sized cutthroats.

It would be your big loss to head back the next day without spending at least one day exploring and fishing in the basin. For climbers, the basin acts as a base for several climbs, with 11,214-foot Echo Peak being the most popular and 11,316-foot Hilgard Peak, the highest point in the Madison Range, being the most technical.

In recent years, Hilgard Basin has become increasingly popular. Such a wonderland can only stay undiscovered for so long. However, Hilgard Basin is among the most fragile of hiking areas, so take every precaution not to leave marks of your visit.—*Bill Schneider*

65 Ramshorn Lake

General description: A long day hike or easy overnighter.

General location: Forty-five miles south of Bozeman.

Maps: Crown Butte USGS Quad and Gallatin National Forest, Gallatin Ranger District.

Special attractions: Gentle backcountry and good fishing.

For more information: Write the District Ranger, Gallatin Ranger District, Gallatin National Forest, Gallatin Gateway, MT 59730 or call (406) 763-4434.

This area isn't scenic in the same sense as the Mission Mountains or Glacier National Park. It offers more of a gentle, quiet beauty—not rugged peaks carved by glaciers.

To find the trailhead, drive south through the Gallatin Canyon on U.S. 191 about 40 miles from where it crosses I-90 or 10 miles south of Big Sky. Watch for a sign to 320 Guest Ranch on the left (east) side of the highway. You can see the guest ranch from the road.

Follow this gravel road until it ends one-half mile past the ranch. The trail to Ramshorn Lake starts where the road ends. Although the Forest Service is attempting to resolve the situation, the bridge across the Gallatin River is

Pika, a delightful little denizen of most high rocky slopes. Harry Engels photo.

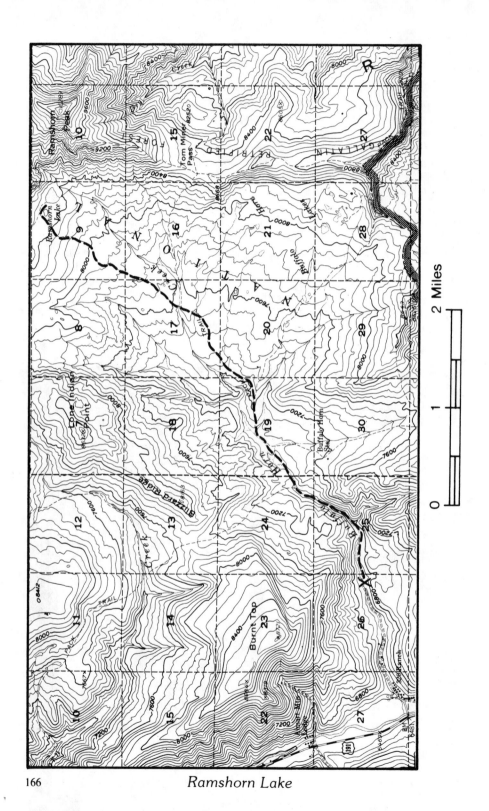

Ramshorn Lake

still privately-owned. So thank somebody at the 320 Ranch for allowing access.

It a gradual uphill for six miles to Ramshorn Lake—a fairly easy hike except, perhaps, the last mile where the trail gains elevation rapidly. It goes through heavy timber all the way with a few open parks—particularly around the four-mile mark where there is a series of big meadows.

The trail is well-maintained and receives considerable use by horses from the guest ranch. Motorized vehicles are restricted on the lower portions of the trail in summer.

The trail follows Buffalo Horn Creek most the way. So drinking water is usually available.

Although the area doesn't seem to support many deer, elk are everywhere. Also, watch for bighorn sheep, moose, and black bear. Since Ramshorn Lake lies just north of Yellowstone National Park, a few grizzly bears inhabit the area.

The lake has all sizes of cutthroat trout, including some over three pounds. But as usual, they're hard to catch.

The best campsite is at the lower end of the lake near the outlet. There's plenty of firewood and good drinking water.

For rock climbers, 10,269-foot Ramshorn Peak (just east of the lake) offers an easy scramble.

For rockhounds, there are some extremely interesting geologic formations about one-half mile from the lake on the way to Ramshorn Pass, just north of Ramshorn Peak. Petrified wood can be found on Ramshorn Peak.

The trail brings hikers into the Porcupine-Buffalo Horn-Hyalite Wilderness Study Area. The fate of this area is being cast, so you might want to pass your ideas for future management onto the Forest Service.—*Bill Cunningham*

66 *Hyalite Lake*

General description: A long, day hike or moderate overnighter to an alpine lake.

General location: Twenty miles south of Bozeman.

Maps: Fridley Peak USGS Quad and Gallatin National Forest, Bozeman Ranger District.

For more information: Write the District Ranger, Bozeman Ranger District, Gallatin National Forest, P.O. Box 130, Bozeman, MT 59715 or call (406) 587-4259.

To find the trailhead, drive south from Bozeman on State Highway 243 (marked #345 on the Montana State Highway Map) for about seven miles before turning left on a gravel road to Hyalite Basin. This junction is marked with Forest Service signs. Drive about 12 miles to the Hyalite Reservoir, then turn left and drive around the north side of the reservoir. When the road forks, turn right and go past Window Rock Ranger Station to the end of the road.

While walking 5.5 miles south and 1,800 feet up this well-maintained trail, you pass 11 waterfalls cascading in stairstep fashion out of a red-rocked, mountain bowl. Although none of them are large waterfalls, each has its own unique character, as their names suggest: Grotto, Arch, Twin, Silken

Grotto Falls on the way to Hyalite Lake in the Gallatin Range. U.S. Forest Service photo.

Skein, Champagne, Chasm, Shower, Devil's Slide, Apex, S'il Vous Plait, and Alpine. The progression of waterfalls lures the hiker onward to see the next cascade. The hike seems to pass quickly, although you may spend four or five hours before climbing out of the timber into the wide bowl which holds Hyalite Lake.

This trail is justly popular with the people in the Bozeman area, but as is so often the case, the usage is mostly at the lower end by dayhikers who come for a short walk to see a couple of the waterfalls. By the time you reach the lake, you may have the surrounding country to yourself.

Do not count on trout for dinner; the lake is too shallow to stay liquid in some winters. Instead, enjoy the spectacular vistas, which include Fridley Peak to the southeast and Hyalite Peak just to the southwest. A large meadow stretches around the lake and expands out to the base of Fridley Peak. Possible campsites are numerous; the only problem is deciding which view you favor the most.

Birds seem to like the basin. On the edges of the timber, Clark's nut-crackers and grey jays flash their black and white patterns; Stellar jays catch the eye with their irridescent blue crests. And out in the meadows hover

Hyalite Basin in the Gallatin Range. Mike Sample photo.

hummingbirds, attracted by the profusion of wildflowers. Especially abundant is the paintbrush, lupine, fleabane, and four o'clocks.

In the evening, you may hear or see a deer come down for a drink at the lakeshore. Spotting an occasional elk, mountain goat, or bear is a possibility. Most assuredly, a few marmots will whistle their attention to you as you explore the bow.

Winter releases its grip on the Hyalite Basin quite late by lowland standards. The snowbanks may not melt off the trail until late June. And winter may return quickly, making late September and October trips a gamble.

While at the lake, the hiker should consider a couple of short, but interesting, sidetrips which depart from the outlet of the lake. One is an easy two-mile walk to the top of Hyalite Peak (10,299 feet) for views down into Horseshoe Basin and out into the Yellowstone River country. The other is a two-mile hike across a neighboring cirque and up a ridge to the Hyalite/Squaw Creek Divide. Both provide high vantage points from which to enjoy the beautiful Gallatin Range.—*Mike Sample*

(Because of their close proximity, the hikes to Hyalite and Emerald and Heather lakes are on the same map—page 172.—Editor.)

67 *Emerald and Heather Lakes*

General description: A long day hike or moderate overnighter to two beautiful mountain lakes.
General location: Twenty miles south of Bozeman.
Maps: Fridley Peak USGS Quad and Gallatin National Forest, Bozeman Ranger District.
For more information: Write the District Ranger, Bozeman Ranger District, Gallatin National Forest, P.O. Box 130, Bozeman, MT 59715 or call (406) 587-4259.

To find the trailhead, drive south from Bozeman on State Highway 243 (marked #345 on the Montana State Highway map) for about seven miles before turning left on a gravel road to Hyalite Basin. This junction is marked with Forest Service signs. Drive 12 miles to the Hyalite Reservoir, then turn left and drive around the north side of the reservoir. At a fork in the road, turn left onto the East Fork Road and continue past the turnout for the short hike to Palisade Falls until the road ends at the trailhead. (Note: the Fridley Peak Quad map does not show this last two mile segment of the road.)

Although somewhat rocky in places, the trail is generally well-maintained. Over the 5.5-mile gradual uphill pull to Emerald Lake, the hiker emerges from the thick forest to gain increasingly expansive views of the rugged cliffs to the east. These cliffs eventually pinch in and meet the mountainous ridgeline from the west to form the walls of the cirque which holds Emerald and Heather Lakes and a few unnamed potholes.

Once at Emerald Lake, the hiker has a wide choice of campsites in the meadows interspersed around the lake with sparse stands of subalpine timber. A rough trail departs from the west side of Emerald and travels less

170

Emerald Lake in the Gallatin Range. Mike Sample photo.

than a half-mile up 250 feet more in elevation to Heather Lake. From the trailhead to Heather Lake the trail climbs a total of about 2,000 feet, yet there aren't any prohibitively steep pitches.

Heather Lake does not have as many potential campsites as does Emerald. The wall of the cirque falls sharply down to the shore of Heather on the west side, while rock shelves and snowbanks protrude on the other shores. Both lakes offer fair fishing for pan-sized trout.

The 11-mile round trip should require only about five hours of hiking— not including time spent relishing the beauty of these high altitude lakes. The hike may be too much for small children.

The trail follows the East Fork of Hyalite Creek most of the way, so unlike many hikes, drinking water is readily available. Wait until July to try this hike, however, as the area remains clogged with snow through June.

About 1.5 miles from the trailhead, the East Fork tumbles over Horsetail Falls—a sight well worth seeing. The falls are plainly visible from the trail; the sound of falling water will be a tonic for anyone who has stayed out on the plains too long.

Perhaps the highlight of the trip is the incredible display of wildflowers. Color is everywhere, even rivalling Glacier National Park's natural flower beds. You'll find glacier lilies, columbine, lupine, paintbrush, alpine forget-me-not, shooting stars, and many more.

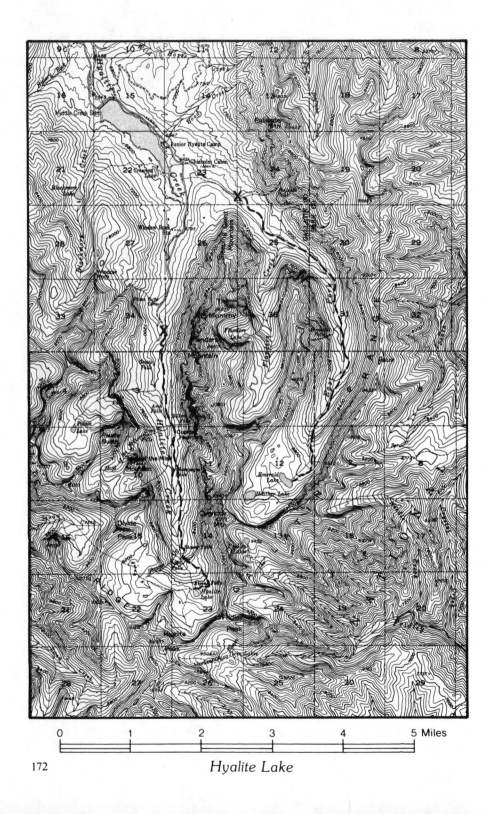

Hyalite Lake

0   1   2   3   4   5 Miles

These lakes are just north of Yellowstone National Park, but the chance of stumbling into a grizzly bear is remote. Nonetheless, take the standard precautions (page 7). However, the chances of seeing deer, black bear, elk, or mountain goats are good.

Although the trail receives above average use, most hikers apparently have taken care not to leave signs of their passing. But please pay special attention to wilderness camping manners, as this is fragile, beautiful, alpine country.—*Mike Sample*

68 *Big Snowies Crest*

General description: A long, but fairly easy, hike on a flat ridge in a little-known mountain range.

Maps: Crystal Lake, Jump Off Peak and Half Moon Canyon USGS Quads and Lewis & Clark National Forest Map.

General location: Twenty miles south of Lewistown.

Special attractions: Flat, alpine prairie, ice cave, unrestricted views of eastern Montana from the Missouri River to the Beartooth Plateau.

For more information: Write the District Ranger, Musselshell Ranger District, Lewis & Clark National Forest, Box F, Harlowton, MT 59036 or call (406) 632-4391.

Mule deer, perhaps the most common big game animal along wilderness trails. Harry Engels photo.

The Big Snowies consist of one massive, broad-based ridge flanked by cirques and streams. The main western segment of this ridge runs for 12 miles and ranges from 8,500-8,700 feet in elevation.

The trail to the ridge can be reached by turning south from U.S. 87 onto the Crystal Lake Road about eight miles west of Lewistown (or five miles east of Moore). From there, it's about 22 miles to Crystal Lake. The trailhead for trail #405 is at the south end of the lake near the campground. The trail climbs over 2,000 feet in 3.2 miles to the crest of the Big Snowies. At this point, the hard-hiking becomes a stroll across level prairie-style, tundra interspersed with mangled thickets of trees.

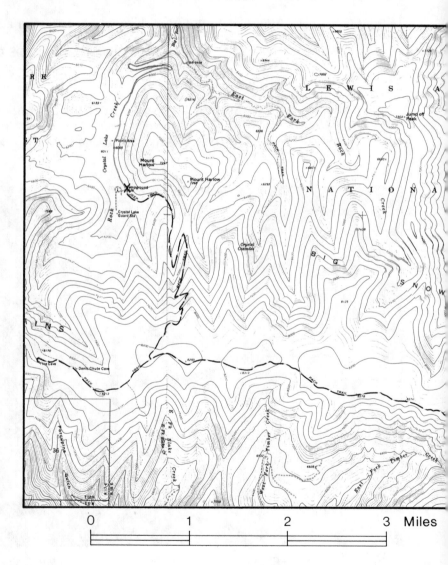

0   1   2   3 Miles

Here, at the top, trail #405 junctions with the Crest Trail #493. Take this trail and follow it either way along the ridge. It isn't always easy to follow and is often marked only by rock cairns. If you lose the trail, stay on the high ground until it materializes again.

There is no water anywhere along the Crest Trail. Day-hikers must carry up what they need. Overnighters can usually melt snow for their water, if they wish. Massive snowdrifts form near the top of the Crest and last through September.

For a good day hike to a rare ice cave (which is only 1.5 miles past the Crest Trail junction) go 1.2 miles to the west, then look carefully for a trail

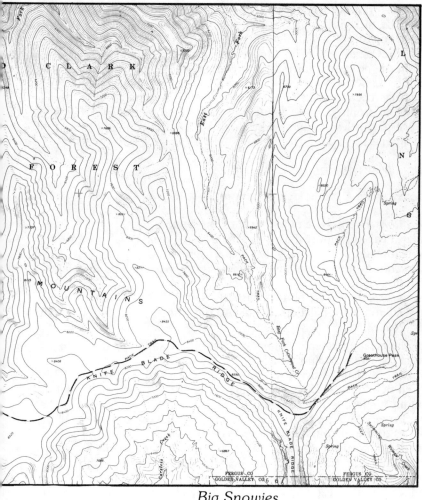

Big Snowies

(#524) branching off to the south. In .3 mile this trail leaves the Crest and goes out on the south slope through scattered trees and rocks to the cave. This cave is one room-full of ice from a combination of water seeping out of the rock and snow blowing in through the entrance. A flashlight is helpful but not necessary.

For a good overnighter, try Greathouse Peak, 10 miles past the Crest Trail junction, going east. This "peak" at 8,730 feet is the high point of the range. Getting there is one surprise after another. The trail crosses large expanses of alpine grasses which give incredible visual harmony to the endless prairies off to either side, 4,000 feet below. Then, there is a stretch called "Knife Edge Ridge" where the mile-wide Crest narrows to a few feet and drops off abruptly on either side. Finally, the trail dips into a primitive little pass where there is a four-way trail junction. Stay on the obvious ridge trail to reach the top of Greathouse Peak. From here, you can retrace your route back to Crystal Lake or choose one of four trails which descend directly from the peak area to trailheads you'll need a good map and a little luck to find by vehicle.

This area has been studied for designation as wilderness. It is a strange area, gentle yet primitive and remote—an easy place to traverse, but also where a spirit of timeless wildness prevails. If uniqueness counts, it would be a superb wilderness. —*Pat Caffrey*

69 Crazy Mountains

General description: A moderately strenuous 23-mile, four-day hike crossing two high ridges.
General location: Twenty-five miles north of Big Timber.
Maps: Crazy Peak, Campfire Lake, and Amelong Creek USGS Quads and Gallatin National Forest, Big Timber Ranger District.
Special attractions: Rugged, alpine scenery, refreshing streams and lakes, and mountain goats.
For more information: Write the District Ranger, Big Timber Ranger District, Gallatin National Forest, Box A, Big Timber, MT 59011 or call (406) 932-2650.

Some of the most spectacular, alpine scenery in the state remains virtually untouched in the Crazy Mountains.

The Crazies stand majestically above the plains near Livingston and Big Timber. Well-developed glacial scouring has produced the enchanting valleys which contain numerous high elevation lakes. Beautifully sculptured peaks and serrated ridges radiating from the core of the range rise over 11,000 feet, offering views of the surrounding mountains and prairie.

This hike is designed for at least three nights, giving participants a glimpse of how pleasant life can be in the heart of goat country, the Crazy Mountains.

The trailhead on the east side of this hike is at Half Moon Campground, which is located about 25 miles northwest of Big Timber. Drive 12 miles north of Big Timber on U.S. 191 until you see the road turning left up the Big Timber Canyon. This gravel road winds for another 10-12 miles across private property, eventually through two gates before you arrive at the

Outstanding scenery along the Big Timber Canyon trail in the Crazy Mountains. Bruce Chesler photo.

Forest Service's Half Moon Campground below Big Timber Canyon where trail #119 begins.

The trail begins with a moderately steep climb up Big Timber Canyon. After less than one mile, drop your pack and take a short, side trip to Big Timber Falls, a roaring waterfall set deep in the canyon rock. The marked trail takes off to the left and goes one-half mile to the falls. Then, return to your pack and continue up the trail.

Two well-constructed bridges are traversed at the 2-3 mile mark, providing ample support in crossing Big Timber Creek even during high runoff periods. Another mile along the trail, Granite Peak stands out as the dominant feature of the landscape. This peak is also the location of a long side trip possibility. At the base of the mountain, a trail turns off left to Blue Lake.

The Blue Lake trail almost immediately crosses Big Timber Creek on a log-jam. Then, it switchbacks up for a mile along a rock slide, through forest, and past a couple of abandoned cabins before reaching a vantage over Blue Lake, a mountain gem with a fair supply of small rainbow trout for anglers. The trail ends at this point with a view of Crazy Peak, highest in

177

the range. However, cross-country hiking will provide access to alpine lakes—Blue, Granite, and Thunder lakes, all over 8,000 feet. Pear and Druckmiller lakes, also nearby, set in a deep cirque approaching 9,000 feet. A base camp set up at Granite Lake could occupy the backcountry enthusiast

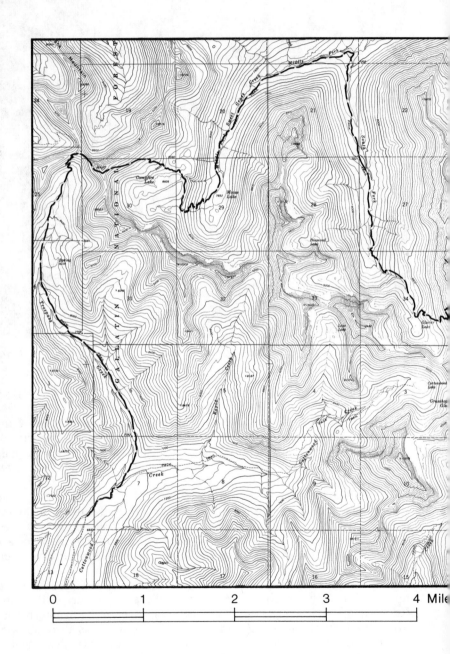

0   1   2   3   4 Mile

for many days with climbing, fishing, and deep thought around the shores of these incredible lakes.

Meanwhile back at the way of Twin Lakes, the trail skirts Granite Peak for about one mile. Moderate climbing and a route crossing an avalanche

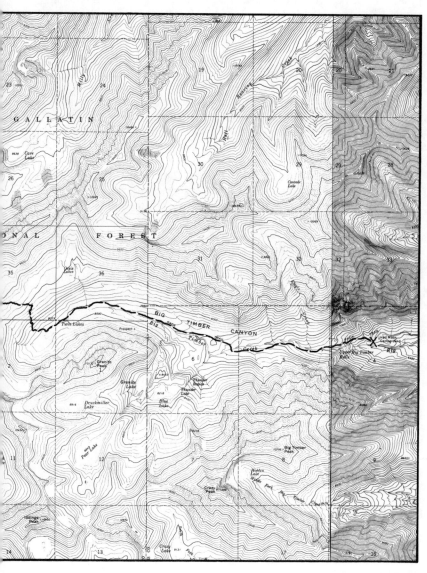

Crazy Mountains

path are encountered after five miles of traveling from Half Moon Campground. The trail breaks out into open meadows beside the Lower Twin Lake. Camp on one of the drier sites. Take in the hard-to-beat views of the surrounding mountains. Or follow the trail around the first lake, and look for a cozy campsite along the stream that separates Twin Lakes. There is an adequate supply of firewood at both sites.

From Upper Twin Lake, the trail begins a steep ascent. Plan on at least an hour for this 2,000-foot trudge. Switchbacking across the high, open country, hikers are treated to wildflowers and cascading brooks. The stiff climb is more than rewarded on top with an awesome view of the Big Timber Creek drainage and surrounding ridges. From this pass, a short scramble along the ridge to the north will put you on top of Conical Peak.

Dropping down one mile into the South Fork of Sweetgrass Creek drainage, the trail reaches Glacier Lake. This alpine lake is fed by sheer waterfalls and a long summer snowmelt. Due to the irregular rocky topography, campsites along this beautiful lake are hard to find. Stay around the area for lunch, drink some of its sparkling chilled water, and watch the icebergs float across the bluegreen lake.

The trail leaves Glacier Lake and drops steadily for over a mile through the trees until a crossing of the South Fork is necessary. No bridge is located at this point, and the crossing can be dangerous during spring runoff.

Another one-fourth mile downstream you cross a series of meadows which may temporarily obscure the trail, as will rock slides in the area. There are some choice campsites located in this part of the valley. Plan on spending your second night at either the meadows or at the stream's junction with the Middle Fork of Sweetgrass Creek two miles downstream. The Middle Fork has fair fishing for small cutthroat.

Where the South Fork joins the Middle Fork, the trail begins heading upstream through forested slopes on the way to Moose and Campfire lakes. The next two miles wind upstream to Moose Lake. Above Moose Lake, the trail switchbacks 800 feet up in one mile to Campfire Lake. Don't get this large body of water confused with the small trailside pools that lie in depressions nearby. Campfire Lake is a big, irregular-shaped beauty which reflects the surrounding peaks and ridges nicely and has good fishing for 12-14 inch rainbows. Campsites around this lake have been abused in the past, so be extra careful, particularly with your fire, if you must have one. And consider packing out trash left by thoughtless visitors.

From Campfire Lake, the trail climbs another 1,000 feet to the divide separating the Middle Fork of Sweetgrass Creek and Trespass Creek drainages. At this 9,500-foot vantage point, the well-defined Crazy Mountain high country is at eye level. Goat tracks cross rock and snowfields, which lie precipitously above green valleys and shining lakes. The Bridgers, Absarokas, Castles, and Spanish Peaks are all visible on a clear day—an inspiring view to say the least. From this point, the lakes of the Sweetgrass drainage shine invitingly in the morning sun, and to the east, the endless expanse of prairie overwhelms visitors unaccustomed to such vistas.

Dropping steeply into the basin at the head of Trespass Creek, the trail winds across talus slopes and through lush meadows for about two miles before entering the trees. The remaining five miles of this hike follows the east side of Trespass Creek, crossing two small tributaries of this stream. Just below the junction of Trespass and Cottonwood Creek trails, there is a ford of Trespass Creek which poses no great difficulty. Less than a mile farther, the Trespass/Cottonwood pack trail turns into a rugged jeep road. Follow this to the head of the Cottonwood Creek Road, near Ibex Guard Station, 15 miles northeast of Clyde Park on a good gravel road, locally called the Cottonwood Creek Road. Your pre-trip preparations should have arranged for a waiting vehicle or a ride at the rock barrier at the end of the Cottonwood Creek Road.

You may find it hard to believe—after this backcountry adventure—that there is no formal wilderness proposal for the Crazy Mountains. The reason? Most of the mountain range is "checkerboarded" with private land, some of which is currently being explored for oil and gas potential. If you want the Crazy Mountains to remain wild, make your feelings known.
—*Bruce Chesler*

70 *Cottonwood Lake*

General description: A moderate overnighter or long day hike.
General location: Forty miles northeast of Livingston in the Crazy Mountains.
Maps: Campfire Lake and Crazy Peak USGS Quads and Gallatin National Forest, Livingston Ranger District.
For more information: Write the District Ranger, Livingston Ranger District, Gallatin National Forest, 1202 W. Front, Livingston, MT 59047 or call (406) 222-1892.

The first mile of this trail retraces the last mile of the Crazy Mountain Traverse hike (page 176). Although the two hikes could be combined, it would turn into a long, strenuous backpack.

To find the trailhead for the Cottonwood Lake trip, take U.S. 89 14 miles north of Livingston to Clyde Park. About a half-mile past Clyde Park turn right on a heavily used gravel road (locally known as the Cottonwood Creek Road) and follow it northeast for 15 miles to the Ibex Guard Station Junction. Instead of turning left to the guard station, continue going straight up the Cottonwood Creek Road. The trail begins about two miles past the guard station junction where the road is blocked to motorized vehicles, except motorcycles and snowmobiles, with a barrier of large rocks.

In the last few miles, you go through three gates. However, don't fret; this is a public road. Be sure to close the gates.

The first mile (almost to the Trespass Creek trail junction) is actually an abandoned jeep road. At the Trespass Creek trail junction, veer right for a five-mile, steep climb to the 8800-foot Cottonwood Lake.

At about the two-mile mark, the trail passes through a large opening which is—believe it or not—a proposed site of a subdivision including a plan to "improve" the trail into an access road for the future home owners. The "checkerboarding" between private and public land in the Crazy Mountains and in other Montana national forests makes this development possible.

Where the trail crosses the stream and leaves this private land, check out

181

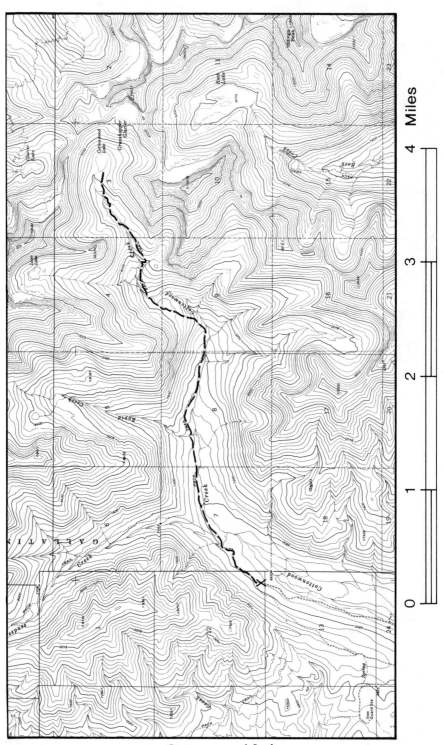

Miles

0 1 2 3 4

Cottonwood Lake

the narrow canyon, with several waterfalls, which isn't visible from the trail. It's about 200 yards upstream from the stream crossing.

The trail is heavily used and well-maintained—with one exception. Towards the end of the hike, the trail passes through some glacial moraine, sometimes disappearing in the rocks. However, at this point in the hike you really don't need a trail as you can look ahead and see where the lake is.

The Crazies get lots of snow, so wait until late summer for this trip. The trail has at least four good sources of drinking water, but there's a 1.5-mile dry stretch between the outlet of Lone Lake to a group of small ponds just before Cottonwood Lake.

The lower end of the lake has several excellent campsites. However, don't forget your stove, as firewood is scarce and should only be used in an emergency. The lake has a good population of pan-sized cutthroat.

If you have extra time at the lake, try a couple of exciting side trips. Perhaps the best is to head east from the lake for a two-hour climb up to Grasshopper Glacier. The unusually large glacier lies on the major north/south crest in the Crazy Mountains and offers a spectacular view into the Big Timber Creek drainage which is dotted with lakes. You can also see 11,214-foot Crazy Peak, the highest in the Crazy Mountains.

This is a difficult, but not technical climb. With caution it can be made by most hikers.

For a shorter side trip, take an easy 15-minute scramble south from the lake up a rocky slope to the divide between Rock Creek Lake and Cottonwood Lake. From here, you can see many of the major peaks in the Crazies.

When you get back from the hike, take a few minutes to encourage the Forest Service to hurry up efforts to resolve the land use conflicts created by checkerboard ownership.—*Bill Cunningham*

71   *Middle Fork, Lost Fork of the Judith*

General description: A fairly demanding three-day overnight loop.

General location: One hundred miles southeast of Great Falls in the Little Belt Mountains.

Maps: Sand Point and Ettien Springs USGS Quads and Lewis & Clark National Forest, Judith Ranger District.

Special attractions: Large roadless area with major streams and 1,000-foot limestone cliffs.

For more information: Write the District Ranger, Judith Ranger District, Lewis & Clark National Forest, Box 484, Stanford, MT 59479 or call (406) 566-2238.

Of all the large roadless areas in Montana, the Middle Fork of the Judith may be the least popular with hikers—not because it doesn't have good hiking, because it does, but because few wilderness travelers know about it. The 81,000-acre *de facto* wilderness has great stream fishing for native cutthroat, a large big game population, and vistas to rival any wildland.

To find the trailhead, take U.S. 12 east from White Sulphur Springs for about 18 miles until you reach the small town of Checkerboard. Go about one mile east of Checkerboard and turn left (north) on a gravel road (Forest

0   1   2   3 Miles

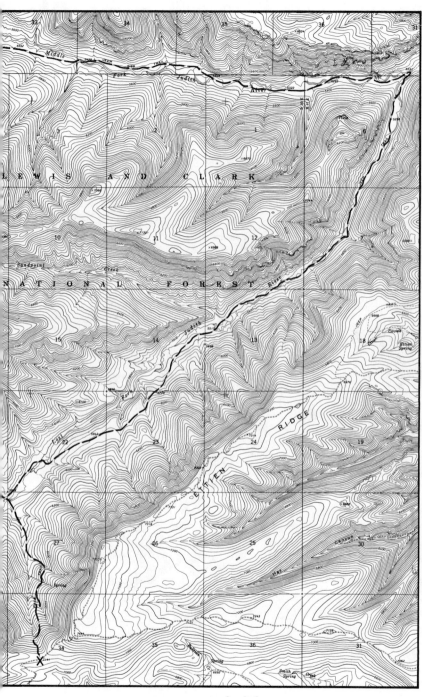

Judith

Road #274) to the Whitetail Guard Station, about 10 miles north of the highway. Go past the guard station and stay on this road. There are several road junctions, but you'll stay on the track by sticking with the major, heavily traveled road. Go about five miles past the guard station to the trailhead for Trail #433 to Burris Cabin.

Unlike most hikes, this trail loses elevation rapidly from the trailhead, as it drops from the ridgetop three miles to the Lost Fork of the Judith and the

Mule deer in velvet. Harry Engels photo.

Burris Cabin, an abandoned homestead. As will become obvious, there has been extensive abuse by motorcycles along this section.

If you started late in the day, you might want to camp along the Lost Fork above Burris Cabin. There's plenty of good sites, complete with firewood and a beautiful stream filled with native cutthroat.

Right at Burris Cabin, the trail junctures with the trail following the length of the Lost Fork. Take the trail northwest up Burris Creek for about five miles until you reach Sand Point, a 8,211-foot knob on the divide separating the Lost Fork and the Middle Fork drainages.

After relishing the view for a few minutes, go northwest for about a half-mile to a trail junction. Take a right here and head down (north) about three miles into the Middle Fork of the Judith River.

You come out on the bottomland at the Middle Fork Ranch, now abandoned. Don't camp on this private land. Take a right and head downstream selecting one of many good campsites along the Middle Fork.

Like the Lost Fork, the Middle Fork offers excellent cutthroat fishing and scenery, especially towering, limestone cliffs. From the Middle Fork Ranch, you're actually walking on a lightly traveled jeep road for about six miles downstream until you reach the point where the Lost Fork joins the Middle Fork. Take a right at this trail junction and follow the Lost Fork about seven miles upstream to the Burris Cabin, where you must retrace your steps three miles uphill to your vehicle.

All told, this is about a 30-mile loop trail that introduces hikers to much of the Middle Fork of the Judith Wilderness Study Area. The Forest Service is presently contemplating the fate of the area, so contact the Lewis & Clark National Forest in Great Falls with your suggestions for future management. —*Bill Cunningham*

72 *Highwood Baldy*

General description: A strenuous day hike.

General location: Thirty miles east of Great Falls in the Highwood Mountains.

Maps: Highwood Baldy and Arrow Peak USGS Quads and Lewis & Clark National Forest, Judith Ranger District.

Special attractions: An outstanding view of the high plains from the summit of Baldy Mountain.

For more information: Write the District Ranger, Judith Ranger District, Lewis & Clark National Forest, Stanford, MT 59479 or call (406) 566-2238.

The Highwoods are one of Montana's isolated mountain ranges that rise like islands from a grass ocean. Hiking in them can be as pleasant as straddling the Continental Divide.

Find the trailhead by taking U.S. 87 east from Great Falls for about three miles, then turn north on paved county road #228. Follow this road north for a few miles before it turns east. After about 15 miles of pavement, the road turns to gravel and follows Highwood Creek to Highwood Guard Station. The trail takes off from the campground right by the guard station. There are several intersections on the roads to Highwood Guard Station, so be sure to take your Lewis & Clark Forest map.

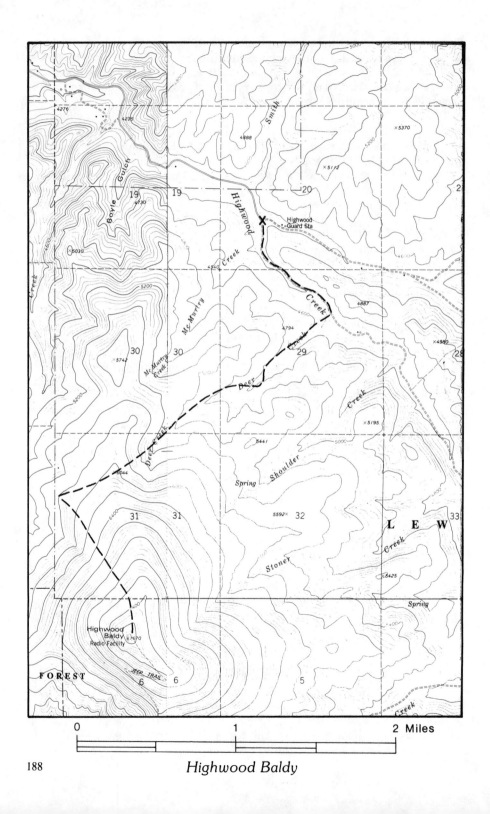

0   1   2 Miles

            Highwood Baldy

For about the first two miles, the trail is well-maintained and has available water. Actually, the first mile is an old jeep road. As you approach Mount Baldy, it gets steep, primitive, dry, and difficult to follow. Be sure to bring water.

Where the jeep road ends at the one-mile mark lies a trail junction with the Deer Creek and Highwood Creek trails. Take the Deer Creek Trail to the top of Baldy.

It's about three miles and 2,600-foot elevation gain to the summit of Baldy. Only experienced hikers should try this hike. It's a six-mile round trip that takes even good hikers a full day.

During July and August, mosquitoes and deer flies can be a problem along the first mile of this hike where the jeep road parallels Highwood Creek. There is no bear danger.

August through October is best for this hike. If you can hit it just as the aspen and cottonwoods turn gold, you can experience east-of-the-divide scenery at its very best.

Motorized vehicles aren't allowed on this trail. The area—especially the last half of the hike—is as wild as any wilderness area. Wildlife is fairly abundant, and most wildflowers common east of the divide as well as high-mountain species can be found.

The high point of the trip—in more ways than one—is Mount Baldy. From the 7,600-foot summit, hikers get an awe-inspiring view of the prairie environment, the high plains of Montana.

From Baldy, ambitious hikers can add four miles to their hike with a cross-country side trip to Pinewood Peak, to the west and easily visible from the summit of Baldy. If you try for both summits in one day, make sure you have enough time; don't get caught in the dark.

Few hikers make this an overnight backpack. But some camp overnight at the trailhead at Highwood Guard Station campground. This is a vehicle campground maintained by the Forest Service and offers some fishing for small brook trout in Highwood Creek. Some hikers also stay overnight two miles up the road at Briggs Creek in Train Creek Campground, which is fairly heavily used by recreational vehicle campers.—*Larry Thompson*

73 *Bear Paw Baldy*

General description: A short, but rugged, day hike to the highest point in the Bear Paw Mountains.

General location: Twenty-five miles south of Havre on the Rocky Boy Indian Reservation.

Maps: Warrick USGS Quad.

Special attraction: A super view of nearly all the isolated mountain ranges of central Montana.

The hike to Mount Baldy in the Bear Paw Mountains resembles the trip to Mount Baldy in the Highwood Mountains east of Great Falls. However, this hike is shorter and the view slightly more impressive.

The trailhead is easy to find. Simply follow Highway 234 south from Havre for about 25 miles until you reach Teepee Campground near Rocky

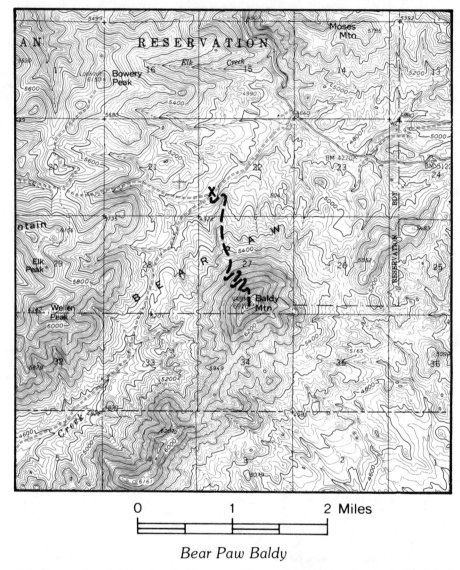

Bear Paw Baldy

Boy Recreation Area, a local ski resort. The trail begins at the far end of the campground.

It's a mere 1.5 miles to the summit of Baldy, but only experienced hikers should try it. The trail is poorly maintained, rocky, without water, and has a 2,200-foot elevation gain.

The entire hike is on the Rocky Boy Indian Reservation. The area is very rugged and remote—too rugged, in fact, for motorized vehicles. After leaving the Teepee Campground, all signs of man disappear.

Although few—if any—hikers make this an overnight backpack, many

190

stay at Teepee Campground and try some of the excellent fishing in the beaver ponds in lower Beaver Creek. A tribal fishing permit is required.

The view from the top of Mount Baldy is unsurpassed. Be sure to pick a clear day (August through October) for this hike, so you can get the full impact of this vista. Almost all the isolated mountain ranges in eastern Montana are visible.

If you have extra time, you might try hiking cross country for about three miles (six miles round trip) into the headwaters of Eagle Creek. You will pass through some unusually moist, dense forests for eastern Montana.—
Larry Thompson

74 *Pine Creek Lake*

General description: A steep four-miler up the east side of Paradise Valley to a beautiful mountain lake.
General location: Fifteen miles south of Livingston.
Maps: Emigrant and Mount Cowen USGS Quads and the Gallatin National Forest, Livingston Ranger District.
For more information: Write the District Ranger, Livingston Ranger District, Gallatin National Forest, 1202 W. Front, Livingston, MT 59047 or call (406) 222-1892.

To begin this hike, drive south of Livingston five miles. Then, turn east (left) onto the old highway at the sign "East River Road" and go about eight more miles. Past the cabin community of Pine Creek 0.7 miles, turn east (left) on a gravel road marked with Forest Service signs and go to the end of this road, where there is a Forest Service campground and the trailhead for this hike.

On this broad, well-maintained trail, the first mile is deceptively flat. At the end of this flat stretch, you stand at the foot of beautiful Pine Creek Falls. This is far enough for some who have heard about the next three miles. In those three miles, the trail climbs more than 3,000 feet. But for others, the allure of a mountain lake held in a glacial cirque is too much to resist. Draw some water at the falls because the trail is usually dry.

Because the trail climbs 1,000 feet per mile, most people take between three and four hours to reach the lake. On the bright side, coming out takes only two. Therefore, this could be a day hike. But there is a good campsite near the outlet and good fishing for pan-sized cutthroat to keep the backpacker occupied. Plan on using your stove, as firewood is scarce.

The lake lies beneath 10,941-foot Black Mountain in an obvious glacial cirque. On the north side of the lake, the bedrock shows pronounced striations where the glacier shoved its rocky load across the granite. At the outlet, a broad slab impounds the lake.

The best time to visit the Pine Creek Lake is from July 15th to September 30. Any earlier will mean wading through snowdrifts on the last part of the trail; in October, those drifts may reappear quickly. If you prize solitude, wait until after Labor Day; before school starts the trail is heavily used by youth camps.

Other than marmots and pika and overly friendly ground squirrels, you probably won't see much wildlife.

191

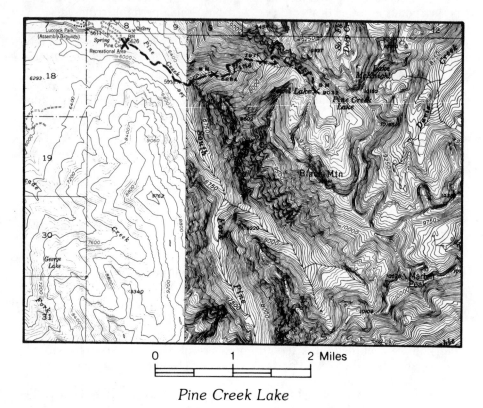

0   1   2 Miles

Pine Creek Lake

If you have extra time, hike around to the east end of the lake and climb the divide to look into Lake McKnight and the Davis Creek drainage. There is no trail into McKnight Lake and the country is so rough and remote that few hikers ever walk its shores.

One of the pleasures of camping at Pine Creek Lake is the chance of seeing alpenglow on the peaks. As the sun moves lower in the west and begins to set behind the Gallatin Range, the atmosphere deflects a portion of the color in the spectrum, leaving a pronounced reddish hue to the last few moments of sunlight. When the conditions are right and this red light bounces off the polished rock surfaces just north of the outlet, the effect is startling. With only a little poetic license, one could say it looks like the peaks are on fire.—*Mike Sample*

75 *Elbow Lake, Mount Cowan*

General description: A rugged overnighter.
General location: Twenty miles south of Livingston in the Absaroka Mountains, now part of the Absaroka-Beartooth Wilderness.
Maps: Emigrant and Mount Cowen USGS Quads and Gallatin National Forest, Livingston Ranger District.

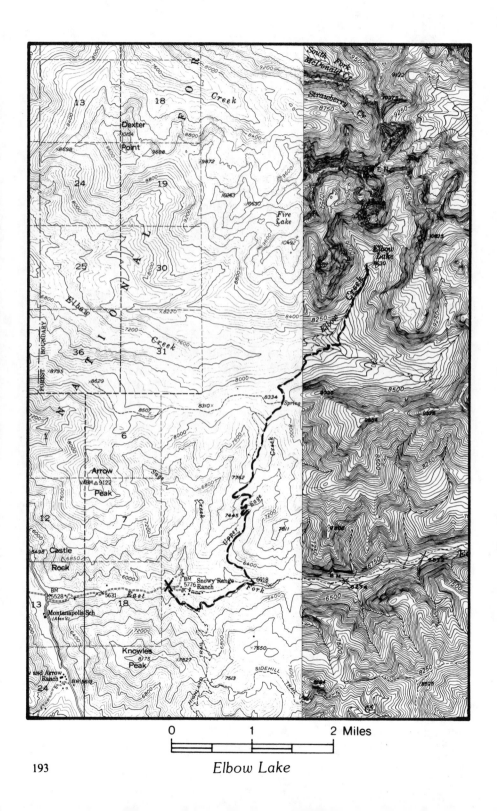

Elbow Lake

Special attractions: Mount Cowen, an incredible mass of rock and the highest point in the Absaroka Range.

For more information: Write the District Ranger, Livingston Ranger Station, Gallatin National Forest, 1202 W. Front, Livingston, MT 59047 or call (406) 222-1892.

The rugged North Absaroka Range forms the east wall of the Paradise Valley south of Livingston along the Yellowstone River. Of all these perilous peaks, 11,206-foot Mount Cowen is the highest.

To find the trailhead, drive south of Livingston on U.S. 89 for five miles and turn left on the East River Road. Follow this paved road for 16 miles to Pray. Here, turn east on a heavily traveled road up Mill Creek that heads for Chico Hot Springs. Two miles inside the National Forest boundary, take a left on the road up the East Fork of Mill Creek. Go about two miles and park at the trailhead a quarter-mile before the Snowy Range Ranch.

The trail skirts around the south side of Snowy Range Ranch for about a mile before hitting the trail up Upper Sage Creek. Be careful not to get on the Highland Trail which heads south shortly after the trailhead.

Take the trail up Sage Creek and stay on it all the way to Elbow Lake, in the southern shadow of formidable Mount Cowen. It's a nine-mile grind, going from 5776 to 8630 feet in elevation. The trail is easy to follow, but you should carry water, as there are several long, dry stretches.

Camp at the lower end of Elbow Lake or just below the outlet. The lake is filled with fat cutthroat. The feeling of remoteness will be with you since this is part of the Absaroka-Beartooth Wilderness and few people make this tough, dead-end hike.

The obvious side trip is climbing Mount Cowen. This is a very tough climb, so make sure you know what you're doing. As you sit in your camp, the sublime reflection of Mount Cowen in the mirror-like lake might make the climb irresistible.—*Art Foran*

76 Lake Pinchot

General description: A week-long backpacking vacation.

General location: Fifty miles south of Big Timber, in the Absaroka-Beartooth Wilderness.

Maps: Mount Douglas and Cutoff Mountain USGS Quads, the Forest Service's Beartooth Hike Lake Country map, and Gallatin National Forest, Big Timber Ranger District.

For more information: Write the District Ranger, Big Timber Ranger Station, Gallatin National Forest, Box A, Big Timber, MT 59011 or call (406) 932-2650.

Reaching Lake Pinchot and investigating the nearby treasures of the Lake Plateau region of the Absaroka-Beartooth Wilderness is more than a hike. Actually, it's more like a vacation.

Don't even think about hiking into this area and out the next day. Instead, plan on at least two days in addition to two days to get in and out. Bring plenty of food—because once you're there, you'll probably decide to stay at least a week.

The trailhead is at Box Canyon Guard Station, 49 miles south of Big

Wounded Man Lake in the Lake Plateau section of the Absaroka-Beartooth Wilderness. Bill Schneider photo.

Timber on the Boulder River Road, of which the last 24 miles are bumpy and dusty. Park at the guard station and take the Trail #27 marked "Rainbow Lakes 12 miles."

The trail gradually climbs through timber and open parks along the East Fork of the Boulder River for about 3.5 miles before crossing on a sturdy bridge. If you started late, you may wish to stay the first night at an excellent campsite just before the bridge.

After crossing the East Fork, the trail follows the river for a quarter-mile before climbing away through heavy timber. Along the river, you'll notice several trout-filled pools, so be prepared to fight off temptations to stop and rig up your fly-casting gear.

After two more miles, Trail #27 goes straight toward Slough Creek Divide. You turn left on trail #28.

About 200 yards after the junction, you pass little Lake Kathleen on your left. Then, two miles later you reach another junction, where Trail #30 breaks off to the right and heads for Columbine Pass. You stay left on Trail #28.

Just before you reach the next junction at the 11-mile mark, you pass along the left side of a large, wet meadow. Watch for moose.

At the 11-mile junction, you have several options. Depending on how tired you are and where you intend to camp, you can (1) go straight for another two miles over the Stillwater Divide to Lake Pinchot, (2) turn left and switchback up a steep hill one mile to Rainbow Lakes, or (3) veer right for a very steep, half-mile climb to 9472-foot Fish Lake, one of the highest in Lake Plateau.

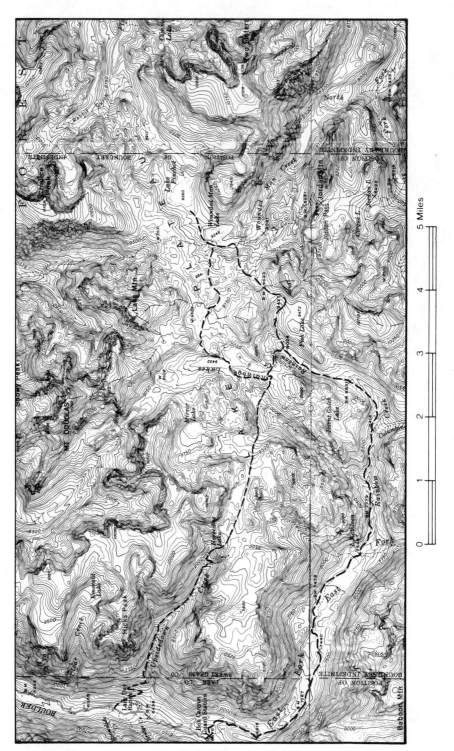

Lake Pinchot

Lake Pinchot is probably the best choice for a base camp for such an extended trip. However, the immediate area has hundreds of excellent campsites along lakes. Thus, you might choose to make a temporary camp and look for a site that is especially appealing.

Once you've established your base camp, start taking advantage of the numerous adventures all around you. For anglers, there are two dozen lakes within the reach of an easy day hike. For climbers, there are 11,298-foot Mount Douglas, 11,153-foot Chalice Peak, and other summits to reach.

Most of the lakes have rainbow trout or hybrids. However, Fish Lake has cutthroat. Although a few lakes are barren, most have good fishing with some rainbows over two pounds.

On the way home, take the trip between Lake Pinchot and Rainbow Lakes. In addition to passing by Wounded Man Lake, you go through a collection of gem-like lakes on an alpine plateau. It's only a two-mile hike. The trail is heavily used and signed, but it doesn't show on the maps. It leaves the main trail on the northwest corner of Wounded Man Lake and comes out between Middle and Upper Rainbow lakes.

To avoid returning to your vehicle on the same trail, you can take the Upsidedown Creek trail that can be found at the foot of Lower Rainbow Lake. This may be slightly shorter, but it involves steep, downhill hiking. It hits the Boulder River Road about two miles north of Box Canyon Guard Station.

The only unpleasant part of this hike is the first day—hiking 12-14 uphill miles with a loaded pack. If you endure this, however, you will almost certainly say it was worth it.

The area is about as heavily used as any hiking area in Montana. However, the large number of campsites dilutes the crowd to a tolerable level.

The climate in this high country often leaves something to be desired, with rain fairly common. So bring good rain gear.

The climate also restricts the hiking season to about one month—the last week in July and the first three weeks in August. Before this time, expect to be hiking through last year's snowbanks. And after it, be prepared for early season snowstorms.

A week in this hiker's wonderland will undoubtedly be an always-remembered vacation. So expect a few remorseful moments when you realize that you must return to your hectic lifestyle back home. For the first few days at home, civilization will never be so unpleasant.—*Bill Schneider*

77 Aero Lakes

General description: A long day hike or moderate overnighter to two high altitude lakes with outstanding fishing.

General location: Three miles northeast of Cooke City near the northeast entrance to Yellowstone National Park.

Maps: Cooke City USGS Quad and Custer National Forest, Beartooth Ranger District.

For more information: Write the District Ranger, Beartooth Ranger District,

Custer National Forest, P.O. Box 1029, Red Lodge, MT 59068 or call (406) 446-2103.

The Beartooth Plateau—now part of the Absaroka-Beartooth Wilderness— is the largest contiguous area in the U.S. over 10,000 feet in elevation and has hundreds of lakes ranging in size from potholes to major lakes like the Aero Lakes.

To reach the trailhead from Cooke City, drive east two miles to a turnoff marked with a large Forest Service sign as the Goose Lake jeep road. Drive northeast about two miles up this dirt road to a cluster of old buildings. An inconspicuous trailhead on the right shoulder of the road has an old Forest

The hoary marmot, not as common as its cousin, the yellow-bellied marmot, but still commonly seen in certain high country hiking areas. Harry Engles photo.

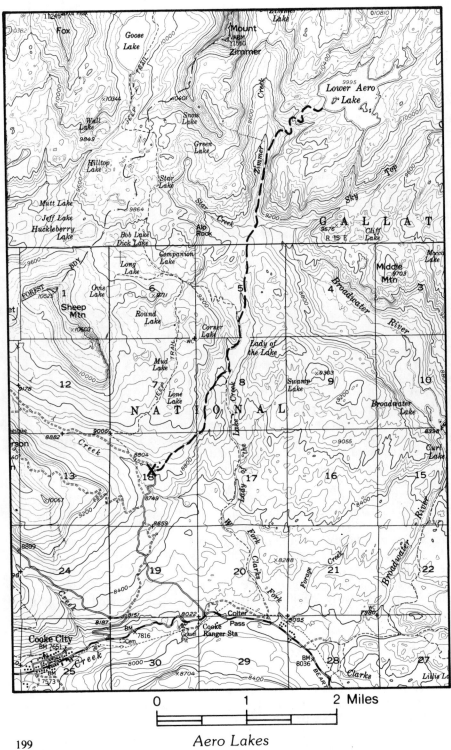

Aero Lakes

Service sign directing you to Lady of the Lake—which is also the trail to Aero Lakes.

Once at Lady of the Lake (1.5 miles from trailhead), turn left and walk up the meadow on the north side of the lake where two trails depart.

The left trail heads north and then turns west to Long Lake. You take the right trail, which leads almost due north one mile to the junction of Star and Zimmer creeks. Continue north along Zimmer Creek another mile until you see a crude trail switchback up the steep right side of the canyon. If you are following Zimmer Creek and see a stream coming in from the left, you have gone too far up the drainage.

The scramble up the switchbacks is steep, but short. Suddenly, you emerge from the timber and stand above Lower Aero Lake. Be sure to notice the dramatic contrast between the treeless ridge and plateau with the timbered country just below.

It's about five miles into Aero Lakes. The trail isn't shown on the maps, but it's fairly obvious on the ground because of the fairly heavy use it receives.

The shoreline around Lower Aero is rocky and punctuated with snowbanks. There are a number of places to camp, but perhaps the best is on the grassy north side where a point juts out into the lake. Don't expect a campfire on this treeless site.

To proceed on to Upper Aero Lake, follow the stream which connects the two lakes. Another good camping spot is just below the outlet of the upper lake. This provides a good view of the lake and the prominent Mount Villard with its spiney ridges. It also makes a good base camp for fishing both lakes and for exploring east to Rough Lake and then north up the Sky Top Lake chain.

Fishing is one of the prime reasons for coming to the Aero Lakes. The fishing here, like most mountain lakes, is tempermental, but both lakes offer outstanding fishing in number and size. Upper Aero Lake has cutthroats, while Lower Aero has both cutthroat and brook trout. They are stocked every four years and thus have two age classes of fish—the young, upcoming trout and the lunkers.

At this altitude, the summer season is very short; the ice may not free lakes until mid-July. Because the tundra is quite wet on the plateau, there tends to be a prodigious number of mosquitoes when the wind isn't blowing. Bug dope is mandatory until the first hard frost.

Enjoy the Absaroka-Beartooth Wilderness for what it is—wild and spectacular. At Aero Lakes, you're at least five miles from the nearest machine. At night, no city lights or heavy auto fumes block your view of the stars. There are nearly a million acres of pristine land around you, more than enough for a lifetime of wandering.—*Mike Sample*

78 Rock Island Lake

General location: An easy day hike or overnighter.
General location: Ten miles east of Cooke City, just north of the Montana border in the Absaroka-Beartooth Wilderness.

Maps: Cooke City USGS Quad and Custer National Forest, Beartooth Ranger District.

For more information: Write the District Ranger, Beartooth Ranger District, Custer National Forest, P.O. Box 1029, Red Lodge, MT 59068 or call (406) 446-2103.

The 10,000-foot Beartooth Plateau may be the finest hiking area in Montana. Without doubt, it is one of the most popular, and Rock Island Lake is no exception. However, the area has so many scenic destinations, the troops of hikers soon dilute into the wilderness environment and the goal to "get away from it all" is still preserved.

Since most hikes seem to end at a mountain lake, the Beartooth Plateau is lucky to be so well-endowed. Rock Island Lake is one of many high altitude lakes in the area, plus one of the largest and easiest to reach.

Start this hike at a well-marked trailhead along U.S. 212 about five miles east of Cooke City. From the highway, it's only about 3.5 miles to Rock Island Lake. There are two trail junctions before you reach the lake, but they're well-marked. Likewise, the trail is heavily used. So there's no chance of going astray on the way to this 8166-foot lake.

Rock Island Lake differs from many high elevation lakes. Instead of forming a small, concise oval in the end of a cirque, it sprawls in every direction. A hiker will tire simply trying to walk all the way around it.

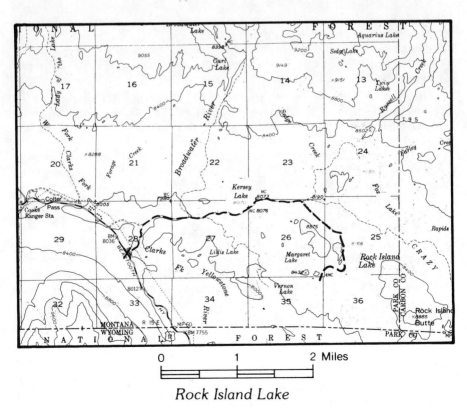

Rock Island Lake

For hikers planning overnight stays, the lake has several good campsites—especially two choice spots on the south shore east of a section of rocky shoreline. The lake contains large brook trout that—like most big fish—take patience and skill to catch.

The selection of side trips in this area is incredible. You can go in for a day or stay a week, going to a new lake or seeing new sights every day.

Because Rock Island Lake is so accessible—seven miles round trip on a near-level trail—it would be a perfect choice for a family planning to try out the Absaroka-Beartooth Wilderness. Drinking water is readily available on the trail and at the lake, but the mosquitoes are bad in early summer. Although you could find enough wood for a campfire at the lake, consider using a stove for cooking. This area receives heavy use, and if every hiker had a fire, it would soon show signs of overuse.—*Bill Schneider*

79 *Tempest Mountain and Granite Peak*

General description: A long, steep backpack to Tempest Mountain, a traditional launching point for ascents of Montana's highest peak, strictly for experienced, well-conditioned hikers.

General location: In the heart of the Beartooth Mountains 80 miles southwest of Billings.

Maps: Alpine and Cooke City USGS Quads and Custer National Forest, Beartooth Ranger District.

Special attractions: An excellent chance to view or climb Montana's highest mountain, 12,799-foot Granite Peak.

For more information: Write the District Ranger, Beartooth Ranger District, Custer National Forest, P.O. Box 1029, Red Lodge, MT 59068 or call (406) 446-2103.

Hikers have a choice of two trailheads for this hike. Both are found by driving south from Columbus on State Highway 307 and after 14 miles taking a left (still on 307) at Absarokee. A few miles out of Absarokee, the road forks.

For the most commonly used route, take the right fork on State Highway 419 along the West Roadbud. Stay on this road through Fishtail to the Mystic Lake power plant where the trail begins.

The alternative route takes the left fork and stays on State Highway 307 until Roscoe where you turn right and go up the East Rosebud to Alpine, just below East Rosebud Lake where the trail starts.

Either trailhead gets you to the same place, the saddle between Prairieview Mountain and Froze-to-Death Mountain. The Mystic Lake route is two miles shorter with 400 feet less elevation to gain, but includes a very steep series of switchbacks. The East Rosebud route has a less steep gradient, more scenery, and more potential campsites for those hikers who don't wish to get to the shoulder of Tempest Mountain in one day. Either way, this hike is definitely for rugged types; just reaching the saddle where the two trails meet is a climb of 3,500 feet from Mystic or 3,900 from East Rosebud Lake.

Once at the saddle, the hiker turns southwest and follows a series of cairns around the north side of Froze-to-Death Mountain. The destination is a

Granite Peak, the highest summit in Montana. Mike Sample photo.

group of rock shelters at approximately the 11,600-foot level of Tempest Mountain. Tempest Mountain is really a plateau, and the rock shelters are on the west edge 1.6 miles north of Granite Peak. The shelters are rock walls (perhaps three-feet high) built over the years to protect campers from the strong winds which frequently blast the area. Behind these walls are some of the few square feet of flat ground to place sleeping bags without making uncomfortable adjustments to this rocky "moonscape."

By the time the hiker reaches the rock shelters, he has traversed approximately ten miles from the trailhead and climbed more than 5,000 feet. He crossed timberline just before reaching the saddle. No plants or

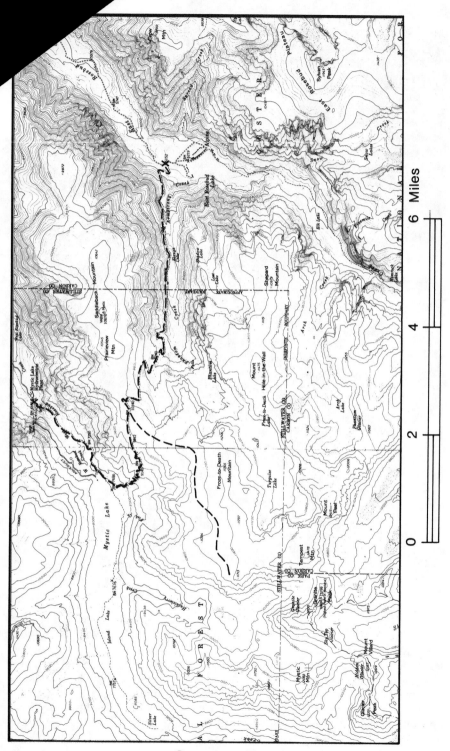

Granite Peak

grasses can survive the climate and elevation at the rock shelters except hardy lichens. Rock, ice, and sky are the predominate elements.

There are some advantages to hiking and camping in such an austere place. The wind is so prevalent that few mosquitoes ever attempt takeoffs from ground zero. The bear danger is nil. And of course, the high altitude grants superb views in all directions.

Along the west edge of the plateau leading up to Tempest, the view of Granite Peak is awesome. Granite buttresses rise almost vertically from the Huckleberry Creek canyon to form a broad wall nearly a half mile wide. The north face is heavily etched with fissures running almost straight up between the buttresses. Granite Glacier clings to the center of the wall. At the top, a series of pinnacles builds from the west side up to the peak.

To those who are skilled in technical climbing, Granite is an easy ascent in good weather, but for those with little experience, it is dangerous. Probably the best advice is to go with someone who knows what he is doing and who has the proper equipment. Especially important is a good climbing rope for crossing several precipitous spots. The easiest approach is across the ridge which connects Granite to Tempest and then up the east side.

Check with the Forest Service for more information before attempting this climb. In recent years, not one summer has passed without mishaps and close calls, mostly due to bad judgement. One sobering concern is the extreme difficulty in rescuing an injured person from Granite.

People have tried this hike and climb at almost all times of the year, but August and early September are the most logical choices. Even then, sudden storms with sub-zero wind chills are a real possibility. Snow can happen anytime. And the thunderstorms around Granite Peak are legendary. Be prepared with warm and windproof clothing and preferably a shelter which will hold together and stay put in strong wind.

Whether or not you climb Granite, take the time to walk up to the top of Tempest. To the north and 2,000 feet below are Turgulse and Froze-to-Death Lakes. On a clear day, one can see perhaps 100 miles out onto the Great Plains. Directly to the south are two unnamed lakes high in the Granite Creek drainage. And if one moves a little east towards Mount Peal, he can look southwest over Granite Peak's shoulder to Mount Villard and Glacier Peak, both over 12,000 feet.

As one might guess, there is little wildlife at this altitude. Nearer the saddle where there is grass and other hardy alpine plants, mountain goats are commonly spotted. An occasional golden eagle soars through this country looking for marmots and pika. Down closer to the trailheads a few mule deer and a rare bear make their summer homes.

If you use the East Rosebud trailhead, you may wish to take an alternate way back. From the east edge of the plateau to the west-northwest of Turgulse Lake, you can drop down into the bowl which holds Turgulse and hike past Froze-to-Death Lake and Phantom Lake (good fishing for cutthroats) and then sidehill back to rejoin the trail above Slough Lake. There is no trail for most of this route and some investigating between Froze-to-Death and Phantom may be necessary, but it is an interesting way out for the adventuresome. And high adventure is what this hike is all about in the first place.—*Mike Sample*

205

80 *Sundance Pass*

General description: A fairly rugged, three-day hike for more experienced hikers.

General location: On the northeast side of the fabulous Beartooth Range, about ten miles southwest of Red Lodge.

Maps: Alpine and Mount Maurice USGS Quads and Custer National Forest.

Special attractions: Spectacular mountain scenery, especially the view from Sundance Pass, and excellent fishing.

For more information: Write the District Ranger, Beartooth Ranger District, Custer National Forest, Box 1029, Red Lodge, MT 59068 or call (406) 446-2103.

In addition to being one of the choicest backpacking trips in the Beartooth Mountains, the Sundance Pass hike is only a short drive from the Billings area.

Find the trailhead by taking U.S. 212 southwest from Red Lodge for about ten miles and take a right at the Lake Fork of Rock Creek. A short, paved road leads to a turn-around and the trailhead.

This is a fairly difficult (3,900-foot elevation gain), 21-mile, point-to-

Keyser Brown Lake from the Sundance Pass trail. U.S. Forest Service photo.

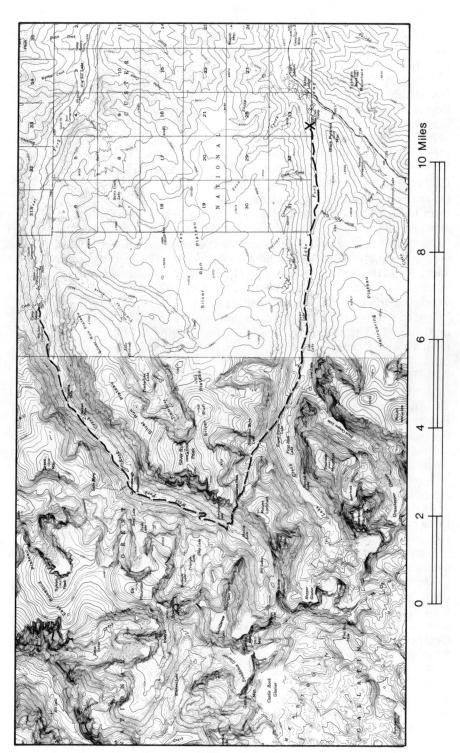

Sundance Pass

point hike that ends at Camp Senia in the West Fork of Rock Creek just south of Red Lodge. Most hikers who take this trip arrange for somebody to pick them up at Camp Senia or leave a vehicle there.

Although many hikers take three days for this trip, it can easily be extended by taking scenic side trips. The main route passes by three lakes— Keyser Brown, September Morn, and Sundance, but several others can be the targets of side trips.

Black Canyon Lake lies just below Grasshopper Glacier and is a short side trip. First and Second Rock lakes can be reached by a fisherman's trail from Keyser Brown Lake. Dude Lake is one mile on a rough, steep trail from Quinnebaugh Meadows. And there's a steep, but good, trail from Quinnebaugh Meadows to Lake Mary. Occasionally, the saddle to the north from Lake Mary is used as a cross country route to Crow, Sylvan, and East Rosebud lakes.

The lakes on the main route and on the side trips offer good fishing, mostly for pan-sized trout. Fishing seems best in Black Canyon and Dude lakes, with the former having large—but hard to catch—cutthroat trout. Stream fishermen often try their luck in Lake Fork and West Fork of Rock Creek, but it's poor fishing for small trout.

It's best to wait for this hike, as Sundance Pass usually isn't snow-free until July 15. This delay also avoids the peak season for mosquitoes and no-see-ums which can be quite bad in this area, especially on the West Fork side.

Besides superb fishing, the hike has spectacular scenery. From Sundance Pass, for example, hikers can see 12,000-foot mountains and the Beartooth Plateau, the largest contiguous area above 10,000 feet in North America. Hikers are also treated to glaciers and obvious results of glaciation, exposed Pre-cambian rock, and waterfalls.

Hikers have a good chance of spotting wildlife, particularly pika, ground squirrels, and marmots. Also watch for mountain goats, deer, golden eagles, and gyrfalcons. Goats are frequently seen from First and Second Rock lakes. An occasional black bear will be spotted, but bear danger is very low.

As with wildlife, wildflowers are present, but not terribly abundant. Fireweed, stonecrop, bluebells, and four o'clocks are some of the most common species.

Water is plentiful except near Sundance Pass. And the trail is well-marked and maintained throughout.

The main route has several good campsites: Keyser Brown Lake (heavily used, but good fishing for pan-sized trout), September Morn Lake (lightly used and good fishing for pan-sized trout), Sundance Lake (seldom used with no fish, but very scenic view of 12,548-foot Whitetail Peak), Quinnebaugh Meadows (poor fishing, but great view of 3,000-foot cliff off Silver Run Plateau), and any number of good campsites along the Lake Fork or West Fork of Rock Creek.

Since this area is part of the Beartooth Wilderness, motorized vehicles aren't allowed. Unlike some sections of the Beartooth Range, this area receives light to moderate use. Large church groups frequently camp at Lake Mary and Keyser Brown Lake, but otherwise the area isn't crowded.—*Mike Sample*

Afterword

The Wilderness Challenge

Many hikers, I suspect, view the "wilderness challenge" as the adventure of braving wild country with only what they carry on their backs. They briefly flee the comfortable life to risk survival along some austere divide, and return home the victor.

It almost seems like our *right* to at least have the opportunity to visit a place on earth that has been primarily affected by the forces of nature, where the imprint of man's hand is substantially unnoticeable.

Yes, we can "challenge" it. We can climb the highest peak, float the wildest river, seek out the most hidden of the mountain's secrets. In Montana, we can even challenge the mighty grizzly bear, the wilderness king, and temporarily become the most feared creature on the mountain.

This challenge lures us to the blank spots on the map. It seems ingrained in our birthright—and most likely will for generations to come.

But today's hikers face an even more fierce, more difficult, more time-consuming, and more frustrating challenge. Now, we must rise to the challenge of saving the last wilderness.

Never has the oft-quoted adage of Will Rodgers—"They ain't makin' any more of it."—been so relevant. Another famous thinker, Aldo Leopold, also emphasized the point by writing, "Wilderness is a resource that can shrink, but not grow."

How true. But it must grow to help dilute the rapidly increasing number of hikers.

I suppose the day will come when most wilderness areas have restrictions on the number of human visitors. However, increasing the size of the wilderness resource would certainly make this day a more distant probability.

It's also true that the label "wilderness," when officially designated by Congress, can attract hikers, leading to more crowded conditions. However, limitations on recreational use is undoubtedly preferable to the alternative—gradual destruction.

In years past, I spent many wonderful days in my favorite roadless areas—which were almost unknown—never meeting another hiker and relishing the uncommon solitude. Too bad it never lasts. These areas are now severely threatened with various development schemes which would be much worse than seeing other hikers. Much worse.

In pioneer times, land could be logged, mined, or homesteaded, then abandoned, slowly reclaiming its wild character. Indeed, this has happened in many places throughout Montana. And of course, this is still scientifically possible, but as we all know, ever more unlikely.

Knowing this, it hurts to hear politicans talk of "balance," as they prepare to give their guarded support to the violation of another unprotected roadless area. In the lower 48 states, the ratio is now 99 percent nonwilderness and 1 percent wilderness, as legally defined by the Wilderness Act of 1964.

Yet, in almost every speech by wilderness opponents or politicians trying to please everybody, we hear cries for balance.

"I'm in favor of wilderness," they predictably say, "but not in this area. We need balance; we can't have all wilderness."

I wonder how many of these podium-thumpers really understand the existing inequity. If every remaining acre of roadless country south of Canada became part of the Wilderness Preservation System (created by the Wilderness Act of 1964), we *wouldn't even come close* to balance. The pitiful 1 percent might, at best, climb to 3 percent.

Here lies our challenge—to make America understand the wisdom of wilderness, to keep the bulldozer out of the last remnants of wild America, to preserve for future hikers a few examples of what it used to be like.

This challenge can't be taken lightly. Compared to winning congressional protection for a threatened roadless area, climbing the highest peak or surviving the elements is remarkably easy.

In a time when economics dictates most decision-making, pleas to designate wilderness aren't always eagerly received. But wilderness can be an economic bonanza to a community, especially for Montana's third largest industry—recreation and tourism.

Claims that wilderness destroys the local economy illustrate only one of the many myths plaguing wilderness preservation efforts. Other myths include: Only the rich, elite, young, and strong use wilderness. Domestic livestock grazing isn't possible or practical in wilderness. Wilderness locks out sportsmen and other recreationists. Wilderness is bad for wildlife. Wilderness isn't multiple-use. Wilderness locks up vital minerals. We have too much wilderness already.

These are pure myths, and quite the opposite is true in each case. So if you're confronted with these false statements, get the facts and set the record straight. Don't let it pass without a reply; there's too much at stake. The integrity of the last American wilderness is on the line. And even more important, the decisions on what to do with the remaining roadless areas will be made in the next few years.

The Montana Wilderness Assn.—and other conservation groups listed at the end of this section—have the facts to support pro-wilderness claims and dispel myths. They even have detailed information on many of the unprotected areas mentioned in this guide. Making the decision-makers relate to these facts is your challenge.

I dislike projecting wilderness as a giant battleground. But in reality, that's a fair description. The battle over wilderness has been—and will be in the future—as bitterly fought as any domestic political issue.

Hikers—and other people who use and adore wilderness—must be the soldiers in this war. Otherwise, the day when the last roadless area is protected as wilderness will soon dawn.—*Bill Schneider*

Conservation Organizations

Montana Wilderness Association
Box 635
Helena, MT 59601

American Wilderness Alliance
4260 E. Evans
Denver, CO 80222

Sierra Club
330 Bush St.
San Francisco, CA 94108

The Wilderness Society
1901 Pennsylvania Ave. N.W.
Washington, D.C. 20006

Montana Wildlife Federation
Box 4373
Missoula, MT 59801

Madison/Gallatin Alliance
P.O. Box 875
Bozeman, MT 59715

Appendix I

Always check the checklist

Hikers can—and will, of course—take almost anything they choose into the mountains. But without a complete checklist it's remarkably easy to forget an essential item. The following list is "over complete"—there are items on it that hikers rarely use. Still, it's always good sense to take a final look at a checklist before loading the pack into the car. The extra minute is usually worth it.

Clothing

____Shirt
____Pants
____Underwear (extras)
____Windshirt
____Vest
____Belt and/or suspenders
____Jacket or down parka
____Turtleneck
____Poncho or rainsuit
____Gloves
____Hat
____Bandana
____Walking shorts
____Sweater
____Swimming suit
____Balaclava or headband

Footwear

____Boots
____Socks (extras)
____Boot wax

____Moccasins or sneakers
      (for around camp)

Bedroom

____Tent
____Poles
____Tent stakes
____Cord/guy lines
____Fly
____Ground cloth
____Sleeping bag
____Sleeping pad or air mattress

Hauling

____Backpack
____Day or belt pack

Cooking

____Matches (extras)
____Matches (waterproof)
____Waterproof match case
____Stove

_____Fuel bottles (filled)
_____Funnel
_____Foam pad for stove
_____Cleaning wire for stove
_____Cleaning pad for pans
_____Fire starter
_____Cook kit
_____Pot gripper
_____Spatula
_____Cup
_____Bowl/plate
_____Utensils
_____Dish rag
_____Dish towel
_____Plastic bottle

Food and drink

_____Cereal
_____Bread
_____Crackers
_____Cheese
_____Margarine
_____Powdered soups
_____Salt/pepper
_____Main course meals
_____Snacks
_____Hot chocolate
_____Tea
_____Powdered milk
_____Drink mixes

Photography

_____Camera
_____Film (extras)
_____Extra lenses
_____Filters
_____Close-up attachments
_____Tripod
_____Lens brush/paper
_____Light meter
_____Flash equipment

Fishing

_____Rods
_____Reels

_____Flies
_____Dry fly floater (silicone)
_____Lures
_____Leader
_____Extra line
_____Swivels
_____Hooks
_____Spit shot/sinkers
_____Floats
_____Bait

Miscellaneous

_____Pocket or Swiss Army knife
_____Whetstone
_____Compass
_____Topo map
_____Other maps
_____Sunglasses
_____Flashlight
_____Batteries (extra)
_____Bulbs
_____Candle lantern
_____First aid kit
_____Snakebite kit
_____Survival kit
_____Repair kit
_____Suntan lotion
_____Insect repellent
_____Zinc Oxide (for sunburn)
_____Toilet paper
_____Space blanket
_____Binoculars
_____Nylon cord
_____Plastic bags
_____Rubber bands/ties
_____Whistle
_____Salt tablets
_____Emergency fishing gear
_____Wallet/I.D. cards
_____Dime
_____Ripstop tape
_____Notebook & pencils
_____Field guides
_____Toothpaste & tooth brush
_____Dental floss

____Mirror

____Garbage bag

____Book

____Towel

____Safety pins

____Scissors

____Trowel

____Water purification tablets

____Car key

____Signal flare

____Watch

____Extra parts for stove, pack and tent

____Solar still kit

____Rubber tubing

Appendix II

Finding Maps

For the hikes listed in this book, hikers need only two types of maps—USGS Quadrangles and various Forest Service maps. The FS maps can be obtained by writing the address listed with each hike. The topographic maps are available at the following locations.

Kalispell, MT 59901
Books West
Main & First Streets

The Sportsman
Junction Highway 2 & 93

Lewistown, MT 59457
Don's, Inc.
207 West Main Street

Livingston, MT 59047
Dan Bailey's Fly Shop
209 West Park St.

Missoula, MT 59801
Missoula Blueprint
1613 South Ave. West

Sportsman's Surplus
Trempers Shopping Center
2301 Brooks

The Trailhead
501 S. Higgins Ave.

Polson, MT 59860
Golden Engineering
6 Fourth Ave. E.

West Yellowstone, MT 59758
Pat Barnes Tackle Shop
105 Yellowstone Ave.

Bud Lilly's Trout Shop
39 Madison Ave.

Eagles Trading Post
Three Canyon St.

Whitefish, MT 59937
Charlie's Sporting Goods
232 Central Avenue

Big Timber, MT 59011
Bob's Sport Shop
230 McLeod

Billings, MT 59101
Selby's
114 N. 26 Avenue

Montana Oil & Gas Commission
15 Poly Drive

Bozeman, MT 59715
Beaver Pond
1716 West Main

Powderhorn
35 East Main

Selby's
232 East Main

Butte, MT 59701
Montana Bureau of Mines & Geology
Main Hall-Montana Tech.
W. Park

Great Falls, MT 59401
Blend's Copy Shop
509 First Avenue North

Helena, MT 59601
Base Camp
334 N. Jackson

State Publishing Co.
Airport Road